Latest
World Changes

GAZETTEER-INDEX OF NEW NATIONS

	AREA (sq. mi.)	AREA (sq. km.)	POPULATION
Armenia	11,506	29,800	3,283,000
Azerbaijan	33,436	86,600	7,029,000
Belarus	80,154	207,600	10,200,000
Bosnia & Hercegovina	19,940	51,129	4,124,256
Croatia	22,050	56,538	4,601,469
Estonia	17,413	45,100	1,573,000
Georgia	26,911	69,700	5,449,000
Kazakhstan	1,048,300	2,715,100	16,538,000
Kyrgyzstan	76,641	198,500	4,291,000
Latvia	24,595	63,700	2,681,000
Lithuania	25,174	65,200	3,690,000
Macedonia	9,889	25,713	1,909,136
Moldova	13,012	33,700	4,341,000
Russia	6,592,812	17,075,400	147,386,000
Slovenia	7,898	20,251	1,891,864
Tajikistan	55,251	143,100	5,112,000
Turkmenistan	188,455	488,100	3,534,000
Ukraine	233,089	603,700	51,704,000
Uzbekistan	173,591	449,600	19,906,000
Yugoslavia	38,989	102,173	11,371,275

	CAPITAL and LARGEST CITY	MAP	INDEX REF.
Armenia	Yerevan 1,199,000	A	E 5
Azerbaijan	Baku 1,150,000	A	E 5
Belarus	Minsk 1,589,000	A	C 4
Bosnia & Hercegovina	Sarejevo 448,500	B	B 1
Croatia	Zagreb 681,173	B	A 1
Estonia	Tallinn 482,000	A	C 4
Georgia	Tbilisi 1,260,000	A	E 5
Kazakhstan	Alma-Ata 1,128,000	A	F 5
Kyrgyzstan	Bishkek 616,000	A	H 5
Latvia	Riga 915,000	A	C 4
Lithuania	Vilnius (Vilna) 582,000	A	C 4
Macedonia	Skopje 506,547	B	C 2
Moldova	Kishinev 665,000	A	C 5
Russia	Moscow 8,769,000	A	H 4
Slovenia	Ljubljana 305,211	B	A 1
Tajikistan	Dushanbe 595,000	A	G 6
Turkmenistan	Ashkhabad 398,000	A	F 6
Ukraine	Kiev 2,587,000	A	C 5
Uzbekistan	Tashkent 2,073,000	A	G 5
Yugoslavia	Belgrade 1,470,073	B	C 1

Russia and Neighboring Countries

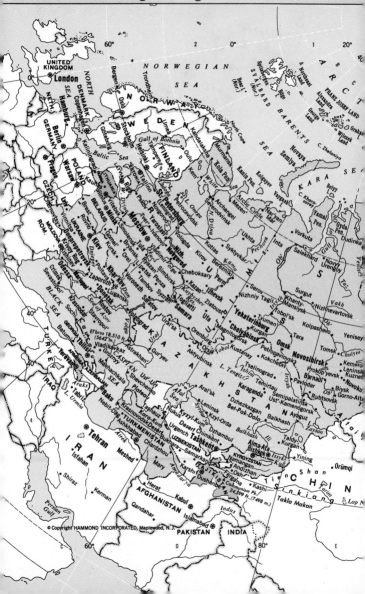

Map A

Russia and Neighboring Countries

CONIC PROJECTION

SCALE OF MILES
0   200   400   600   800

SCALE OF KILOMETERS
0   200   400   600   800

Capitals of Countries .... ⊗
International Boundaries .... ▬ ▬ ▬

MONGOLIA

CHINA

NORTH KOREA

SOUTH KOREA

JAPAN

Longitude 120° East of Greenwich

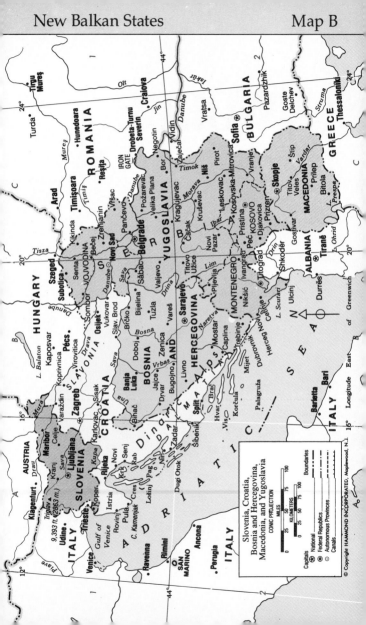

Slovenia, Croatia,
Bosnia and Hercegovina,
Macedonia, and Yugoslavia

CONIC PROJECTION

MILES

0   25   50   75   100

KILOMETERS

0   25   50   75   100

Capitals   Boundaries
⊛ National
⊕ Federal Republics
⊙ Autonomous Provinces
Canals

© Copyright HAMMOND INCORPORATED, Maplewood, N.J.

HAMMOND

WORLD ATLAS

COLLECTORS EDITION

Hammond Incorporated

Maplewood, New Jersey

PRINTED IN THE UNITED STATES OF AMERICA

Library of Congress Cataloging-in-Publication Data

Hammond Incorporated.
   Hammond world atlas.–Collectors ed.
      p.   cm.
   Includes indexes.
   ISBN 0-8437-1603-7
   1. Atlases.   2. Zip code–United States.   I. Title.   II. Title:

   World atlas.
   G1021.H279   1991 <G&M>
   912–dc20
                                                          90-27290
                                                             CIP
                                                             MAP

Contents 3

5-15	Gazetteer—Index of the World
16-17	World—Languages
18-19	World—Occupations
20-21	World—Natural Vegetation
22-23	World—Climates
24-25	World—Time Zones
26-27	World—Air Distances
28-32	World—Statistics
33	Arctic Ocean
34-35	World—Political
36-37	World—Physical
38-39	World—Population
40-41	North America
42-43	Canada
44-45	United States
46-47	Mexico
48-49	Central America
50-51	West Indies
52-53	Cuba, Hispaniola & Jamaica
54-55	Puerto Rico & Lesser Antilles
56-57	South America—Northern Part
58-59	South America—Southern Part
60-61	Africa—Northern Part
62-63	Africa—Southern Part
64-65	Europe
66-67	United Kingdom & Ireland
68-69	Norway, Sweden, Finland & Denmark
70-71	Germany
72-73	Netherlands, Belgium & Luxembourg
74-75	France
76-77	Spain & Portugal

Contents

78–79	Italy
80–81	Switzerland
82–83	Austria, Czechoslovakia & Hungary
84–85	Balkan States
86–87	Poland
88–89	U.S.S.R.—European Part
90–91	U.S.S.R.
92–93	Asia
94–95	Near & Middle East
96–97	Turkey, Syria, Lebanon & Cyprus
98–99	Israel & Jordan
100–101	Iran & Iraq
102–103	Southern Asia
104–105	China & Mongolia
106–107	Japan & Korea
108–109	Philippines
110–111	Burma, Thailand, Indochina & Malaya
112–113	Southeast Asia
114–115	Australia & New Zealand
116–117	Pacific Ocean
118	Antarctica
119–124	Flags of the World
125	Road Atlas—Contents, Symbols
126–180	Highway Maps—United States
181	Highway Map—Mexico
182–191	Highway Maps—Canada
192	Highway Mileage Table
193–224	Index

This alphabetical list of continents, countries, states, possessions, etc., gives the areas, populations, index references and page numbers on which they are shown on the largest scale. The index reference letter and number indicates the square on the respective map in which the named area is located.

*Member of the United Nations. †Does not appear on map.

Country	Area (Sq. Miles)	(Sq. Kilometers)	Population	Page No.	Index Ref.
*Afghanistan	250,775	649,507	17,672,000	102	A1
Africa	11,707,000	30,321,130	537,000,000	60-63	
Alabama, U.S.A.	51,705	133,916	3,893,978	128	
Alaska, U.S.A.	591,004	1,530,700	401,851	129	
*Albania	11,100	28,749	2,590,600	85	C3
Alberta, Canada	255,285	661,185	2,237,724	191	
*Algeria	919,591	2,381,740	18,666,000	60	C2
American Samoa	77	199	32,297	117	J7
Andorra	188	487	39,940	77	G1
*Angola	481,351	1,246,700	7,262,000	62-63	D6
Anguilla	35	91	6,519	51	F3
Antarctica	5,500,000	14,245,000	...	118	
*Antigua and Barbuda	171	443	77,000	51	G3
*Argentina	1,072,070	2,776,661	30,097,000	58-59	B-D5-8
Arizona, U.S.A.	114,000	295,260	2,718,425	130	
Arkansas, U.S.A.	53,187	137,754	2,286,419	131	
Armenian S.S.R., U.S.S.R.	11,506	29,800	3,031,000	89	F6
Aruba, Netherlands	75	193	55,148	50	D4
				55	O
Ascension Island, Saint Helena	34	88	719	62	A5
Ashmore and Cartier Islands, Australia†	61	159	939	114	B2
Asia	17,128,500	44,362,815	2,819,196,000	92-93	
*Australia	2,966,136	7,682,300	14,576,330	114-115	
Australian Capital Territory	927	2,400	221,609	115	D4
*Austria	32,375	83,851	7,555,338	82	B-C3
Azerbaidzhan S.S.R., U.S.S.R.	33,436	86,600	6,028,000	89	G6
Azores, Portugal	902	2,335	264,400	35	J4
*Bahamas	5,382	13,939	350,798	50	C1
*Bahrain	240	622	358,857	95	G4
Baker Island, U.S.A.	1	2.6	....	117	J5
Balearic Islands, Spain	1,936	5,014	558,287	77	G3
*Bangladesh	55,126	142,776	87,119,965	103	E2

Gazetteer–Index of the World

Country	Area (Sq. Miles)	(Sq. Kilometers)	Population	Page No.	Index Ref.
*Barbados	166	430	248,983	51	G4
				55	S
*Belgium	11,781	30,513	9,848,647	73	
*Belize	8,867	22,966	145,353	48	B1
*Benin	43,483	112,620	3,338,240	60	C4
Bermuda, U.K.	21	54	67,761	41	M6
				51	H3
*Bhutan	18,147	47,000	1,301,000	103	D2
*Bolivia	424,163	1,098,582	6,082,000	56	C4
Bonaire, Neth. Antilles	112	291	8,087	51	E4
				55	M
Bophuthatswana, S. Africa	15,570	40,326	1,200,000	63	E7
*Botswana	224,764	582,139	936,600	63	E7
Bouvet Island, Norway	22	57	....	35	K8
*Brazil	3,284,426	8,506,663	119,098,992	56-57	
British Columbia, Canada	366,253	948,596	2,744,467	190	
British Indian Ocean Territory	29	75	2,000	93	F6
*Brunei	2,226	5,765	192,832	122	E5
*Bulgaria	42,823	110,912	8,942,976	84	D3
*Burkina Faso	105,869	274,200	7,919,895	60	B3
*Burma (Myanmar)	261,789	678,034	36,747,000	110	A2
*Burundi	10,747	27,835	4,028,420	63	F5
*Byelorussian S.S.R. (White Russian S.S.R.), U.S.S.R.	80,154	207,600	9,560,543	89	C4
California, U.S.A.	158,706	411,049	23,667,837	132-133	
*Cambodia (Kampuchea)	69,898	181,036	7,200,000	111	D4
*Cameroon	183,568	475,441	9,432,000	60	D4
*Canada	3,851,787	9,976,139	24,343,181	42-43	
Canary Islands, Spain	2,808	7,273	1,170,224	76	B4
				35	J4
Cape Province, S. Africa	261,705	677,816	5,543,506	63	E8
*Cape Verde	1,557	4,033	296,093	35	J5
Cayman Islands, U.K.	100	259	19,000	50	B3
Celebes, Indonesia	72,986	189,034	7,732,383	113	G6
*Central African Republic	242,000	626,780	2,442,000	61	D-E4
Central America	197,480	511,475	25,000,000	48-49	
Ceylon, see Sri Lanka					

Country	Area (Sq. Miles)	(Sq. Kilometers)	Population	Page No.	Index Ref.
*Chad	495,752	1,283,998	4,309,000	60-61	D3
*Channel Islands, U.K.	75	194	129,363	67	E6
*Chile	292,257	756,946	11,275,440	56	B4
				58	B-C5-8
*China, People's Rep. of	3,691,000	9,559,690	1,036,000,000	104-105	
China, Republic of (Taiwan)	13,971	36,185	18,029,798	105	F3
Christmas Island, Australia	52	135	3,184	93	H6
Ciskei, S. Africa	2,988	7,740	635,631	63	E8
Clipperton Island, France	2	5.2	....	41	H8
Cocos (Keeling) Islands, Australia	5.4	14	555	93	G6
*Colombia	439,513	1,138,339	27,867,326	56	B2
Colorado, U.S.A.	104,091	269,596	2,889,735	134	
*Comoros	719	1,862	345,000	63	G6
*Congo	132,046	342,000	1,912,429	62	D5
Connecticut, U.S.A.	5,018	12,997	3,107,576	136	
Cook Islands, New Zealand	91	236	17,754	117	K7
Coral Sea Islands, Australia	8.5	22	....	116	E-F7
				115	D2†
Corsica, France	3,352	8,682	289,842	75	B7
*Costa Rica	19,575	50,700	2,379,000	48	C3
Crete, Greece	3,218	8,335	456,642	85	D5
*Cuba	44,206	114,494	9,706,369	50	B2
				52-53	
Curaçao, Neth. Antilles	178	462	145,430	50	E4
				55	N
*Cyprus	3,473	8,995	655,000	96	E5
*Czechoslovakia	49,373	127,876	15,470,000	82-83	
Delaware, U.S.A.	2,044	5,294	594,317	139	F2
*Denmark	16,629	43,069	5,114,000	69	B3
District of Columbia, U.S.A.	69	179	638,432	139	D1
*Djibouti	8,880	23,000	330,000	61	G3
*Dominica	290	751	74,089	51	G4
				54-55	K
*Dominican Republic	18,704	48,443	5,647,977	50	D3
				52-53	Q-S7
East Germany, see Germany					
*Ecuador	109,483	283,561	9,251,000	56	B3
*Egypt	386,659	1,001,447	45,915,000	61	F2
				94	B2

Gazetteer–Index of the World

Country	Area (Sq. Miles)	Area (Sq. Kilometers)	Population	Page No.	Index Ref.
*El Salvador	8,260	21,393	4,999,000	48	B2
*England, U.K.	50,516	130,836	46,220,995	66-67	
*Equatorial Guinea	10,831	28,052	300,000	60	C4
Estonian S.S.R., U.S.S.R.	17,413	45,100	1,466,000	88	C3
*Ethiopia	471,776	1,221,900	33,680,000	61	F-G4
Europe	4,057,000	10,507,630	723,804,000	64-65	
*Faeroe Islands, Denmark	540	1,399	45,000	64	D2
Falkland Islands & Dependencies, U.K.	6,198	16,053	1,813	58-59	D8
*Fiji	7,055	18,272	671,712	116	H7
*Finland	130,128	337,032	4,869,858	68-69	E2
Florida, U.S.A.	58,664	151,940	9,746,421	140-141	
*France	210,038	543,998	54,334,871	74-75	
French Guiana	35,135	91,000	73,022	57	D2
French Polynesia	1,544	4,000	166,753	117	M8
*Gabon	103,346	267,666	555,000	62	D5
*Gambia	4,127	10,689	695,886	60	A3
Gaza Strip	139	360	400,000	94	G3
Georgia, U.S.A.	58,910	152,577	5,463,087	142	
Georgian S.S.R., U.S.S.R.	26,911	69,700	5,015,000	89	F6
*Germany	137,753	356,780	78,039,155	70-71	
*Ghana	92,099	238,536	12,205,574	60	B4
Gibraltar, U.K.	2.28	5.91	29,648	76	D4
*Great Britain & Northern Ireland (United Kingdom)	94,399	244,493	55,638,495	66-67	
*Greece	50,944	131,945	9,740,417	85	C4
Greenland, Denmark	840,000	2,175,600	52,000	40	P2
*Grenada	133	344	103,103	51	F4
				55	R
Guadeloupe & Dependencies, France	687	1,779	328,400	51	F3
				54-55	H
Guam, U.S.A.	209	541	105,979	116	E4
*Guatemala	42,042	108,889	6,043,559	48	B2
*Guinea	94,925	245,856	5,143,284	60	A3
*Guinea-Bissau	13,948	36,125	810,000	60	A3
*Guyana	83,000	214,970	793,000	56	D2
*Haiti	10,694	27,697	5,053,792	50	D3
				52	P6
Hawaii, U.S.A.	6,471	16,760	964,691	129	
Heard & McDonald Islands, Australia	113	293	....	35	M8

Country	Area (Sq. Miles)	(Sq. Kilometers)	Population	Page No.	Index Ref.
*Holland, see Netherlands					
Honduras	43,277	112,087	4,092,000	48	C2
*Hong Kong, U.K.	403	1,044	4,986,560	105	E3
Howland Island, U.S.A.	1	2.6	....	117	J5
*Hungary	35,919	93,030	10,664,000	83	E-F3
*Iceland	39,768	103,000	237,000	64	C2
Idaho, U.S.A.	83,564	216,431	944,038	143	
Illinois, U.S.A.	56,345	145,934	11,427,414	144	
*India	1,269,339	3,287,588	685,184,692	102-103	
Indiana, U.S.A.	36,185	93,719	5,490,260	145	
*Indonesia	788,430	2,042,034	147,490,298	112-113	C-H6-7
Iowa, U.S.A.	56,275	145,752	2,913,808	146	
*Iran	636,293	1,648,000	43,414,000	100-101	
*Iraq	172,476	446,713	14,110,000	100	
*Ireland	27,136	70,282	3,537,000	67	B-C4
Ireland, Northern, U.K.	5,452	14,121	1,507,065	67	C3
Isle of Man, U.K.	227	588	64,679	67	D3
*Israel	7,847	20,324	3,980,000	98-99	
*Italy	116,303	301,225	56,243,935	78-79	
*Ivory Coast (Côte d'Ivoire)	124,504	322,465	7,920,000	60	B4
*Jamaica	4,411	11,424	2,095,878	50,53	
Jan Mayen Island, Norway	144	373	....	35	J2
*Japan	145,730	377,441	121,047,916	106-107	
Jarvis Island, U.S.A.	1	2.6	....	117	L6
Java, Indonesia	48,842	126,500	73,712,411	112	D-E7
Johnston Atoll, U.S.A.	0.91	2.4	327	117	K4
*Jordan	35,000	90,650	2,152,273	98-99	
Kalaallit Nunaat (Greenland), Denmark	840,000	2,175,600	49,773	40	P2
*Kampuchea (Cambodia)	69,898	181,036	5,756,141	132-133	
Kansas, U.S.A.	82,277	213,097	2,364,236	147	
Kazakh S.S.R., U.S.S.R.	1,048,300	2,715,100	14,684,000	90	E-F3
Kentucky, U.S.A.	40,409	104,659	3,660,257	148-149	
*Kenya	224,960	582,646	19,536,000	63	F4
Kermadec Islands, New Zealand	13	33	5	117	J9
Kirgiz S.S.R., U.S.S.R.	76,641	198,500	3,529,000	90	D3
Kiribati	291	754	56,213	117	J6
Korea, North	46,540	120,539	18,317,000	106	C2

Gazetteer–Index of the World

Country	Area (Sq. Miles)	Area (Sq. Kilometers)	Population	Page No.	Index Ref.
*Korea, South	38,175	98,873	37,448,836	106	C3
*Kuwait	6,532	16,918	1,695,128	94	F4
*Laos	91,428	236,800	3,584,803	110	D3
Latvian S.S.R., U.S.S.R.	24,595	63,700	2,521,000	88	C3
*Lebanon	4,015	10,399	2,688,000	96	F6
*Lesotho	11,720	30,355	1,339,000	63	E7
*Liberia	43,000	111,370	2,220,000	60	B4
*Libya	679,358	1,759,537	3,356,000	60-61	D2
*Liechtenstein	61	158	26,130	81	E1
Lithuanian S.S.R., U.S.S.R.	25,174	65,200	3,398,000	88	B3
Louisiana, U.S.A.	47,752	123,678	4,206,098	150	
Loyalty Islands, New Caledonia	414	1,072	14,518	116	G8
*Luxembourg	999	2,587	364,606	73	H8
Macau, Portugal	6	16	261,680	140	E3
*Madagascar	226,657	587,041	9,400,000	63	G6-7
Madeira Islands, Portugal	307	796	262,800	76	A2
Maine, U.S.A.	33,265	86,156	1,125,030	151	
*Malawi	45,747	118,485	6,839,000	63	F6
Malaya, Malaysia	50,806	131,588	11,138,227	111	C7
*Malaysia	128,308	332,318	13,435,588	111	C6
				112	D5
*Maldives	115	298	173,000	93	F5
*Mali	464,873	1,204,021	7,719,000	60	B2
*Malta	122	316	360,000	79	E7
Man, Isle of, U.K.	227	588	66,000	67	D3
Manitoba, Canada	250,999	650,087	1,026,241	189	
Marquesas Islands, French Polynesia	492	1,274	5,419	117	N6
Marshall Islands	70	181	30,873	116	G4
Martinique, France	425	1,101	328,566	50	G4
				54-55	J
Maryland, U.S.A.	10,460	27,091	4,216,941	139	
Massachusetts, U.S.A.	8,284	21,456	5,737,081	136-137	
*Mauritania	419,229	1,085,803	1,681,000	60	A3
*Mauritius	790	2,046	993,000	35	M7
Mayotte, France	144	373	47,300	63	G6
McDonald Islands, Australia, see Heard & McDonald Islands					
*Mexico	761,601	1,972,546	67,395,826	46-47	
Michigan, U.S.A.	58,527	151,585	9,262,070	152	

Country	Area (Sq. Miles)	Area (Sq. Kilometers)	Population	Page No.	Index Ref.
*Micronesia, Fed. States of	271	702	73,755	116	F5
Midway Islands, U.S.A.	1.9	4.9	468	116	H3
Minnesota, U.S.A.	84,402	218,601	4,075,970	153	
Mississippi, U.S.A.	47,689	123,515	2,520,631	154	
Missouri, U.S.A.	69,697	180,515	4,916,759	155	
Moldavian S.S.R., U.S.S.R.	13,012	33,700	3,947,000	89	C5
Monaco	368 acres	149 hectares	27,063	75	G6
*Mongolia	606,163	1,569,962	1,732,000	104-105	C-E1
Montana, U.S.A.	147,046	380,849	786,690	156	
Montserrat, U.K.	40	104	12,073	51	G3
*Morocco	172,414	446,550	20,419,555	60	B1
*Mozambique	303,769	786,762	12,615,000	63	F6-7
Myanmar, see Burma					
*Namibia	317,827	823,172	1,009,000	62-63	D7
Natal, South Africa	33,578	86,967	5,722,215	63	F7
Nauru	7.7	20	7,254	116	G6
Navassa Island, U.S.A.	2	5	....	50	C3
Nebraska, U.S.A.	77,355	200,349	1,569,825	157	
*Nepal	54,663	141,577	15,022,839	102	D2
*Netherlands	15,892	41,160	14,529,430	72-73	
Netherlands Antilles	390	1,010	246,000	51	E4,F3
Nevada, U.S.A.	110,561	286,353	800,493	132-133	
New Brunswick, Canada	28,354	73,437	696,403	182	
New Caledonia & Dependencies, France	7,335	18,998	145,368	116	G8
Newfoundland, Canada	156,184	404,517	567,681	43	L5
New Hampshire, U.S.A.	9,279	24,033	920,610	158	
New Jersey, U.S.A.	7,787	20,168	7,365,011	159	
New Mexico, U.S.A.	121,593	314,926	1,303,445	135	
New South Wales, Australia	309,498	801,600	5,126,217	115	D4
New York, U.S.A.	49,108	127,190	17,558,072	160-161	
*New Zealand	103,736	268,676	3,307,084	115	F4
*Nicaragua	45,698	118,358	3,058,000	48	C2
*Niger	489,189	1,267,000	5,868,000	60	C3
*Nigeria	357,000	924,630	82,887,000	60	C4
Niue, New Zealand	100	259	3,578	117	K7
Norfolk Island, Australia	13.4	34.6	2,175	116	G8
North America	9,363,000	24,250,170	395,000,000	40-41	
North Carolina, U.S.A.	52,669	136,413	5,881,385	162-163	

Gazetteer–Index of the World

Country	Area (Sq. Miles)	(Sq. Kilometers)	Population	Page No.	Index Ref.
*North Dakota, U.S.A.	70,702	183,118	652,717	164	
Northern Ireland, U.K.	5,452	14,121	1,507,065	66	C3
Northern Marianas, U.S.A.	184	477	16,780	116	E4
Northern Territory, Australia	519,768	1,346,200	123,324	114	C3
*North Korea	46,540	120,539	18,317,000	106	C3
Northwest Territories, Canada	1,304,896	3,379,683	45,741	42-43	E-J2
*Norway	125,053	323,887	4,141,000	68-69	
Nova Scotia, Canada	21,425	55,491	847,442	182-183	
Oceania	3,292,000	8,526,280	23,000,000	116-117	
Ohio, U.S.A.	41,330	107,045	10,797,624	166-167	
Oklahoma, U.S.A.	69,956	181,186	3,025,495	168	
*Oman	120,000	310,800	919,000	95	H6
Ontario, Canada	412,580	1,068,582	8,625,107	186-187	
Orange Free State, S. Africa	49,866	129,153	1,833,216	63	E7
Oregon, U.S.A.	97,073	251,419	2,633,149	167	
Orkney Islands, Scotland	376	974	17,675	66	E1
*Pakistan	310,403	803,944	83,782,000	102	B-C1-2
Palau	188	487	12,116	116	D5
Palmyra Atoll, U.S.A.	3.85	10	...	117	K5
*Panama	29,761	77,082	1,830,175	49	D-E3
*Papua New Guinea	183,540	475,369	3,010,727	116	E6
Paracel Islands, China	...	...	...	112	E2
*Paraguay	157,047	406,752	3,026,165	58-59	D5
Pennsylvania, U.S.A.	45,308	117,348	11,864,751	170-171	
*Peru	496,222	1,285,215	17,031,221	56	B3-4
*Philippines	115,707	299,681	48,098,460	108-109	
Pitcairn Islands, U.K.	18	47	54	117	O8
*Poland	120,725	312,678	37,003,000	86-87	
*Portugal	35,549	92,072	9,883,014	76	
Prince Edward Island, Canada	2,184	5,657	122,506	183	D2
Puerto Rico, U.S.A.	3,515	9,104	3,196,520	51	E3
				54	D2
*Qatar	4,247	11,000	257,000	95	G4
Québec, Canada	594,857	1,540,680	6,438,403	184-185	
Queensland, Australia	666,872	1,727,200	2,295,123	115	D3
Réunion, France	969	2,510	515,814	35	L7
Rhode Island, U.S.A.	1,212	3,139	947,154	137	D3
Rhodesia, see Zimbabwe					
*Romania	91,699	237,500	22,553,074	84	C-D2

Country	Area (Sq. Miles)	Area (Sq. Kilometers)	Population	Page No.	Index Ref.
*Russian S.F.S.R., U.S.S.R.	6,592,812	17,075,400	137,551,000	88-91	
*Rwanda	10,169	26,337	5,046,000	63	F5
Sabah, Malaysia	29,300	75,887	1,002,608	112	F4
Saint Helena & Dependencies	162	420	5,147	35	J6
Saint Kitts and Nevis	104	269	44,404	51	F3
Saint Lucia	238	616	115,783	51	G4
Saint Pierre & Miquelon, France	93.5	242	6,041	43	L6
*Saint Vincent & the Grenadines	150	388	124,000	51	G4
				55	P
Sakhalin, U.S.S.R.	29,500	76,405	655,000	91	H3
San Marino	23.4	60.6	22,000	78	D3
*São Tomé & Príncipe	372	963	86,000	62	C4
Sarawak, Malaysia	48,202	124,843	1,294,753	112	E5
Sardinia, Italy	9,301	24,090	1,450,483	79	B4-5
Saskatchewan, Canada	251,699	651,900	968,313	188-189	
*Saudi Arabia	829,995	2,149,687	9,319,000	94	E-F4-5
Scotland, U.K.	30,414	78,772	5,117,146	66	D-E2-3
*Senegal	75,954	196,720	6,316,000	60	A3
*Seychelles	145	375	64,332	93	E6
Shetland Islands, Scotland	552	1,430	18,494	66	G1
Sicily, Italy	9,926	25,708	4,628,918	79	D-E6
*Sierra Leone	27,925	72,325	3,571,000	60	A4
*Singapore	226	585	2,413,945	111	E6
Society Islands, French Polynesia	677	1,753	117,703	117	L7
*Solomon Islands	11,500	29,785	285,796	116	G6
*Somalia	246,200	637,658	4,895,000	61	G4
*South Africa	455,318	1,179,274	23,385,645	63	E7-8
South America	6,875,000	17,806,250	263,000,000	56-59	
South Australia, Australia	379,922	984,000	1,285,033	114	C3
South Carolina, U.S.A.	31,113	80,583	3,122,814	162-163	
South Dakota, U.S.A.	77,116	199,730	690,768	165	
South Korea	38,175	98,873	37,448,836	106	C3
South-West Africa, see Namibia					
*Spain	194,881	504,742	37,746,260	76-77	
Spratly Island	...	...	....	112	E4
*Sri Lanka	25,332	65,610	14,848,369	104	D4

Gazetteer–Index of the World

Country	Area (Sq. Miles)	(Sq. Kilometers)	Population	Page No.	Index Ref.
*Sudan	967,494	2,505,809	20,564,364	61	E-F5
Sulawesi (Celebes), Indonesia	72,986	189,034	7,732,383	113	G6
Sumatra, Indonesia	164,000	424,760	19,360,400	112	B-C5-6
*Suriname	55,144	142,823	354,860	57	D2
Svalbard, Norway	23,957	62,049	3,431	68	A1
*Swaziland	6,705	17,366	605,000	63	F7
*Sweden	173,665	449,792	8,381,941	68-69	
*Switzerland	15,943	41,292	6,365,960	80-81	
*Syria	71,498	185,180	9,172,000	97	G-H5
Tadzhik S.S.R., U.S.S.R.	55,251	143,100	3,801,000	90	D4
Tahiti, French Polynesia	402	1,041	95,604	117	L7
Taiwan	13,971	36,185	18,029,798	105	F3
*Tanzania	363,708	942,003	21,015,000	63	F5
Tasmania, Australia	26,178	67,800	418,957	115	D5
Tennessee, U.S.A.	42,144	109,153	4,591,120	148-149	
Texas, U.S.A.	266,807	691,030	14,227,574	172-173	
*Thailand	198,455	513,998	44,278,000	110	C3
Tibet, China	463,320	1,200,000	1,790,000	104	B2
*Togo	21,622	56,000	2,702,945	60	C4
Tokelau, New Zealand	3.9	10	1,552	116	J6
Tonga	270	699	96,592	117	J8
Transkei, South Africa	16,910	43,797	2,000,000	63	E8
Transvaal, South Africa	109,621	283,918	10,673,033	63	E7
*Trinidad and Tobago	1,980	5,128	1,058,320	51	G5
Tristan da Cunha, Saint Helena	38	98	323	35	J7
Tuamotu Archipelago, French Polynesia	341	883	9,052	117	M7
*Tunisia	63,378	164,149	6,886,000	60	C1
*Turkey	300,946	779,450	51,420,757	96-97	
Turkmen S.S.R., U.S.S.R.	188,455	488,100	2,759,000	90	C4
Turks and Caicos Islands, U.K.	166	430	7,436	50-51	D-E2
Tuvalu	9.78	25.33	7,349	116	H6
*Uganda	91,076	235,887	12,630,076	61	F4
*Ukrainian S.S.R., U.S.S.R.	233,089	603,700	49,754,642	89	C-E5
*Union of Soviet Socialist Republics	8,649,490	22,402,179	280,000,000	88-91	
*United Arab Emirates	32,278	83,600	1,043,225	95	G5
*United Kingdom	94,399	244,493	55,638,495	66-67	

Country	Area (Sq. Miles)	Area (Sq. Kilometers)	Population	Page No.	Index Ref.
*United States of America	3,623,420	9,384,658	226,549,448	44-45, 126-127	
Upper Volta, see Burkina Faso					
*Uruguay	72,172	186,925	2,968,000	59	D6
Utah, U.S.A.	84,899	219,888	1,461,037	174	
Uzbek S.S.R., U.S.S.R.	173,591	449,600	15,391,000	90	D3
*Vanuatu	5,700	14,763	111,251	116	G7
Vatican City	108.7 acres	44 hectares	733	78	D4
Venda, South Africa	2,510	6,501	450,000	63	E7
*Venezuela	352,143	912,050	14,570,085	56	C2
Vermont, U.S.A.	9,614	24,900	511,456	158	
Victoria, Australia	87,876	227,600	3,832,443	115	D4
*Vietnam	128,405	332,569	52,741,766	110	D3
Virginia, U.S.A.	40,767	105,587	5,346,797	138-139	
Virgin Islands, British	59	153	12,000	51 54	H1 F
Virgin Islands, U.S.A.	132	342	96,569	51 54	H1 F-G
Wake Island, U.S.A.	2.5	6.5	302	116	G4
Wales, U.K.	8,017	20,764	2,790,462	67	E4
Wallis and Futuna, France	106	275	11,000	117	J7
Washington, U.S.A.	68,139	176,480	4,132,204	175	
West Bank	2,100	5,439	800,000	98-99	
Western Australia, Australia	975,096	2,525,500	1,273,624	114	B3
Western Sahara	102,703	266,000	165,000	60	A2
*Western Samoa	1,133	2,934	158,130	117	J7
West Germany, see Germany					
West Virginia, U.S.A.	24,231	62,758	1,950,258	138-139	
*White Russian S.S.R. (Byelorussian S.S.R.), U.S.S.R.	80,154	207,600	9,560,543	89	C4
Wisconsin, U.S.A.	56,153	145,436	4,705,642	176	
World (land)	57,970,000	150,142,300	4,763,000,000	34-35	
Wyoming, U.S.A.	97,809	253,325	469,557	177	
*Yemen	188,321	487,752	8,681,189	94	D6
*Yugoslavia	98,766	255,804	23,018,000	84	B2
Yukon Territory, Canada	207,075	536,324	23,153	42	C3
*Zaire	905,063	2,344,133	30,261,000	63	E5
*Zambia	290,586	752,618	5,679,808	63	E6
*Zimbabwe	150,803	390,580	7,539,000	63	E-F6

LANGUAGES. *Several hundred different languages are spoken in the World, and in many places two or more languages are spoken, sometimes by the same people. The map above shows the dominant languages in each*

Russian

other Indo-European languages

itic & Hamitic Languages

Copyright by C. S. HAMMOND & CO., N. Y.

locality. English, French, Spanish, Russian, Arabic and Swahili are spoken by
many people as a second language for commerce or travel.

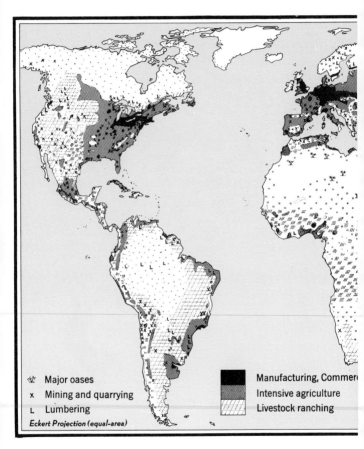

☼ Major oases	Manufacturing, Commer...
x Mining and quarrying	Intensive agriculture
L Lumbering	Livestock ranching

Eckert Projection (equal-area)

OCCUPATIONS. *Correlation with the density of population shows that the most densely populated areas fall into the regions of manufacturing and intensive farming. All other economies require considerable space. The most*

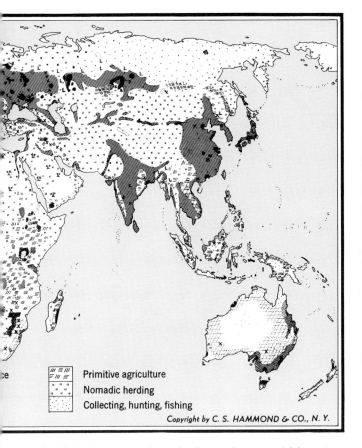

///≡/// *≡///≡* *///≡///*	Primitive agriculture
" " " *" " "* *" " "*	Nomadic herding
.·.·.·.·	Collecting, hunting, fishing

Copyright by C. S. HAMMOND & CO., N. Y.

sparsely inhabited areas are those of collecting, hunting and fishing. Areas with practically no habitation are left blank.

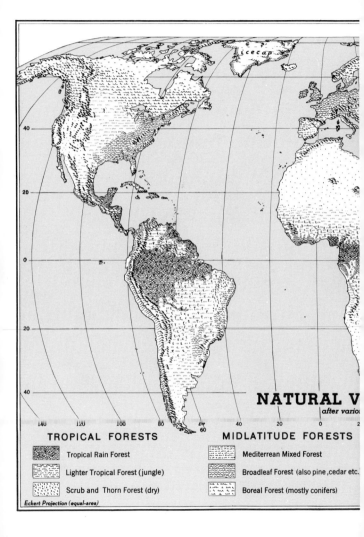

NATURAL V
after vario

TROPICAL FORESTS

Tropical Rain Forest

Lighter Tropical Forest (jungle)

Scrub and Thorn Forest (dry)

Eckert Projection (equal-area)

MIDLATITUDE FORESTS

Mediterrean Mixed Forest

Broadleaf Forest (also pine ,cedar etc.)

Boreal Forest (mostly conifers)

icecap

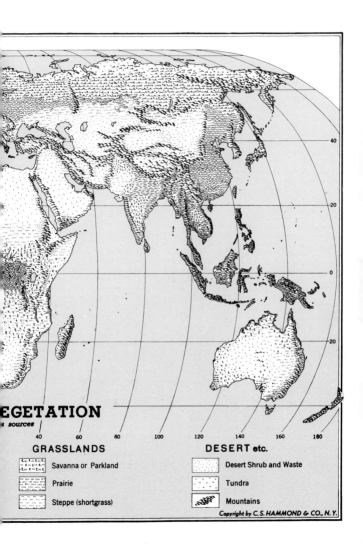

EGETATION

s sources

40 60 80 100 120 140 160 180

GRASSLANDS

Savanna or Parkland

Prairie

Steppe (shortgrass)

DESERT etc.

Desert Shrub and Waste

Tundra

Mountains

Copyright by C. S. HAMMOND & CO., N. Y.

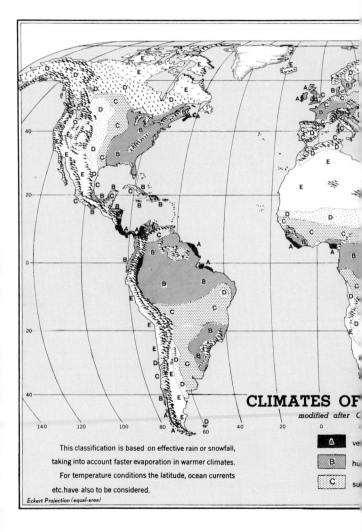

CLIMATES OF

modified after C

This classification is based on effective rain or snowfall,
taking into account faster evaporation in warmer climates.
For temperature conditions the latitude, ocean currents
etc. have also to be considered.

Eckert Projection (equal-area)

A ve

B hu

C su

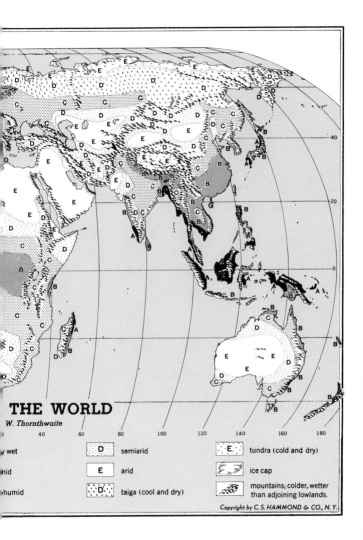

THE WORLD

W. Thornthwaite

40 60 80 100 120 140 160 180

wet	D semiarid	E tundra (cold and dry)
mid	E arid	ice cap
humid	D taiga (cool and dry)	mountains; colder, wetter than adjoining lowlands.

Copyright by C.S. HAMMOND & CO., N.Y.

World–Time Zones

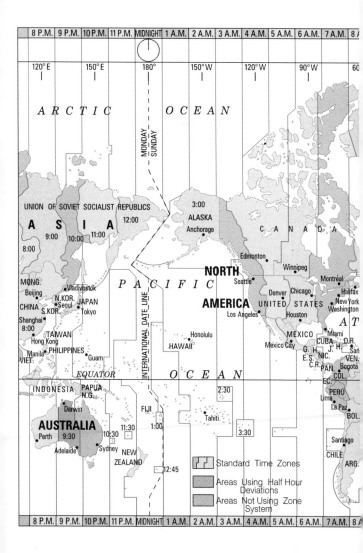

WORLD TIME ZONES

Air Distances Between Major World Cities (in miles)

	Beijing	Cairo	Cape Town	Chicago	Hong Kong	Honolulu	London	Madrid
Amsterdam	4890	2015	5997	4118	5772	7254	222	9
Athens	4757	671	4957	5447	5316	8353	1488	14
Bangkok	2027	4521	6301	8569	1076	6610	5929	63
Beijing	—	4687	8034	6625	1195	5084	5089	57
Buenos Aires ...	11,994	7360	4285	5582	11,478	7554	6907	62
Cairo	4687	—	4510	6116	5057	8818	2158	20
Cape Town	8034	4510	—	8489	7377	11,534	5988	53
Chicago	6625	6116	8489	—	7797	4256	3960	41
Denver	6385	6846	9331	920	7476	3346	4701	50
Frankfurt	4567	1730	5944	4460	5403	7341	628	11
Hong Kong	1195	5057	7377	7797	—	5557	5986	65
Honolulu	5084	8818	11,534	4256	5557	—	7241	78
Houston	7244	7005	8608	942	8349	3902	4860	50
Lisbon	6040	2352	5301	4001	6862	7835	989	3
London	5089	2158	5988	3960	5986	7241	—	7
Los Angeles	6255	7522	9981	1750	7217	2565	5454	58
Madrid	5759	2069	5306	4192	6556	7874	786	—
Melbourne	5632	8700	6428	9667	4605	5501	10,508	10,7
Mexico City	7772	7677	8516	1688	8789	3791	5558	56
Montréal	6541	5403	7920	746	7736	4919	3256	34
Moscow	3627	1770	6277	4984	4443	7049	1556	21
New Delhi	2350	2752	5769	7486	2339	7413	4178	45
New York	6867	5598	7801	714	8061	4969	3473	35
Paris	5138	1973	5782	4145	5992	7452	215	6
Rio de Janeiro ..	10,778	6153	3773	5288	11,002	8295	5751	50
Rome	5076	1305	5231	4823	5773	8040	892	8
San Francisco ..	5934	7436	10,248	1860	6904	2397	5369	58
Seattle	5432	6809	10,205	1737	6481	2681	4799	53
Singapore	2754	5143	6007	9376	1608	6728	6747	70
Stockholm	4197	2084	6422	4288	5115	6873	892	16
Tokyo	1305	5937	9155	6313	1792	3860	5956	67
Washington, D.C.	6965	5800	7892	594	8157	4839	3676	37

Melbourne	Mexico City	Moscow	New Delhi	New York	Paris	Rio de Janeiro	Rome	San Francisco	Tokyo
0,286	5735	1337	3958	3654	271	5938	807	5465	5788
9297	7021	1387	3120	4938	1305	6030	654	6792	5924
4579	9793	4394	1812	8669	5877	9987	5493	7930	2865
5632	7772	3627	2350	6867	5138	10,778	5076	5934	1305
7219	4580	8369	9823	5279	6857	1231	6925	6455	11,411
8700	7677	1770	2752	5598	1973	6153	1305	7436	5937
6428	8516	6277	5769	7801	5782	3773	5231	10,248	9155
9667	1688	4984	7486	714	4145	5288	4823	1860	6313
8755	1438	5501	7730	1631	4900	5866	5887	953	5815
9882	6127	961	3550	4028	589	6237	729	5709	5533
4605	8789	4443	2339	8061	5992	11,002	5773	6904	1792
5501	3791	7049	7413	4969	7452	8295	8040	2397	3860
8979	749	5925	8388	1419	5035	5015	5702	1648	6685
1,049	5396	2433	4844	3377	904	4777	1163	5679	6943
0,508	5558	1556	4178	3437	215	5751	892	5369	5956
7928	1566	6036	7015	2455	5661	6334	6336	349	5476
0,766	5642	2140	4528	3596	652	5045	849	5806	6704
—	8420	8965	6340	10,352	10,442	8218	9940	7850	5070
8420	—	6671	9119	2086	5723	4769	6374	1889	7036
0,390	2315	4397	7012	333	3432	5082	4102	2544	6470
8965	6671	—	2703	4680	1550	7162	1477	5884	4663
6340	9119	2703	—	7319	4103	8747	3684	7691	3638
0,352	2086	4680	7319	—	3638	4805	4293	2574	6757
0,442	5723	1550	4103	3638	—	5681	688	5579	6054
8218	4769	7162	8747	4805	5681	—	5704	6621	11,535
9940	6374	1477	3684	4293	688	5704	—	6259	6140
7850	1889	5884	7691	2574	5579	6621	6259	—	5148
8176	2340	5217	7046	2409	5012	6890	5680	679	4793
3767	10,331	5236	2574	9539	6676	9776	6231	8449	3304
9693	5965	764	3466	3939	964	6638	1229	5372	5091
5070	7036	4663	3638	6757	6054	11,535	6140	5148	—
0,174	1883	4873	7500	203	3841	4783	4496	2444	6792

World Statistics

The Continents

Area in:

	Sq. Miles	Sq. Km.	Percent of World's Land
Asia	17,128,500	44,362,815	29.5
Africa	11,707,000	30,321,130	20.2
North America	9,363,000	24,250,170	16.2
South America	6,875,000	17,806,250	11.8
Antarctica	5,500,000	14,245,000	9.5
Europe	4,057,000	10,507,630	7.0
Australia	2,966,136	7,682,300	5.1

Oceans and Major Seas

	Area in:		Greatest Depth in:	
	Sq. Miles	Sq. Km.	Feet	Meters
Pacific Ocean	64,186,000	166,241,700	36,198	11,033
Atlantic Ocean	31,862,000	82,522,600	28,374	8,648
Indian Ocean	28,350,000	73,426,500	25,344	7,725
Arctic Ocean	5,427,000	14,056,000	17,880	5,450
Caribbean Sea	970,000	2,512,300	24,720	7,535
Mediterranean Sea	969,000	2,509,700	16,896	5,150
Bering Sea	875,000	2,266,250	15,800	4,800
Gulf of Mexico	600,000	1,554,000	12,300	3,750
Sea of Okhotsk	590,000	1,528,100	11,070	3,370
East China Sea	482,000	1,248,400	9,500	2,900
Sea of Japan	389,000	1,007,500	12,280	3,740
Hudson Bay	317,500	822,300	846	258
North Sea	222,000	575,000	2,200	670
Black Sea	185,000	479,150	7,365	2,245
Red Sea	169,000	437,700	7,200	2,195
Baltic Sea	163,000	422,170	1,506	459

Dimensions of the Earth

	Area in Sq. Miles	Sq. Kilometers
Superficial area	196,939,000	510,073,000
Land surface	57,506,000	148,941,000
Water surface	139,433,000	361,132,000

	Miles	Kilometers
Equatorial circumference	24,902	40,075
Polar circumference	24,860	40,007
Equatorial diameter	7,926.68	12,756.4
Polar diameter	7,899.99	12,713.4
Equatorial radius	3,963.34	6,378.2
Polar radius	3,949.99	6,356.7

Maximum distance from Sun	94,600,000 miles	152,000,000 kilometers
Minimum distance from Sun	91,300,000 miles	147,000,000 kilometers

Principal Mountains of the World

	ft./m		ft./m
Everest, Nepal-China	29,028/8,848	Huila, Colombia	18,865/5,750
Godwin Austen (K2),		Citlaltépetl (Orizaba),	
Pakistan-China	28,250/8,611	Mexico	18,855/5,747
Kanchenjunga, Nepal-India	28,208/8,598	El'brus, U.S.S.R.	18,510/5,642
Lhotse, Nepal-China	27,923/8,511	Damavand, Iran	18,376/5,601
Makalu, Nepal-China	27,824/8,481	St. Elias, Alaska-Canada	
Dhaulagiri, Nepal	26,810/8,172	(Yukon)	18,008/5,489
Nanga Parbat, Pakistan	26,660/8,126	Vilcanota, Peru	17,999/5,486
Annapurna, Nepal	26,504/8,078	Popocatépetl, Mexico	17,887/5,452
Gasherbrum, Pakistan-		Dykhtau, U.S.S.R.	17,070/5,203
China	26,740/8,068	Kenya, Kenya	17,058/5,199
Nanda Devi, India	25,645/7,817	Ararat, Turkey	16,946/5,165
Rakaposhi, Pakistan	25,500/7,788	Vinson Massif, Antarctica	16,864/5,140
Kamet, India	25,447/7,756	Margherita (Ruwenzori),	
Gurla Mandhada, China	25,355/7,728	Africa	16,795/5,119
Kongur Shan, China	25,325/7,719	Kazbek, U.S.S.R.	16,512/5,033
Tirich Mir, Pakistan	25,230/7,690	Puncak Jaya, Indonesia	16,503/5,030
Gongga Shan, China	24,790/7,556	Tyree, Antarctica	16,289/4,965
Muztagata, China	24,757/7,546	Blanc, France	15,771/4,807
Communism Peak,		Klyuchevskaya Sopka,	
U.S.S.R.	24,599/7,498	U.S.S.R.	15,584/4,750
Pobeda Peak, U.S.S.R.	24,406/7,439	Dufourspitze (Mte. Rosa),	
Chomo Lhari, Bhutan-		Italy-Switzerland	15,203/4,634
China	23,997/7,314	Ras Dashan, Ethiopia	15,157/4,620
Muztag, China	23,891/7,282	Matterhorn, Switzerland	14,691/4,478
Cerro Aconcagua,		Whitney, California,	
Argentina	22,831/6,959	U.S.A.	14,494/4,418
Ojos del Salado, Chile-		Elbert, Colorado, U.S.A.	14,433/4,399
Argentina	22,572/6,880	Rainier, Washington,	
Bonete, Chile-Argentina	22,541/6,870	U.S.A.	14,410/4,392
Tupungato, Chile-		Shasta, California, U.S.A.	14,162/4,350
Argentina	22,310/6,800	Pikes Peak, Colorado,	
Pissis, Argentina	22,241/6,779	U.S.A.	14,110/4,301
Mercedario, Argentina	22,211/6,770	Finsteraarhorn,	
Huascarán, Peru	22,205/6,768	Switzerland	14,022/4,274
Llullaillaco, Chile-		Mauna Kea, Hawaii,	
Argentina	22,057/6,723	U.S.A.	13,796/4,205
Nevada Ancohuma, Bolivia	21,489/6,550	Mauna Loa, Hawaii,	
Illampu, Bolivia	21,276/6,485	U.S.A.	13,677/4,169
Chimborazo, Ecuador	20,561/6,267	Jungfrau, Switzerland	13,642/4,158
McKinley, Alaska	20,320/6,194	Cameroon, Cameroon	13,350/4,069
Logan, Canada (Yukon)	19,524/5,951	Grossglockner, Austria	12,457/3,797
Cotopaxi, Ecuador	19,347/5,897	Fuji, Japan	12,389/3,776
Kilimanjaro, Tanzania	19,340/5,895	Cook, New Zealand	12,349/3,764
El Misti, Peru	19,101/5,822	Etna, Italy	11,053/3,369
Pico Cristóbal Colón,		Kosciusko, Australia	7,310/2,228
Colombia	19,029/5,800	Mitchell, North Carolina,	
		U.S.A.	6,684/2,037

World Statistics

Longest Rivers of the World

River	Length: mi./kms.	River	Length: mi./kms.
Nile, Africa	4,145/6,671	Orinoco, S. Amer.	1,600/2,575
Amazon, S. Amer.	3,915/6,300	Zambezi, Africa	1,600/2,575
Chang Jiang (Yangtze), China	3,900/6,276	Paraguay, S. Amer.	1,584/2,549
Mississippi-Missouri-Red Rock, U.S.A.	3,741/6,019	Kolyma, U.S.S.R.	1,562/2,514
		Ganges, Asia	1,550/2,494
Ob'Irtysh-Black Irtysh, U.S.S.R.	3,362/5,411	Ural, U.S.S.R.	1,509/2,428
Yenisey-Angara, U.S.S.R.	3,100/4,989	Japurá, S. Amer.	1,500/2,414
Huang He (Yellow), China	2,877/4,630	Arkansas, U.S.A.	1,450/2,334
Amur-Shilka-Onon, Asia	2,744/4,416	Colorado, U.S.A.-Mexico	1,450/2,334
Lena, U.S.S.R.	2,734/4,400	Negro, S. Amer.	1,400/2,253
Congo (Zaire), Africa	2,718/4,374	Dnieper, U.S.S.R.	1,368/2,202
Mackenzie-Peace-Finlay, Canada	2,635/4,241	Orange, Africa	1,350/2,173
Mekong, Asia	2,610/4,200	Irrawaddy, Burma	1,325/2,132
Missouri-Red Rock, U.S.A.	2,564/4,125	Brazos, U.S.A.	1,309/2,107
Niger, Africa	2,548/4,101	Ohio-Allegheny, U.S.A.	1,306/2,102
Paraná-La Plata, S. Amer.	2,450/3,943	Kama, U.S.S.R.	1,262/2,031
Mississippi, U.S.A.	2,348/3,778	Red, U.S.A.	1,222/1,966
Murray-Darling, Australia	2,310/3,718	Don, U.S.S.R.	1,222/1,967
Volga, U.S.S.R.	2,194/3,531	Columbia, U.S.A.-Canada	1,214/1,953
Madeira, S. Amer.	2,013/3,240	Saskatchewan, Canada	1,205/1,939
Purus, S. Amer.	1,995/3,211	Peace-Finlay, Canada	1,195/1,923
Yukon, Alaska-Canada	1,979/3,185	Tigris, Asia	1,181/1,901
St. Lawrence, Canada-U.S.A.	1,900/3,058	Darling, Australia	1,160/1,867
Rio Grande, Mexico-U.S.A.	1,885/3,034	Angara, U.S.S.R.	1,135/1,827
Syrdar'ya-Naryn, U.S.S.R.	1,859/2,992	Sungari, Asia	1,130/1,819
São Francisco, Brazil	1,811/2,914	Pechora, U.S.S.R.	1,124/1,809
Indus, Asia	1,800/2,897	Snake, U.S.A.	1,000/1,609
Danube, Europe	1,775/2,857	Churchill, Canada	1,000/1,609
Salween, Asia	1,770/2,849	Pilcomayo, S. Amer.	1,000/1,609
Brahmaputra, Asia	1,700/2,736	Magdalena, Colombia	1,000/1,609
Euphrates, Asia	1,700/2,736	Uruguay, S. Amer.	994/1,600
Tocantins, Brazil	1,677/2,699	Platte-N. Platte, U.S.A.	990/1,593
Xi (Si), China	1,650/2,655	Ohio, U.S.A.	981/1,578
Amudar'ya, Asia	1,616/2,601	Pecos, U.S.A.	926/1,490
Nelson-Saskatchewan, Canada	1,600/2,575	Oka, U.S.S.R.	918/1,477
		Canadian, U.S.A.	906/1,458
		Colorado, Texas, U.S.A.	894/1,439
		Dniester, U.S.S.R.	876/1,410

Largest Islands

	Area in:	
	Sq. Mi.	Sq. Km.
Greenland	840,000	2,175,600
New Guinea	305,000	789,950
Borneo	290,000	751,100
Madagascar	226,400	586,376
Baffin, Canada	195,928	507,454
Sumatra, Indonesia	164,000	424,760
Honshu, Japan	88,000	227,920
Great Britain	84,400	218,896
Victoria, Canada	83,896	217,290
Ellesmere, Canada	75,767	196,236
Celebes, Indonesia	72,986	189,034
South I., New Zealand	58,393	151,238
Java, Indonesia	48,842	126,501
North I., New Zealand	44,187	114,444
Newfoundland, Canada	42,031	108,860
Cuba	40,533	104,981
Luzon, Philippines	40,420	104,688
Iceland	39,768	103,000
Mindanao, Philippines	36,537	94,631
Ireland	31,743	82,214
Sakhalin, U.S.S.R.	29,500	76,405
Hispaniola, Haiti & Dom. Rep.	29,399	76,143
Hokkaido, Japan	28,983	75,066
Banks, Canada	27,038	70,028
Ceylon, Sri Lanka	25,332	65,610
Tasmania, Australia	24,600	63,710
Devon, Canada	21,331	55,247
Novaya Zemlya (north isl.), U.S.S.R.	18,600	48,200
Marajó, Brazil	17,991	46,597
Tierra del Fuego, Chile & Argentina	17,900	46,360
Alexander, Antarctica	16,700	43,250

Principal Natural Lakes

	Area in:		Max. Depth in:	
	Sq. Miles	Sq. Km.	Feet	Meters
Caspian Sea, U.S.S.R.-Iran	143,243	370,999	3,264	995
Lake Superior, U.S.A.-Canada	31,820	82,414	1,329	405
Lake Victoria, Africa	26,724	69,215	270	82
Lake Huron, U.S.A.-Canada	23,010	59,596	748	228
Lake Michigan, U.S.A.	22,400	58,016	923	281
Aral Sea, U.S.S.R.	15,830	41,000	213	65
Lake Tanganyika, Africa	12,650	32,764	4,700	1,433
Lake Baykal, U.S.S.R.	12,162	31,500	5,316	1,620
Great Bear Lake, Canada	12,096	31,328	1,356	413
Lake Nyasa (Malawi), Africa	11,555	29,928	2,320	707
Great Slave Lake, Canada	11,031	28,570	2,015	614
Lake Erie, U.S.A.-Canada	9,940	25,745	210	64
Lake Winnipeg, Canada	9,417	24,390	60	18
Lake Ontario, U.S.A.-Canada	7,540	19,529	775	244
Lake Ladoga, U.S.S.R.	7,104	18,399	738	225
Lake Balkhash, U.S.S.R.	7,027	18,200	87	27
Lake Maracaibo, Venezuela	5,120	13,261	100	31
Lake Chad, Africa	4,000-10,000	10,360-25,900	25	8
Lake Onega, U.S.S.R.	3,710	9,609	377	115
Lake Eyre, Australia	3,500-0	9,000-0	—	—
Lake Titicaca, Peru-Bolivia	3,200	8,288	1,000	305
Lake Nicaragua, Nicaragua	3,100	8,029	230	70
Lake Athabasca, Canada	3,064	7,936	400	122
Reindeer Lake, Canada	2,568	6,651	—	—
Lake Turkana (Rudolf), Africa	2,463	6,379	240	73
Issyk-Kul', U.S.S.R.	2,425	6,281	2,303	702
Lake Torrens, Australia	2,230	5,776	—	—
Vänern, Sweden	2,156	5,584	328	100
Nettilling Lake, Canada	2,140	5,543	—	—
Lake Winnipegosis, Canada	2,075	5,374	38	12
Lake Mobutu Sese Seko (Albert), Africa	2,075	5,374	160	49
Kariba Lake, Zambia-Zimbabwe	2,050	5,310	295	90
Lake Nipigon, Canada	1,872	4,848	540	165
Lake Mweru, Zaire-Zambia	1,800	4,662	60	18
Lake Manitoba, Canada	1,799	4,659	12	4
Lake Taymyr, U.S.S.R.	1,737	4,499	85	26
Lake Khanka, China-U.S.S.R.	1,700	4,403	33	10
Lake Kioga, Uganda	1,700	4,403	25	8

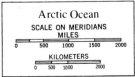

Arctic Ocean

SCALE ON MERIDIANS
MILES

0   500   1000   1500   2000

KILOMETERS

0   500   1000   2000

World–Political

A 120° B 150° C 180° D 150° E 120° F

1

80°

ARCTIC
OCEAN

SEVERNAYA
ZEMLYA

C. Chelyuskin

LAPTEV
SEA

NEW
SIBERIAN ISLANDS

EAST
SIBERIAN SEA

Nordvik

SVERDRU

Pr. Patrick I.

QUEEN ELIZA

McClure St.
Banks

Melville I.
Parry

Pt. Barrow

BEAUFORT
SEA

Amundsen G.

Victoria
I.

2

60°

Arctic Circle

Srednekolymsk

Lena

UNION OF SOVIET

Yakutsk

Magadan

Anadyr

UNITED STATES

Nome Yukon

Fairbanks ALASKA
Anchorage

Gt.
Bear L.

NORT

Gt.
Slave L.

CAN

SOCIALIST REPUBLICS

Krasnoyarsk
Irkutsk

Khabarovsk

SEA OF
OKHOTSK

BERING SEA

Juneau

G. of
Alaska

AMER

Edmonton

Vancouver
Seattle

Ulaanbaatar
MONGOLIA

Amur

Sakhalin
Island

Kuril Is.

ALEUTIAN IS.

Minneapolis
Chi

GOBI

Shenyang

Sea of
Japan

NORTH

Denver

UNITED S.

40°

CHINA

Beijing

Nanjing

KOR

JAPAN

San Francisco

Chongqing

Tianjin

Osaka

Tokyo

PACIFIC

Los Angeles

Housto

Lhasa

Shanghai

Taipei

East
China
Sea

Tropic of Cancer

Midway Is. (U.S.)

HAWAIIAN IS.

Mexico
City

20°

BURMA

Guangzhou

Taiwan (Formosa)

U.S.
HAWAII

Honolulu

CENTRA

HONG KONG
(U.K.)

NORTHERN
MARIANAS
(U.S.)

Wake I.
(U.S.)

AMER

Rangoon

PHILIPPINES

Bangkok

South
China
Sea

Manila

Guam
(U.S.)

MARSHALL
IS.

Ho Chi Minh
City

MALAYSIA

Borneo

FED. STATES
OF MICRONESIA

Equator

Kiritimati

0°

6

SINGAPORE

Celebes

Jakarta

INDONESIA

Java

New Guinea

PAPUA
NEW
GUINEA

NAURU

SOLOMON
IS.

TUVALU

KIRIBATI

SOUTH

Galápa
(E

20°

INDIAN

Darwin

CORAL SEA

VANUATU

SAMOA Samoa

FIJI

New
Caledonia
(Fr.)

TONGA

Society Is.
(Fr.)

Marquesas Is.
(Fr.)

Tahiti

TUAMOTU
ARCH.

PACIFI

OCEAN

Townsville

AUSTRALIA

Brisbane

Tropic of Capricorn

Easter I.
(Chile)

7

Perth

Adelaide

Sydney
Canberra

TASMAN
SEA

Melbourne

Auckland

OCEAN

40°

Tasmania

Hobart

NEW
ZEALAND

Wellington

N

8

60°

Longitude East of Greenwich

Longitude West of Greenwich

A 120° B 150° C 180° D 150° E 120° F

World–Political

MERCATOR PROJECTION

Capitals of Countries............. ●

The dramatic map above is a photograph of a sculptured
three-dimensional terrain model. In addition to depicting
traditional landforms, the model also includes canyons,
trenches, rises and ridges of ocean floor topography.

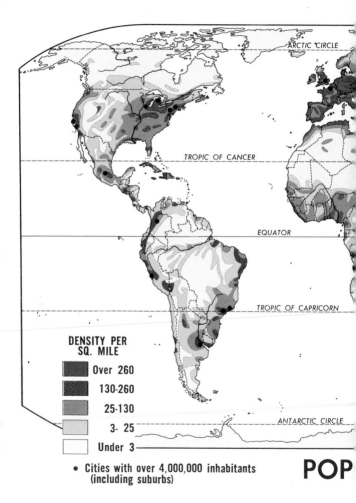

ARCTIC CIRCLE

TROPIC OF CANCER

EQUATOR

TROPIC OF CAPRICORN

DENSITY PER
SQ. MILE

Over 260

130-260

25-130

3- 25

Under 3

ANTARCTIC CIRCLE

• Cities with over 4,000,000 inhabitants
(including suburbs)

POP

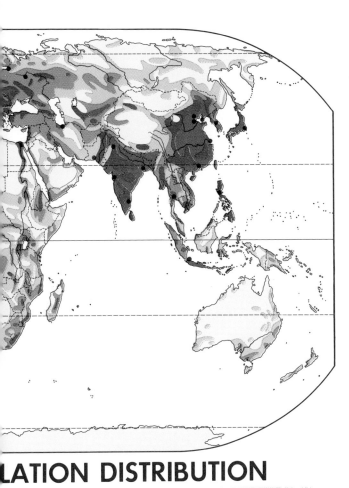

LATION DISTRIBUTION

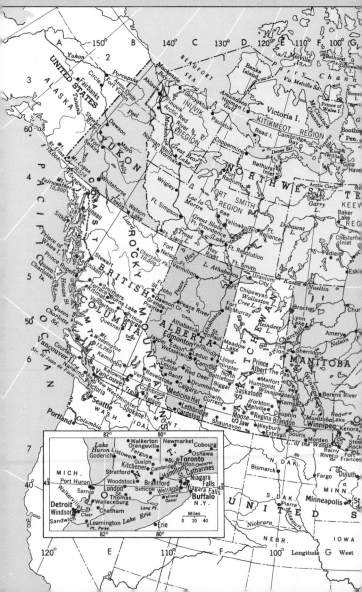

A 125° B 120° C 115° D 110° E 105° F 100°

P A C I F I C   O C E A N

Vancouver I.
Juan de Fuca Str.
C. Flattery
Vancouver
Victoria
Bellingham
Everett
Seattle
Tacoma
Olympia
WASHINGTON
Yakima
Richland
Spokane
Coeur
d'Alene
Kalispell

Calgary
Lethbridge
Medicine Hat
Saskatchewan
Moose
Jaw
Regina
Saskatoon
L.
Winnipegosis
Lake
Manitoba
Brandon
Winnip

C A N A D A

Portland
Salem
Corvallis
Eugene
Coos
Bay
Grants Pass
Medford
Klamath Falls
The
Dalles
La Grande
Pendleton
Walla Walla
Baker
Bend
OREGON
Columbia
Lewiston
Snake

Havre
Ft. Peck
Res.
Missouri
Great Falls
Helena
MONTANA
Butte
Anaconda
Bozeman
Yellowstone
Livingston
Billings
Miles
City
Sheridan

Sakakawea
Williston
Minot
Devils
Lake
NORTH
DAKOTA
Dickinson
Bismarck
Jamestown
Fa
L. Oahe
Aberde
SOUTH
DAKOTA
Lead
Rapid
City
Wat
Pierre
Mitch
Sioux

Eureka
Redding
Marysville
Richmond
San
Francisco
Oakland
San Jose
Sacramento
Stockton
Fresno
IDAHO
Boise
Nampa
Arco
Idaho
Falls
Twin
Falls
Burley
Pocatello
Snake
Logan
Ogden
Salt Lake City
Provo
WYOMING
Lander
Casper
Rock
Springs
North Platte
Rawlins
Laramie
Cheyenne
Fort
Collins
Boulder
Scotts-
bluff
NEBRASKA
North
Platte
Grand
Island
Kearney
Hasting
South Platte
Fre
Norfo

Winnemucca
Reno
Sparks
Carson City
NEVADA
Elko
Tooele
Great
Salt
Lake
Ely
UTAH
Price
Green
Colorado
Grand
Junction
COLORADO
Denver
Colorado
Springs
Pueblo
La Junta
Arkansas
Salina
KANSAS
Hutchinson
Dodge
City
Arkans
City

S I E R R A   N E V A D A
C A L I F O R N I A

San Luis
Obispo
Santa
Barbara
Pt.
Conception
Los Angeles
SANTA
BARBARA
IS.
Glendale
Pasadena
San
Bernardino
Long Beach
San Diego

Tonopah
Goldfield
Las
Vegas
Cedar
City
St. George
Lake
Mead
Lake
Powell
Durango
Grand
Canyon
Trinidad
Raton
Los Alamos
Santa
Fe
Gallup
Albuquerque
Las Vegas
Tucumcari
Amarillo
Flagstaff
Prescott
ARIZONA
Phoenix
Mesa
Globe
NEW MEXICO
Clovis
Roswell
Hobbs
Lubbock
Oklahoma
City
OKLA
Lawton
Wichita Falls
Denis
Enid
Abilene
Fort Worth

Tijuana
Yuma
Brawley
Lower
California
Colorado
Tucson
Nogales
Douglas
Heroica Nogales
Silver City
Las
Cruces
El Paso
Carlsbad
San Angelo
San Antc
TEXAS
Waco
Tem.
Austin

M E X I C O
Rio Grande
Ciudad
Juárez
Del Rio
Piedras
Negras
Nuevo
Laredo
Laredo
Falcon
Res.
Corpus
Christi
Matamoros
Ciudad
Victoria

INSET — ALASKA
U.S.S.R.
ARCTIC OCEAN
Barrow
148° 132°
Colville
Brooks Range
Inuvik
MILES
250
KILOM.
250
Kotzebue
Arctic Circle
Ft. Yukon
Fairbanks
Bering Str.
Anadyr
Nome
Unalakleet
A L A S K A
CANADA
Yukon
Mt. McKinley
20,320
Bethel
Anchorage
Cordova
Whitehorse
Bering
Sea
56°
Dillingham
Seward
Juneau
Kodiak
Ketchikan
Aleutian Is.
164°
180°
Aleutian Is.
80°

INSET — HAWAII
160° Kauai 158°
Lihue
Niihau
Oahu
Wahiawa
Honolulu
Molokai
Lanai
Wailuku
Kahoolawe
Maui
Halaula
H A W A I I
Kona
Mauna Loa
Hawaii
Hilo
Pahala
20°
PACIFIC
OCEAN
MILES
0 40 80
160° 158° 156°

United States
POLYCONIC PROJECTION
SCALE OF MILES
0   100   200   300   400
SCALE OF KILOMETERS
0   100   200   300   400
Capitals of Countries _____ ⊛   State Capitals _____ ◉
International Boundaries _____   State Boundaries___ _
Copyright by C. S. HAMMOND & Co., N.Y.

Mexico

Scale reference	
Mexico	
CONIC PROJECTION	

SCALE OF MILES
0   100   200   300

SCALE OF KILOMETERS
0   100   200   300

National Capitals.....☆   State Capitals.....◉

® Copyright HAMMOND INCORPORATED, Maplewood, N.J.

States Indicated by Numbers:

1	Tlaxcala	6	Querétaro
2	Morelos	7	Guanajuato
3	Distrito Federal	8	Aguascalientes
4	México	9	Nayarit
5	Hidalgo	10	Colima

IS. REVILLAGIGEDO
(Colima)

● I. S. Benedicto
● I. Socorro

Central America

Copyright by C. S. HAMMOND & Co., N.Y.

Central America

CONIC PROJECTION

SCALE OF MILES

0 25 50   100   150

SCALE OF KILOMETERS

0 25 50   100   150

Capitals of Countries _ _ _ _ _ ⊛

International Boundaries _ . _ . _

Canals _ _ _ _ _ _ _ _ _

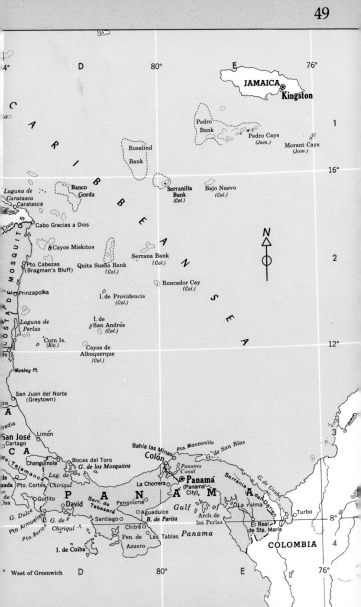

4° D 80° E 76°

C A R I B B E A N

JAMAICA
Kingston

Pedro
Bank

Pedro Cays
(Jam.)

Morant Cays
(Jam.)

1

16°

Rosalind
Bank

Laguna de
Caratasca
Caratasca

Banco
Gorda

Serranilla
Bank
(Col.)

Bajo Nuevo
(Col.)

Coco

Cabo Gracias a Dios

Cayos Miskitos

Serrana Bank
(Col.)

N

2

COSTA DE MOSQUITOS

Pto. Cabezas
(Bragman's Bluff)

Quita Sueño Bank
(Col.)

Roncador Cay
(Col.)

S

Prinzapolka

I. de Providencia
(Col.)

E

Laguna de
Perlas

I. de
San Andrés
(Col.)

A

Corn Is.
(Nic.)

Cayos de
Albuquerque
(Col.)

12°

Monkey Pt.

San Juan del Norte
(Greytown)

A

redia

Limón

San José
Cartago

C A

G. de San Blas

3

de Talamanca

Bocas del Toro
G. de los Mosquitos

Bahía las Minas
Colón

Pta. Manzanillo

G. de Urabá

ada

Pto. Cortés

Changuinola

Chiriquí

Lag. de

Panama
Canal

P A N A M Á

La Chorrera

Panamá
(Panama
City)

Serranía de Darién

Golfito

David

Serr. de
Tabasará

Peñonomé

A M A

G. Dulce

Aguadulce

Gulf of

La Palma

Turbo

Pto. Armuelles

G. de
Chiriquí

Santiago

Chitré
B. de Parita

Arch. de
las Perlas

El Real
de Sta. María

8°

Pta. Burica

I. de Coiba

Pen. de
Azuero

Las Tablas

Panama

COLOMBIA

4

West of Greenwich D 80° E 76°

West Indies

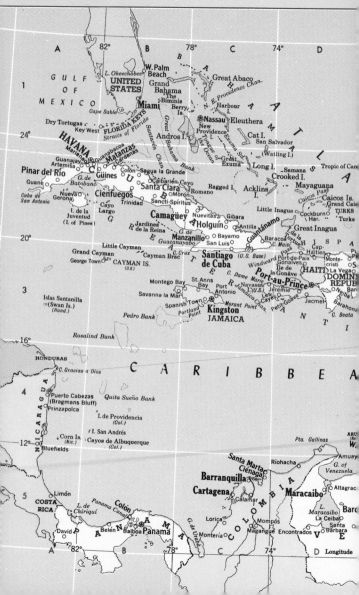

Cuba, Hispaniola & Jamaica

A B C D E

84° 83° 82° Tropic of Cancer 81°

1

23° GULF OF MEXICO

Cay Sal Bank Nicholas Ch.

ARCH. DE SABANA

HAVANA

CIUDAD DE

Marianao LA HABANA

Marie Baut Guanabacoa

Guanajay Santiago Matanzas B. de Matanzas Pen. de Hicacos

Bahía de las Vegas Varadero

Honda LA HABANA Cárdenas

Puerto Artemisa San Antonio de los Baños Unión de Isabela

Esperanza Güines Reyes Santo VILLA

San Diego Jovellanos Gómez de Sagua

Viñales de los Baños Pedro Colón Domingo Sagua

Minas de Consolación Bétancourt la Grande

Metahambre del Sur Cayos las MATANZAS Jagüey Santa Clara Remedios

Los Arroyos Pinar del Río Cayamas Ciénaga Grande CLARA Caiba

La Fe del Río Pta. Ens. de la Cruces Placetas

Guane Gorda Broa Pen. de Occ. de Zapata CIENFUEGOS Palmira Foment.

San Juan y Zapata Pico

Martinez G. de Batabanó Cienfuegos Potrerillo

Guanahacabibes ARCH. DE LOS CANARREOS B. de Cienfuegos (977 m.) Sancti

2

C.-San Nueva- Cayo del B. de Cazones Trinidad Spíritus

Antonio Pen. Las Cayos de Gerona Rosario B. de Tunas de Zaza

C.Corrientes C. Francés Cortés San Felipe La Cochinos

Ens. de la Siguanea Coloma Santa Fé

1,017 m. Cayo

(310 m.) Cantiles Cayo

Isla de la Juventud Largo

(Isle of Pines)

(LA HABANA)

N

3

C A R I B B E A N

S

83° Longitude 82° West of 81° Greenwich 80°

4

74° 73° 72° 71° 70°

Baracoa A T L A N T I C

Pta. Maisí O C E Silver

CUBA Bank

20° Tortuga C. Isabela

(Île de la Tortue) bahía de Puerto Plata

Windward Port-de-Paix St-Louis- Cap- Manzanillo C. Macorís C. Francé.

Passage C. de Môle du-Nord Haïtien Monte Cristi Cord. Septentrional Sosúa Veragua Cabrera Es

5

Jean- Gonaïves Guayubín Dajabón Abajo San Francisco

Rabel Gros Valverde Moca de Macorís

Môle-St.- Morne Trou Ft. Santiago Salcedo Pimentel Sánchez

Nicolas Plaisance Liberté Vega Cotu Yuna Saban

Golfe de la St-Michel-l'Atalaye St-Raphaël Hinche Cordillera de la

Gonâve Petite-Rivière- Dessalines Bánica Pico Duarte Vega Cotu

de-l'Artibonite 10,417 ft. (3175 m.) Salcedo Mont

6

19° Île de la Gonâve Verrettes Artibonite Plat

Grande Mirebalais Elías San D O M I N I C A N R E P U B. Mte. Tina

Jérémie Cayemite Canal de Lascahobas Piño Juan 9,239 ft. San José Bajos

Dame- Anse-à-Galets Léogâne Etang Sa. de Neiba (2816 m.) de Ocoa Haina

Marie C. des Anse-à-Veau Port-au-Prince Saumâtre Neiba Azua San Cay

Irois Massif de Léogâne Pétionville Sa. de Bahoruco Tamayo Cristóbal SANTO

Corail la Hotte Miragoâne Sa. de Neiba B. de Ocoa Baní Nizao DOMINGO

Port-à-Piment Petit-Goâve Jacmel Pol. Pta. Salinas

Tiburon Côteaux Massif de la Selle Duvergé B. de Neiba

Les Cayes Aquin Bainet Barahona

18° Pte. à Gravois Île à Vache Belle-Anse Pedernales

C. Falso Paraíso

Enriquillo

I. Beata C. Beata

7

C A R I B B E A N

Hispaniola

SCALE OF MILES

0 20 40 60 80 100

KILOMETRES

0 20 40 60 80

72° Longitude 71° West of 70° Gree

A B C D E

Puerto Rico & Lesser Antilles

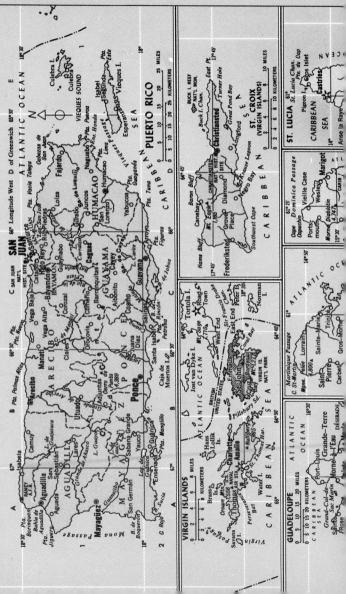

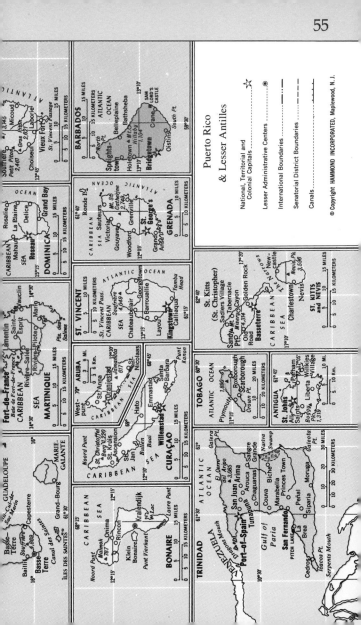

South America—Northern Part

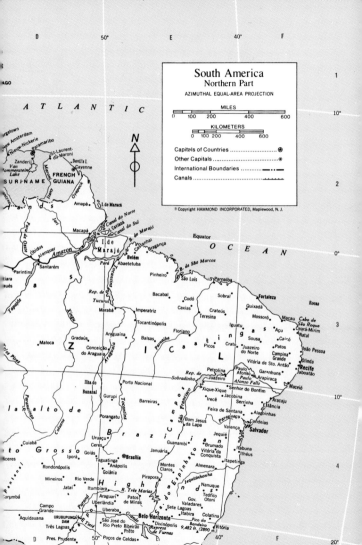

D   50°   E   40°   F

ATLANTIC

South America
Northern Part
AZIMUTHAL EQUAL-AREA PROJECTION

MILES
0   100   200   400   600

KILOMETERS
0   100 200   400   600

Capitals of Countries .... ⊕
Other Capitals .... ⊛
International Boundaries .... ▬ ▪ ▬
Canals .... ▬ ▪ ▬

© Copyright HAMMOND INCORPORATED, Maplewood, N.J.

Georgetown
New Amsterdam
Nieuw Nickerie   Paramaribo
Zanderij
Van   St-Laurent-du-Maroni
Commewijne   Devil's I.
Lake   Cayenne
SURINAME   **FRENCH GUIANA**

Amapá
Canal do Norte
Caxias   Canal do Sul
Macapá
I. de Marajá
B. de Marajá
Óbidos   **Amazon**
Alenquer   Pará
Santarém   Belém
Parintins   Abaetetuba
uaués

Maloca
Gradaús
Conceição
do Araguaia
Ilha de
Bananal

Equator   **OCEAN**

Cametá
Bragança   B. de São Marcos
Pinheiro   São Luís
Bacabal   Parnaíba
Codó   Sobral   **Fortaleza**
Caxias   Crateús   Quixadá
Teresina   Iguatu   Mossoró   Macau
Floriano   Picos   Juazeiro   Patos
Balsas   do Norte   Sousa   Cairó
Araguaína   Crato   Vitória de Sto. Antão
Petrolina   Juazeiro   Paulo
Rep. de   Afonso   Arapiraca
Sobradinho   Xique-Xique   Senhor do Bonfim
Irecê   Jacobina   Aracaju
Feira de Santana   Serrinha   Estância
Bom Jesus   Valença   Candeias
da Lapa   **Salvador**
Jequié   Ilhéus
Guanambi   Itabuna   Itapetinga
Januária   Brumado
Montes   Vitória da   Almenara
Claros   Conquista
Piripora   Nanuque
Teófilo   Otoni

Parintins
Tapajós

Maloca   Z
Gradaús
Conceição
do Araguaia

Ilha de
Bananal
Gurupi   Porto Nacional
Barreiras
Porangatu   B
Uruaçu   r
Cuiabá   Ceres   a
Iporá   Goiás   z   i
Rondonópolis   Taguatinga   l   i
Anápolis   ⊛**Brasília**   a
Goiânia   n
Mineiros   Rio Verde
Jataí   Itumbiara   H   i   g   h
São José do   Uberlândia   Araguari
Rio Preto Ribeirão   Patos   Pirapora
Prêto   de Minas   Divinópolis
Poços de Caldas   Pico do
Bandeira
9,482 ft. (2890 m)

Rocas
Ceará-Mirim   Cabo de
São Roque
Recife
Natal
João Pessoa
Olinda
Jaboatão
Maceió

Rep. de
Tucuruí
Marabá   Imperatriz
Tocantinópolis

Reconcavo
Sete Lagoas
Itabira   Colatina
Gov. Valadares
Belo Horizonte   Vitória
Represa
de Furnas

Grosso
Cáceres
Pantanal
Corumbá
Aquidauana
Três Lagoas
Pres. Prudente   URUBUPUNGA
DAM   Campo
Grande   Paraná   Grande   Tietê

D   50°   40°   F
                                                                20°

1

10°

2

0°

3

10°

4

20°

South America–Southern Part

PACIFIC OCEAN

BOLIVIA

Tropic of Capricorn

I. de San Félix (Chile) I. San Ambrosio (Chile)

I. Alejandro Selkirk I. Robinson Crusoe
JUAN FERNÁNDEZ IS. (Chile)

CHILE

•Pulacayo •Camiri
Ollagüe Tupiza Villa Montes
Tocopilla Villazón Tarija Yacuiba Tartagal
Calama Villazón
Mejillones •Jujuy
Antofagasta •Salta
Volcán Llullaillaco 22,057 ft. (6723 m.)
Taltal •Tatí Viejo
Chañaral Nev. Ojos del Salado 22,572 ft. (6880 m.) S. Miguel de Tucumán
Caldera Santiago del Estero Catamarca
Copiapó •La Rioja
La Serena Cruz del Eje Mar Chiquita
Coquimbo Rafaela Santa Fé
Ovalle Córdoba San Francisco Paraná
San Juan Villa María Bell Ville
Cerro Aconcagua 22,831 ft. (6959 m.) Rosario San Nicolás
Viña del Mar Mendoza San Luis Río Cuarto
Valparaíso **Buenos Aires**
Santiago San Rafael Pergamino
Rancagua Junín Chivilcoy La
Curicó Pehuajó
Talca Malargüe Azul
Linares Santa Rosa Olavarría Ta
Chillán Colorado
Talcahuano Tres Arroyos
Coronel Concepción Bahía Blanca Punta Alta
Los Ángeles Zapala Neuquén Bahía Blanca
Temuco Choele-Choel Río Colorado
Valdivia Negro
San Antonio Oeste Viedma
Osorno Nahuel Huapi Golfo San Matías
Puerto Montt San Carlos de Bariloche Puerto Madryn Pen. Valdés
Ancud Esquel Chubut Rawson
Isla de Chiloé
G. Corcovado Puerto Aisén Comodoro Rivadavia
ARCHIPIÉLAGO DE LOS CHONOS Sarmiento Golfo San Jorge Caleta Olivia
Pen. Taitao Lago Buenos Aires C. Tres Puntas
C. Tres Montes Deseado Puerto Deseado
G. de Penas
I. Campana I. San Martín Puerto Deseado
I. Wellington I. Viedma Chico San Julián
Santa Cruz Santa Cruz
I. Madre de Dios Bahía Grande West Falkland (U.K.) FALK
ARCHIPIÉLAGO REINA ADELAIDA Veintioche de Noviembre Río Gallegos
Strait of Magellan Puerto Natales Tierra del Fuego
I. Desolación Punta Arenas
I. Santa Inés Ushuaia San Diego
I. Clarence I. de los Estados
I. Hoste Bahía Nassau Cape Horn

PAR

60° Fue
Oli
Conc
PA
Bermejo
Presidencia R. Sáenz Peña
Resistencia
Go
Coru
Cua
Norte

4
20°
5
6
7
50°
8

80° A B 70° C 60°
90° A 80° B 70° C 60°

idauana

D Campo Grande
URUBUPUNGÁ DAM
Três Lagoas

Belo Horizonte • Itabira   Colatina
F

50°
Grande
Represa
de Furnas
Pico do • 9,482 ft. (2890 m.)
Bandeira • Cachoeiro de Itapemirim
• Vitória
40°
20°

Bela Vista
Pres. Prudente
Ribeirão • Prêto
Barbacena

edro Juan
Caballero
Dourados
Marília
Bauru
Poços de Caldas
Juiz de Fora •
Campos
C. de São Tomé

UAY
Maringá Londrina
Piracicaba
Campinas
Volta Redonda •
Nova Iguaçu

Sorocaba
São Paulo
Niterói
Rio de Janeiro

Asunción
Iraipú
Res.
Sete Quedas Falls
Curitiba •
I. de
Santos São Sebastião
C. Frio
Tropic of Capricorn

Villarrica
ITAIPÚ
DAM
Iguazú Falls
Iguaçu
Ponta Grossa

carnación
Posadas
Blumenau
Itajaí

kes
BRAZIL
I. de Santa Catarina
Florianópolis
5

Passo Fundo •
Lages •

Uruguaiana
Cruz Alta •
Caxias do Sul •

Alegrete
Santa Maria
Canoas

Cachoeira do Sul • Porto Alegre
Rivera
Santana do Livramento
Lagoa dos Patos

ito
Bagé •
Pelotas •

sandú
Melo
Emb. del
Rio Negro
Rio Grande

ro
cedes
Lagoa Mirim

URUGUAY
•Canelones
A T L A N T I C

de la Plata
•Montevideo
Pta. del Este

C. San Antonio

Mar del Plata
30°

ea
O C E A N

6

40°

N

ISLANDS
by Arg.)
7

nley
sland

South America
Southern Part

AZIMUTHAL EQUAL-AREA PROJECTION

MILES

| 0 | 100 | 200 | 400 | 600 |

KILOMETERS

| 0 | 100·200 | 400 | 600 |

Capitals of Countries .... ⊛

Other Capitals .... ⊛

International Boundaries .... — ·· — ·· —

Canals ....

© Copyright HAMMOND INCORPORATED, Maplewood, N. J.

8

50°

Africa–Northern Part

ATLANTIC

OCEAN

Bay of
Biscay

FRANCE
Paris
Seine
Loire
Rhône
GERMANY
Munich
SWITZ.
AUSTRIA
Vienna
CZE

ANDORRA
Marseille
Corsica
Rome
ITALY
Naples
Sardinia
Sicily

Douro
Lisbon
PORTUGAL
Madrid
SPAIN
Barcelona
Balearic Is.
Guadiana
GIBRALTAR (U.K.)

M E D I T E R

Str. of Gibraltar
Tangier
Ceuta (Sp.)
Tétouan
Melilla (Sp.)
Kenitra
Rabat
Casablanca
El Jadida
Safi
Essaouira
MOROCCO
Meknès
Fès
Oujda
Tlemcen
Oran
Mostaganem
Algiers
Blida
Ech Cheliff
Sidi Bel Abbes
Béjaïa
Skikda
Sétif
Constantine
Batna
Biskra
Tébessa
Annaba
Bizerte
Tunis
TUNISIA
Sousse
Sfax
MALTA

Madeira (Port.)
Porto Santo
Funchal
Desertas

Agadir
Marrakech
Beni Mellal
Jeb. Toubkal
Taroudant
Figuig
Béchar
Ghardaïa
Laghouat
El Bayadh
Guemar
Touggourt
Ouargla
Gabès
Zarzis
Tripoli
Homs
Misurat
Tarhuna
Gharian

Atlas Mountains
A t l a s   M o u n t a i n s

Canary Is. (Sp.)
La Palma
Tenerife
Sta. Cruz
Las Palmas
Gran Canary
C. Bojador

Lanzarote
Fuerteventura
Sidi Ifni
Wadi Dra
Tarfaya
Dra
Erg Iguidi
Tindouf
Adrar
Timimoun
Plateau du Tademaït
In Salah
Grand Erg Occidental
El Golea
Grand Erg Oriental
Ghadames
TRIPOLITANIA
Tripolitan

ALGERIA

WESTERN SAHARA
Dakhla (Villa Cisneros)
Semara

Bordj Omar Driss
Illizi
Hon
Brak
Sebha
Ubari
Murzuk
Ghat
El Gatro
Tejerri
Fezzan
F e z z a n
LI

C. Blanc
Nouadhibou
Atar

El Djouf
Erg Chech
Taoudenni
Tanezrouft
Ahaggar
7,852 ft. (3003 m.)
Tamanrasset
Djanet
Djado Plateau
Djado
Tib

S A H A R A

MAURITANIA
Nouakchott
Boutilimit
Tidjikja
Araouane
Kidal
Héroune
Tlmia
Bilma

MALI
Aluen el Atrous
Goundam
Timbuktu
Gao
Agadès
NIGER

Kosso
St-Louis
Thiès
Dakar
C. Verde
Kaolack
Kaédi
Kankossa
Maghama
Matam
Néma
Niger
Douentza
Mopti
Dori
Tahoua
Dosso
Birni-N'Konni
Zinder
L. Chad
Bol
N'Djamena

SENEGAL
Banjul
GAMBIA
Ziguinchor
GUINEA-BISSAU
Bissau
Bijagós Is.
Kayes
Kita
Banamba
Ségou
Djenné
Koutiala
Sikasso
Bobo Dioulasso
BURKINA FASO
Ouahigouya
Ouagadougou
Sokoto
Gusau
Maradi
Katsina
Kano
Nguru
Maiduguri
Marcua
Bongor
D

GUINEA
Kindia
Conakry
Kankan
Koulikoro
Bamako
Tamale
Kaduna
Zaria
Jos
NIGERIA
Yola
Garoua
Kélo
Dob

SIERRA LEONE
Freetown
Makeni
Bo
Kenema
Macenta
Korhogo
Bouaké
Man
Abengourou
Kumasi
Lake Volta
Benin City
Ilorin
Ogbomosho
Oshogbo
Abeokuta
Ibadan
Enugu
Onitsha
Aba
Calabar
CAMEROON
Ngaoundéré
Bossanga

LIBERIA
Robertsport
Monrovia
Buchanan
Harper
C. Palmes
Bo
Gbarnga
Sanniquellie
Tabou
Grand Lahou
Yamoussoukro
Bouaflé
Gagnoa
IVORY COAST
Abidjan
Agboville
GHANA
Ashanti
Accra
Lomé
Cotonou
Porto-Novo
Lagos
Benin City
Port Harcourt
Cameroon 13,350 ft. (4069 m.)
Foumban
Yaoundé
Bata
EQUAT. GUINEA
GABON
Oyem
Ebolowa
RE CO

Takoradi
Sekondi
Bioko (Fernando Po)
Malabo
São Tomé & Príncipe

ATLANTIC   OCEAN

Gulf of Guinea

Africa
Northern Part
AZIMUTHAL EQUAL-AREA PROJECTION

MILES
0 100 200 400 600 800

KILOMETERS
0 100 200 400 600 800

Capitals of Countries .... ⊗
Other Capitals .... ⊙
International Boundaries .... ▪▪▪▪▪
Other Boundaries .... ▪▪▪▪▪
Canals .... ┼┼┼┼

© Copyright HAMMOND INCORPORATED, Maplewood, N.J.

Africa–Southern Part

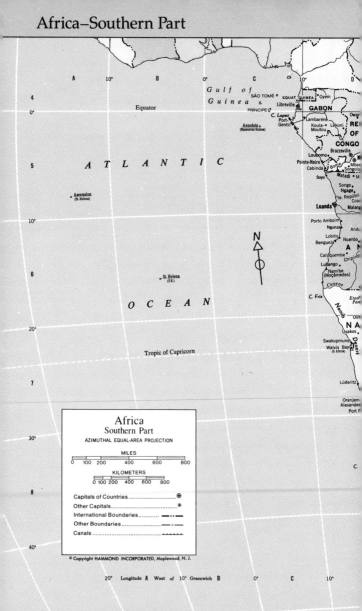

A   10°   B   0°   C   Cb   10°   D

Gulf of SÃO TOMÉ •   EQUAT. GUINEA• Oyem
Guinea &   Libreville•   **GABON**
PRÍNCIPE ○   Owar

Equator   C. Lopez• Port   Lambaréné•   **RE**
Gentil   Koula•   • Lekoni   **OF**
0°   Moutou   **CONGO**
Annobón•   • M
(Equatorial Guinea)   Loubomo•   Brazzaville•
Pointe-Noire •   Boma•   •Mba
Cabinda•   Songolo
• Ascension   Soyo•   Matadi •   • M
(St. Helena)
Songo•
A T L A N T I C   Ngage•
Pte. República•
Luanda   Malanc

10°   Porto Amboim•
Ngunza•   Andu
N   Lobito•   Humbo,   •
•St. Helena   Benguela•   **A**
(U.K.)   Calaquembe•   Chipi
Lubango•
6   Namibe•   •
(Moçâmedes)
Cunene

O C E A N   C. Fria   Etos)
Parl

20°   Out
N A
Usakos•
Tropic of Capricorn   Swakopmund•   **Namib Desert**
Walvis Bay•
(S. Africa)

7   Lüderitz•

Oranjem•
Alexande)
Port f

Africa
Southern Part
AZIMUTHAL EQUAL-AREA PROJECTION

MILES
0 100 200   400   600   800

KILOMETERS
0 100 200   400   600   800

Capitals of Countries .... ⊕
Other Capitals .... ⊛
International Boundaries.......... ▬▬ ▬
Other Boundaries .... ▬ ▬ ▬
Canals .... ┼┼┼┼┼┼

© Copyright HAMMOND INCORPORATED, Maplewood, N. J.

C.

8

30°

40°

20°   Longitude A West of 10° Greenwich B   0°   C   10°

SOUTH AFRICAN BANTUSTANS

1 BOPHUTHATSWANA
2 TRANSKEI
3 VENDA
4 CISKEI

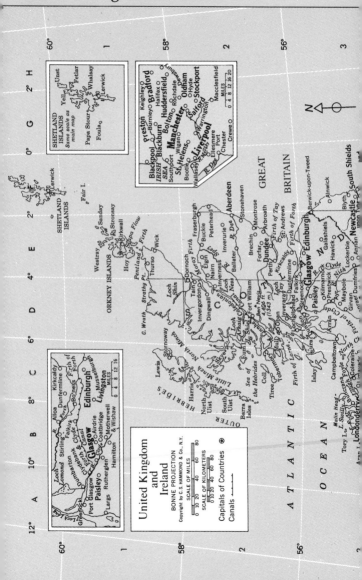

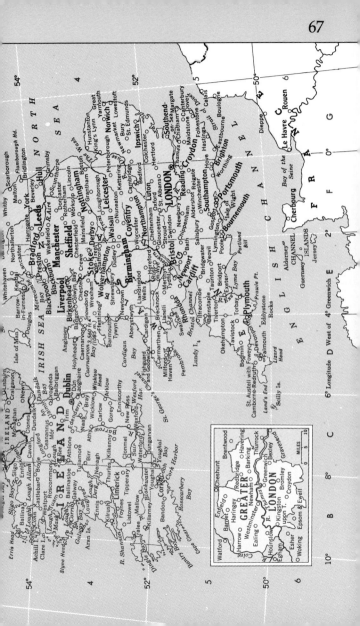

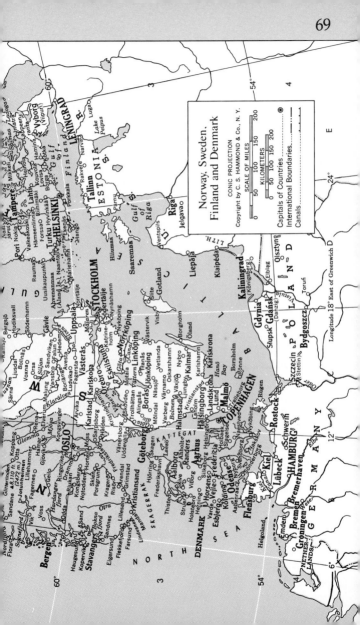

Norway, Sweden,
Finland and Denmark

CONIC PROJECTION

Copyright by C. S. HAMMOND & Co., N. Y.

SCALE OF MILES

0   50   100   150   200

KILOMETERS

0 50 100 150 200

Capitals of Countries .... ⊛
International Boundaries .... —·—·—
Canals ....

Longitude 18° East of Greenwich D

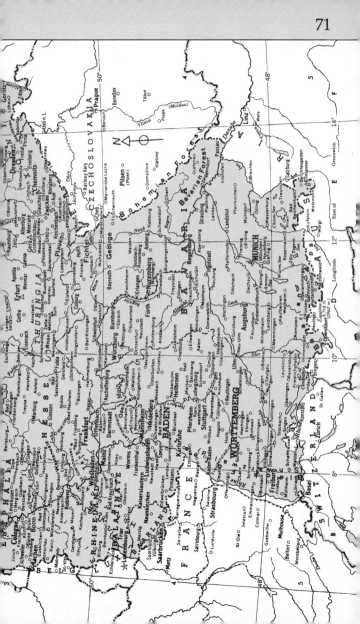

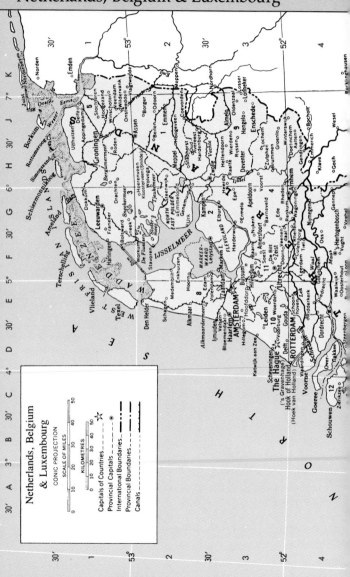

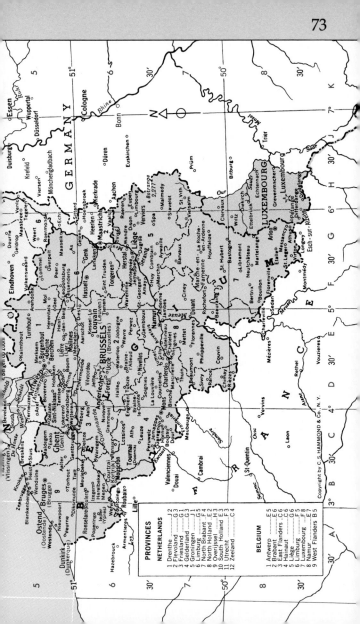

73

PROVINCES

NETHERLANDS

1 Drenthe J2
2 Flevoland G3
3 Friesland G1
4 Gelderland G3
5 Groningen J1
6 Limburg G5
7 North Brabant E5
8 North Holland E2
9 Overijssel H3
10 South Holland E3
11 Utrecht F3
12 Zeeland C4

BELGIUM

1 Antwerp E6
2 Brabant E6
3 East Flanders C6
4 Hainaut C6
5 Liège G6
6 Limburg F6
7 Luxembourg F8
8 Namur E7
9 West Flanders B5

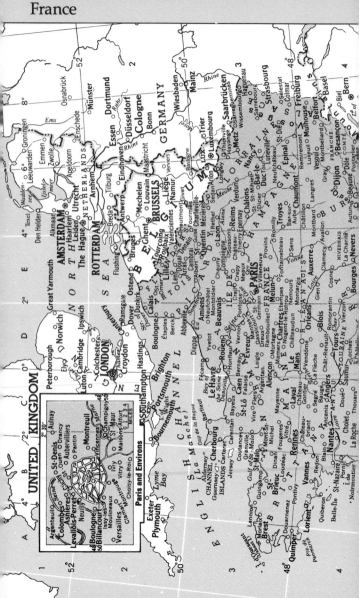

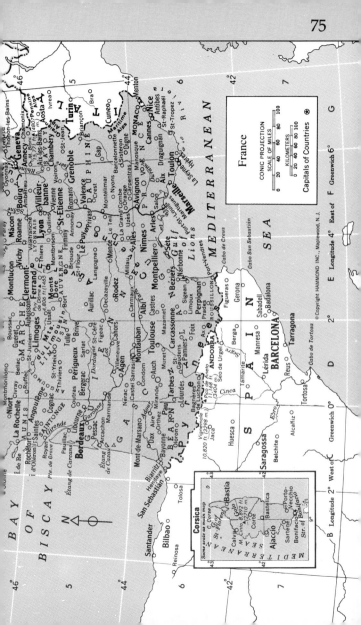

Spain & Portugal

Spain and Portugal

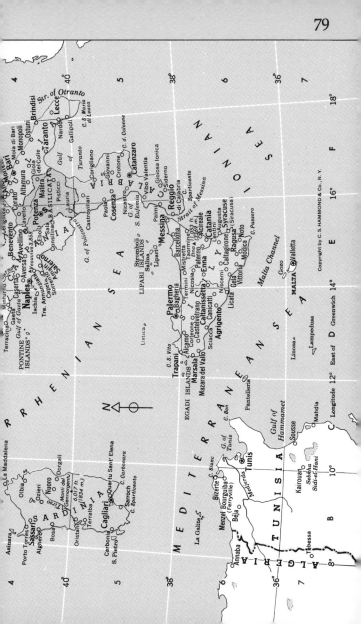

Switzerland

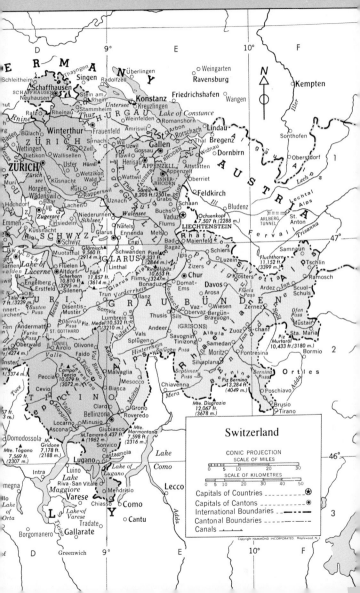

Austria, Czechoslovakia & Hungary

Austria, Czechoslovakia
& Hungary

Conic Projection
SCALE OF MILES
0   20   40   60   80   100
SCALE OF KILOMETRES
0   20   40   60   80   100

Capitals of Countries   ⊛
International Boundaries   ___ ___ ___
Canals   -----

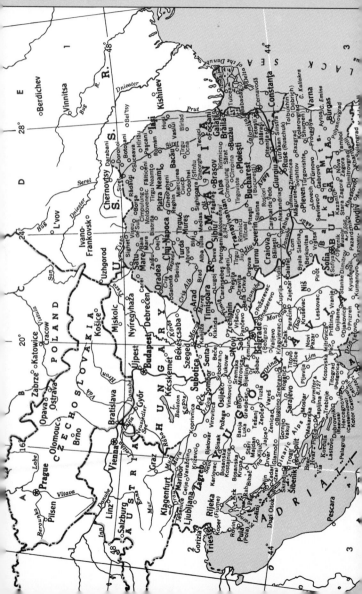

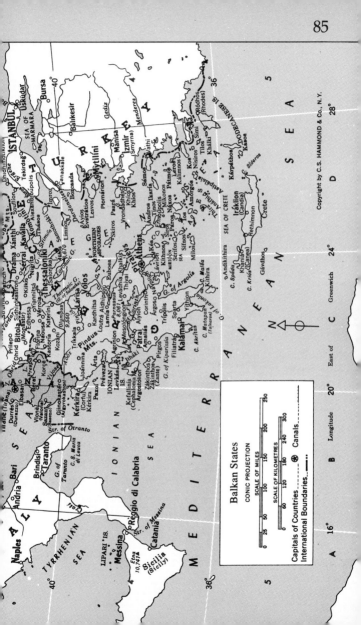

Poland

© Copyright HAMMOND INCORPORATED, Maplewood, N.J.

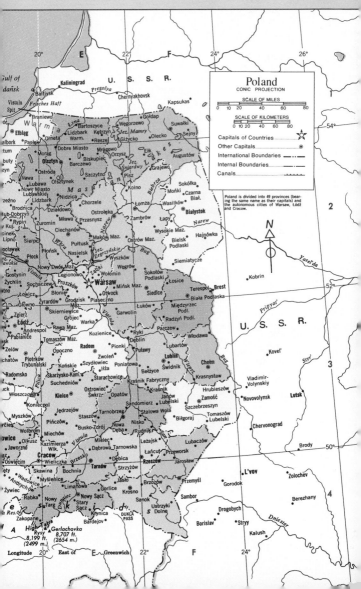

Poland
CONIC PROJECTION

SCALE OF MILES
0 10 20   40   60   80

SCALE OF KILOMETERS
0 10 20   40   60   80

Capitals of Countries..............
Other Capitals.......................
International Boundaries ....
Internal Boundaries........
Canals..............................

Poland is divided into 49 provinces (bearing the same name as their capitals) and the autonomous cities of Warsaw, Łódź and Cracow.

N

Gulf of Danzig

U. S. S. R.

Kaliningrad

Baltiysk
Frisches Haft
Pregolya
Chernyakhovsk
Kapsukas
Vistula Spit

Braniewo
Elbląg
Warmia
Jez. Mamry
Suwałki

Paslek
Orneta
Reszel
Giżycko
Olecko
Sejny

Dobre Miasto
Biskupiec
Orzysz
Ełk
Augustów

Morag
Olsztyn
Barczewo
Szczytno
Jez. Śniardwy

Ostróda
Mazury
Kolno
Grajewo

Iława
Lubawa
Nidzica
Chorzele
Łomża
Sokółka

Brodnica
Działdowo
Ostrołęka
Mońki
Czarna Biał.

Nowe Miasto Lubawskie
Mława
Przasnysz
Zambrów
Wasilków
Białystok

Lidzbark
Żuromin
Ciechanów
Maków Maz.
Narew
Łapy
Hajnówka

Rypin
Sierpc
Pułtusk
Ostrów Maz.
Wysokie Maz.

Lipno
Płońsk
Nasielsk
Wyszków
Bielsk Podlaski

Płock
Nowy Dwór Maz.
Legionowo
Bug
Siemiatycze

Gostynin
Żychlin
Sochaczew
Pruszków
Warsaw
Mińsk Maz.
Sokołów Podlaski

Łowicz
Błonie
Grodzisk
Siedlce
Łosice
Terespol
Brest

Głowno
Żyrardów
Maz.
Piaseczno
Biała Podlaska

Zgierz
Skierniewice
Otwock
Łuków
Międzyrzec Podl.

Łódź
Rawa Maz.
Grójec
Warka
Garwolin
Radzyń Podl.
Kobrin

Pabianice
Andrespol
Kozienice
Ryki
Parczew
Włodawa

Zelów
Tomaszów Maz.
Pionki
Dęblin
Lubartów

Piotrków Trybunalski
Opoczno
Radom
Zwoleń
Puławy
Lublin
Chełm
Kovel'

Radomsko
Końskie
Szydłowiec
Iłża
Poniatowa
Świdnik

Skarżysko-Kam.
Starachowice
Bełżyce
Krasnystaw
Vladimir-Volynskiy

Suchedniów
Kraśnik Fabryczny
Krasnystaw
Lutsk

Włoszczowa
Ostrowiec
Opatów
Kraśnik
Hrubieszów
Novovolynsk

Kielce
Świętokrz.
Sandomierz
Janów Lubelski
Zamość

Końskie
Jędrzejów
Staszów
Tarnobrzeg
Stalowa Wola
Szczebrzeszyn
Chervonograd

Myszków
Pińczów
Nowa Dęba
Nisko
Biłgoraj
Tomaszów Lubelski

Olkusz
Miechów
Busko-Zdrój
Rudnik
Lubaczów

Wolbrom
Kazimierza Wlk.
Mielec
Leżajsk
Przeworsk
Brody

Jaworzno
Dąbrowa Tarnowska
Łańcut
Rzeszów

Oświęcim
Cracow
Wieliczka
Brzesko
Dębica
Strzyżów
Jarosław

Skawina
Bochnia
Tarnów
Jasło
Przemyśl
Gorodok
L'vov
Zolochev

Myślenice
Limanowa
Brzozów
Krosno
Sanok

Żywiec
Rabka
Nowy Targ
Nowy Sącz
Gorlice
Sambor
Drogobych
Berezhany

Zakopane
Tatry
Krynica
Stary Sącz
Ustrzyki Dolne
Borislav
Stryy
Dniester

High
A
Gerlachovka
8,707 ft.
(2654 m.)
Bardejov
DUKLA PASS
Kalush

8,199 ft.
(2499 m.)

Pripyat'
Yatel'da
Styr'

U. S. S. R.

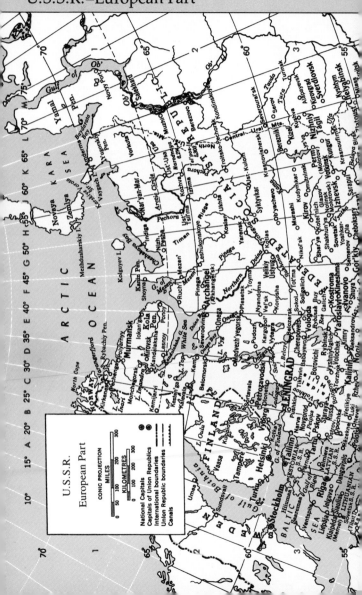

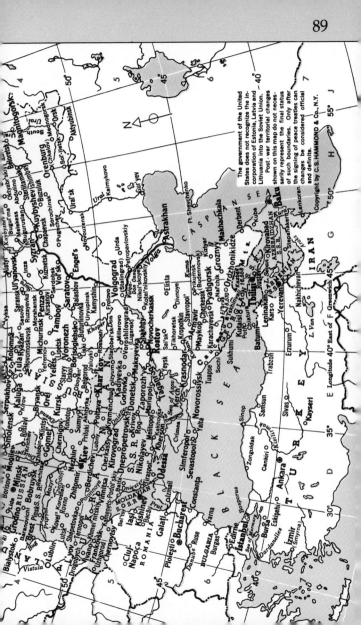

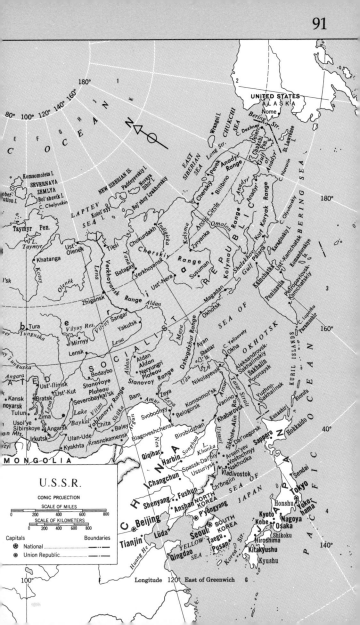

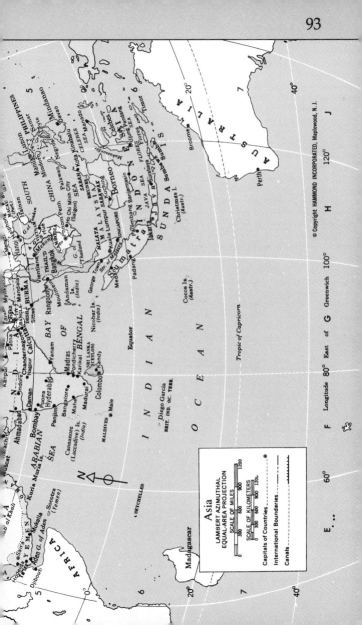

Asia
LAMBERT AZIMUTHAL EQUAL-AREA PROJECTION

SCALE OF MILES
0 300 600 900 1200

SCALE OF KILOMETERS
0 300 600 900 120u

Capitals of Countries ......●
International Boundaries ......
Canals ......

© Copyright HAMMOND INCORPORATED, Maplewood, N.J.

Near and Middle East

© Copyright HAMMOND INC., Maplewood, N.J.

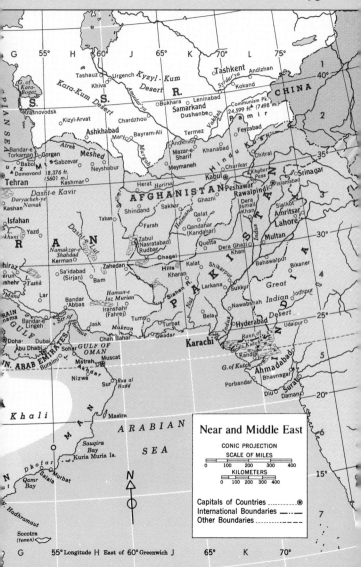

G 55° H 60° J 65° K 70° L 75°

Tashkent • Andizhan
Tashauz ○ Urgench Kyzyl - Kum Syrdar'ya○ Kokand
Khiva Desert Leninabad
Kara-Bogaz S. S. R. CHINA
Krasnovodsk Bukhara Samarkand Communism Pk.
Kizyl-Arvat Chardzhou Dushanbe 24,599 ft. (7498 m.)
Ashkhabad Mary Pamir
Bandar-e ○Gorgan Atrek Bayram-Ali Murgab Termez Feyzabad
Torkaman Babol Sabzevar Meshed Mazar-e Khanabad
Damavond 18,376 ft. Neyshabur Sharif Meymaneh Chitral
Tehran (5601 m.) Herat Harirud Kabul ⊛ Charikar Srinagar
Kashan Dasht-e Kavir AFGHANISTAN Peshawar Rawalpindi⊛ Islamabad
Daryacheh-ye Ghazni Dera Ismail Sialkot
Namak Shindand Sakhar Qalat Khan Amritsar
Isfahan Tabas Dasht-e Farah Qandahar Lahore
○ Yazd R Zabul (Kandahar) Quetta Multan
L. A (Nasratabad) Chaman Dera Ghazi Bikaner
khuni Namakzar-e N Rudbar Kalat Khan Bahawalpur
hiraz Shahdad Zahedan Shikarpur Great
erun Kerman Hills Kharan Larkana Sukkur Jodhpur
ushehr Sa'idabad Bam P Siahan R. Indian Udaipur
Tashk (Sirjan) Hamun-e Nawabshah Desert
AIN Mand Jaz Murian Iranshahr Tump Bela Hyderabad
nama Bandar (Fahrej) Turbat Ahmadabad
○Doha Abbas Jask Makran Gwadar Karachi Randu
Abu Dhabi Lingeh Chah Bahar Rann of Bhavnagar
RAIN Bandar-e Sir○ Muscat Kateh Porbandar Surat
GULF Sohar GULF OF Ras al Kutch Diu Daman
○ Doha Dubai OMAN Hadd Ahmadnagar
N. ARAB EMIRATES Bursimi Matrah ⊛ Sur G. of Kutch
Nizwa Akhdar
Khali Masira
ARABIAN
OMAN SEA
Saugira N
Bay
Dhofar Kuria Muria Is.
Murbat
Qamr Salala
Bay
Hadhramaut
Socotra
(Yemen)

G 55° Longitude H East of 60° Greenwich J 65° K 70°

Copyright by C. S. Hammond & Co., N.Y.

Turkey, Syria, Lebanon & Cyprus
CONIC PROJECTION

MILES
0 25 50 75 100 125 150

KILOMETRES
0 25 50 75 100 125 150

Capitals of Countries ⊛
International Boundaries ∙━∙━∙
Ruins ∴

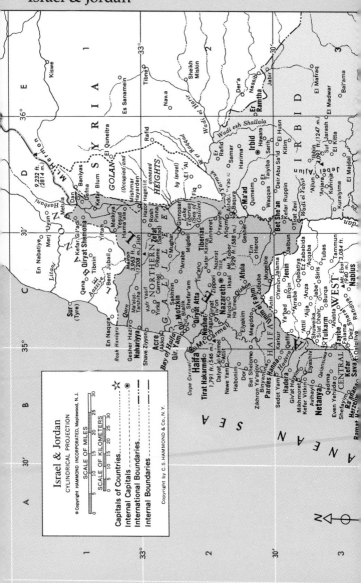

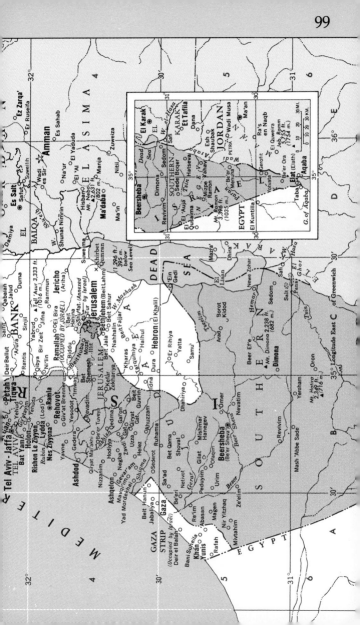

52° H 54 56° K 58° L 60° M 62° N 64°

U. S. S. R.

Kizyl-Arvat
Kara-Kala
eleken Pen.
gurchinskiy

Kavakli
Kami-Dar-ya
Farab-
Pristan'
Chardzhou
Repetek
Burdalyk
Ravnina
Mary
Bayram-Ali

Kara Kum Desert

Ashkhabad
Artyk
Kaakhka
Tedzhen
Murgab
Dushak

Atrek
Gasan-Kuli
Bandar-e-
Torkeman

Bojnurd
Shirvan
Darreh Gaz
Quchan

Gorgan
Gonbad-e Kavus
Jajarm

Takhta-Bazar

Sarakhs
Serakhs

Meshed
Karhai Rud
Bala
Murghab

halus
Amo
Babol
Damavand
18,376

Gorgan
(Asterabad)
S.O Emam-
shahr
Damghan

Sabzevar
Neyshabur
Torbat-e
Heydariyeh
Torbat-e
Jam

Kushka
Tirpul
Kushk

Paropamisus

TEHRAN
Semnan
Firuzkuh
Torud
Qal'eh
Shur

Turan

Kashmar

Khvaf

Obeh
Herat 11,795

Namak

Dasht-e Kavir

Bejestan

Kuh-i-Wala
12,680
Daulatabad
Farsi

ashan
Natanz
Ardestan
Anarak
Na'in
Kuhpayeh

Khvor
Ferdows
Tabas
Qayen
Sseh Kuh
Yazdan
Namaksar
Sabzawar

Anardarra

R
Shahreza
Gavkhuni
Meybod
I
Taft
Yazd
Bafq
A
N
Nay Band

Birjand
Khuri Rud
Tabas
Duruh

Forah Rud
Farah
Juwain
Khash

14,029
Abadeh
Abarqu
Shir
13,369
Anar
Madvar
11,811
Ravar
Shahdad
Namakzar-e
Shahdaa

Dasht-i Lut

Nehbandan

Daryacheh-ye
Sistan
Zabol
SEISTAN
Dasht-i
Margo

Deh Bid
Rafsanjan
Mahan
Kerman

Robat Qila
Zahedan

Helmand
Gaud-i-Zirreh
Rudbar

Chahar Burjak

Shiraz
Zargan
Persepolis
L. Tashk
Bakhtegan
Sa'idabad
Neyriz
Estahbanat
14,340
Laieh Zar
Baft
Bam

Mirjaveh
Chagai Hills
Nok Kundi
PAKISTAN

run
jan
Kor
Mand
Fasa
Bafidar
10,459
Jahrom
Darab
Tarom

Rigan

Bazman
11,447
Khash

Taftan
13,201
Siahan Kuh
Ladgasht
Gasht
Saravan

Talab
Nahang
PAKISTAN

zabad

LARISTAN
Lar
Mehran
Bandar
Abbas
Minab
Hormoz

Hamun-e Jaz
Murian
Bampur
Iranshahr
(Fahrej)
Bampur
Sarbaz

BALUCHISTAN

Tump

Nay Band
Sheykh
Sho'eyb
Qeys
Bandar-e-
Lingeh
Qeshm
Strait
of Hormuz
Raas al Jibal
(To Oman)
Ras Musandam

Nikshahr

Qasr-e
Qand

Dashtiari
MAKRAN
Dashti
Gwadar

GULF
UNITED ARAB
EMIRATES
Dibah
Jask
G. of Oman
Ras-
Meydani
Bir Bala
Chah Bahar
Gavater

52° Longitude 54° East 56° of Greenwich 58° L 60° M 62°

Southern Asia

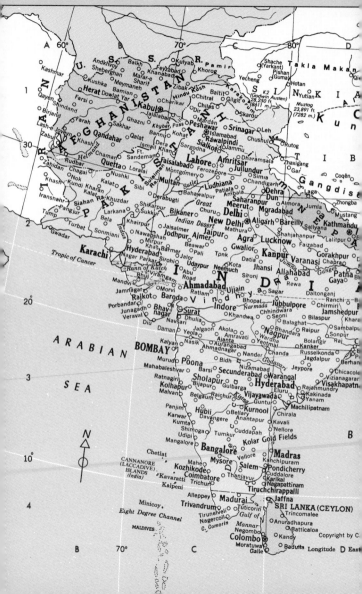

A 60°   70°   C 80° D

U. S. S. R.

Kashmar   Andkhvoy   S. Balkh   R. pamir   Shache   Takla Makan
Sheberghan   Marar-e   Kulyab   Khorog   (Yarkant)
Kushka   Meymaneh   Sharif   Feyzabad   Yecheng   Pishan   Gumay
Qayen   Herat   Dowlat Yar   Zibak   Hotan   Nyutian   K   I   A
Shindand   Bamian   Hindu   Baltit   K2   N   Kun
Farsi   Charikar   Kush   Chitral   Gilgit   (Godwin Austen)   Muztag
Birjand   Kabul   Jalalabad   Chilas   Skardu   28,250 ft.   23,891 ft
Zabul   Ghazni   Khyber Pass   Peshawar   Leh   (8611 m.)   (7282 m.)
Lashe   Joqin   Farah   Sakhar   Bannu   Islamabad   Srinagar   Chushul   Rutog
Zabul   Helmand   Qandahar   Qalat   Ft. Ismail Khan   Rawalpindi   Jammu   Zhaxigang
Rudbar   Chaman   Sandeman   Sargodha   Sialkot   Dharamsala   Coqen   Gangdis
Zahidan   Chagai   Nushki   Quetta   Loralai   Faisalabad   Lahore   Amritsar   Simla   Laga   Zhongba
Khash   Kundi   Kharan   Kalat   Sibi   Montgomery   Ferozepore   Juliundur   Chandigarh   Almora   Jumla   Mustang
Iranshahr   Panjgur   Siahan   Khuzdar   Derabugti   Multan   Bahawalpur   Ludhiana   Patiala   Ambala   Dehra   Saliyana   Kathmandu
Turbat   Bela   Larkana   Sukkur   Bikaner   Great   Patiala   Meerut   Saharanpur   Dun   Almora   Lalitpur   P
Gwadar   Sonmiani   Nawabshah   Jaisalmer   Indian Desert   Delhi   Aligarh   Bareilly   Faizabad
Karachi   Mirpur   Jodhpur   Ajmer   New Delhi   Mathura   Moradabad   Shahjahanpur   Gorakhpur
    Hyderabad   Nagar Parkar   Barmer   Beawar   Jaipur   Agra   Lucknow   Chapra   Patna
Tropic of Cancer   Khas   Pali   Jalor   Udaypur   Gwalior   Kanpur   Varanasi   Ganges   Gaya
    Mandvi   Viramgam   Sirohi   Tonk   Kota   Jhansi   Allahabad   Rewa   Daltonganj   Ranchi
    Rann of Kutch   Bhuj   Road   Neemuch   Sironj   Sagar   Chirmiri   Jamshedpur
20°   Jamnagar   Rajkot   Morvi   Ahmadabad   Ujjain   Vindhya   Bhopal   Jubbulpore   Bilaspur   Raipur   Sambalpur   Khara
    Porbandar   Baroda   Indore   Narmada   Khandwa   Chhindwara   Seoni   Bolangir   Sonpur
    Junagadh   Bhav-   Surat   Dhulia   Jalgaon   Akola   Amravati   Wardha   Nagpur   Bhandara   Kanker   Jeypore   Berhan
    Veraval   nagar   Navsari   Diu   Daman   Yeola   Nasik   Ajanta   Yeotmal   Chanda   Russelkonda   Jagdalpur
    ARABIAN   Kalyan   Ahmadnagar   Aurangabad   Bidh   Nizamabad   Godavari   Chicacole
    BOMBAY   Murud   Poona   Bars   Nander   Vizianagaram
SEA   Mahabaleshwar   Secunderabad   Warangal   Visakhapatn
3   Ratnagiri   Sholapur   Gulbarga   Hyderabad   Rajahmundry
    Kolhapur   Bijapur   Eluru   Kakinada   Yanam
    Panjim   Malvan   Belgaum   Raichur   Vijayawada   Guntur   Machilipatnam
    Karwar   Hubli   Davangere   Bellary   Kurnool   Chirala
    Kumta   Anantapur   Kavali
    Shimoga   Tumkur   Cuddapah   Nellore
    Udipi   Kolar Gold Fields   B
10°   Mangalore   Bangalore   Vellore   Madras
    Chetlat   Mahe   Mysore   Kanchipuram
CANNANORE   Kozhikode   Salem   Pondicherry
(LACCADIVE)   Coimbatore   Cuddalore
ISLANDS   Kavaratti   Trichur   Thanjavur   Karikal
(India)   Kalpeni   Tiruchchirappalli   Nagapattinam
4   Minicoy   Alleppey   Madurai   Jaffna
Eight Degree Channel   Trivandrum   Tuticorin   SRI LANKA (CEYLON)
MALDIVES   Tirunelveli   Gulf of   Trincomalee
    Nagercoil   Mannar   Anuradhapura   Batticaloa
    C. Comorin   Negombo   Copyright by C.
    COLOMBO   Kandy
B   70°   C   Moratuwa   Baduila   Longitude 80° East
    MALDIVES   Galle

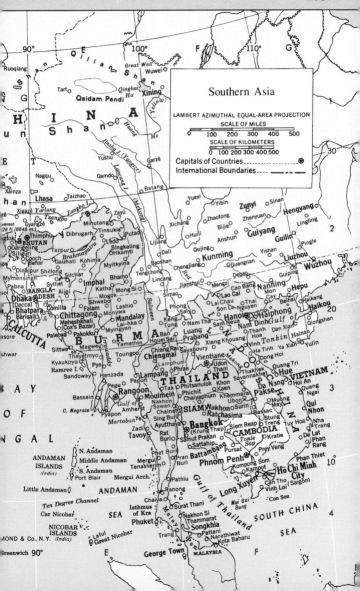

Southern Asia

LAMBERT AZIMUTHAL EQUAL-AREA PROJECTION
SCALE OF MILES

China & Mongolia

China and Mongolia

CONIC PROJECTION
MILES
0 100 200 300 400 500

KILOMETERS
0 100 200 300 400 500

Capitals of Countries _____ ⊕
Provincial Capitals _____ ◉
International Boundaries _ _ . _
Provincial Boundaries _____

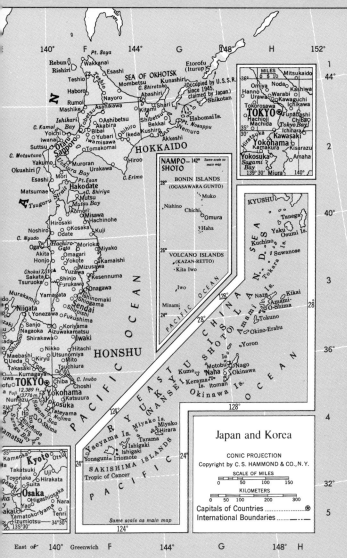

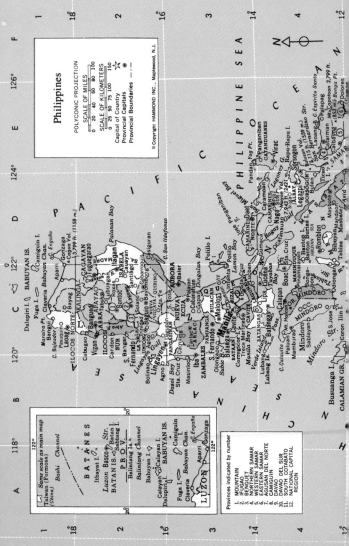

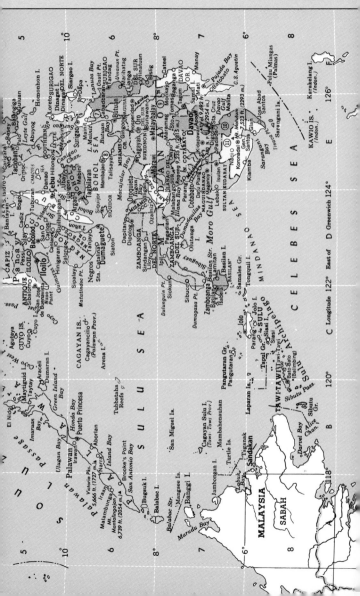

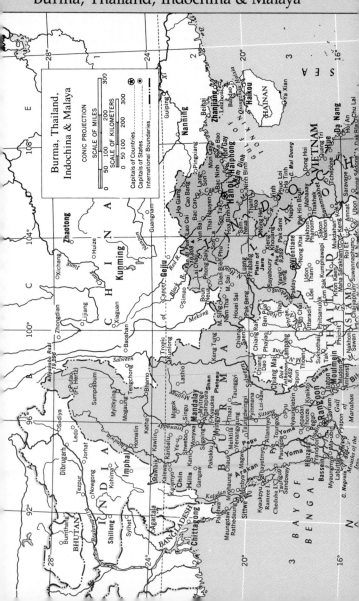

Southeast Asia

Australia & New Zealand

INDONESIA

Java
Bali
Sumbawa
Sumba
Dili
Timor
Kupang

SUNDA IS

ARAFURA SEA

TIMOR SEA

Bathurst I.
Melville I.
Van Diemen Gulf
Darwin
ARNHEM LAND
Pine Creek
Katherine
Roper
Birdum
C. Arr
Groo
Eyla
Car

C. Talbot
Joseph Bonaparte Gulf

Daly
Victoria

Collier B.
C. Leveque
Derby
Fitzroy
Wyndham
Ord

Newcastle Waters
L. Woods

Broome

St. George Range

NORTHERN

Murchison Ra.

Goldfield

Port Hedland
Barrow I.
Roebourne
North West C.
Marble Bar
Goldfield
Fortescue

Great Sandy Desert

L. Mackay

Barrow Creek

TERRITORY

Ashburton

WESTERN

L. Disappointment

Gibson Desert

Alice Springs
Macdonnell Ranges

L. Amadeus

Musgrave Ranges

Simpson Desert

Sh.
Bay
Carnarvon
Dirk Hartog I.
Steep Pt.

Murchison

AUSTRALIA

L. Carnegie

Meekathara
Wiluna
L. Austin
Goldfield

Oodnadatta
Stuarts
Coober Pedy
Range

L. Eyre

SOUTH

Northampton
Geraldton

Leonora
L. Carey

Great Victoria Desert

Marree

AUSTRALI

L. Moore
L. Barlee
Goldfield
Kalgoorlie
Boulder

L. Gairdner

Perth
Fremantle
Northam
Merredin
Narrogin
Norseman

Fowler's Bay
Streaky Bay
Whyalla
Port Pirie

Bunbury
C. Naturaliste
Collie
Esperance
C. Arid

Great

Australian Bight

Port Lincoln
Spencer
Gulf

Northcliffe
Albany

Kangaroo I.

Australia and New Zealand
BONNE PROJECTION
SCALE OF MILES

0   200   400   600   800

SCALE OF KILOMETERS

0   200   400   600   800

National Capitals _ _ _ ⊕   State and Territorial Capitals _ _ _ ⊙

Mount C

PAPUA NEW GUINEA

Port Moresby

Torres Str.

C. York

The

CAPE

Coen

YORK

C. Flattery

PEN.

Cooktown

Cairns

Is.

Barrier

Normanton

Forsayth

Mitchell

Townsville

Charters Towers

Hughenden

Mackay

oulia

Aramac

Longreach

Clermont

Barcaldine

Emerald

Blackall

C. Manifold

Rockhampton

Tropic of Capricorn

Charleville

Roma

Bundaberg

Great Sandy I.

Maryborough

Gympie

St. George

Toowoomba

Ipswich

Brisbane

Bulloo L.

Moree

C. Byron

Lismore

Darling

Bourke

Armidale

Grafton

Broken Hill

Cobar

Tamworth

NEW SOUTH

Dubbo

Orange

Lithgow

Newcastle

Mildura

Blue Mts.

Sydney

WALES

Wagga Wagga

Cootamundra

Wollongong

Albury

Canberra

AUSTRALIAN

CAP. TERR.

VICTORIA

Australia

C. Howe

orsham

Bendigo

Bairnsdale

stlemaine

Ballarat

Melbourne

Geelong

Wonthaggi

Wilson's Promontory

C. Otway

ool

King I.

Bass Str.

Furneaux

Group

Devonport

Launceston

Queenstown

TASMANIA

Hobart

CORAL SEA

SOLOMON

ISLANDS

Honiara

Guadalcanal

10°

N

NEW

CALEDONIA

(Fr.)

Noumea

20°

East of D Greenwich 150°

E

160°

F

170°

150°

160°

D

F

1

2

3

4

TASMAN SEA

North Cape

Whangarei

Auckland

North

Island

Hamilton

Bay of

Plenty

New Plymouth

Gisborne

Wanganui

Tasman

Napier

Hastings

Bay

Palmerston

North

Nelson

Wellington

Cook Str.

Greymouth

Southern

Christchurch

Alps

Timaru

South

Oamaru

Island

Dunedin

Invercargill

Stewart I.

New Zealand

Same scale as main map.

170°

180°

PACIFIC OCEAN

40°

30°

40°

Pacific Ocean

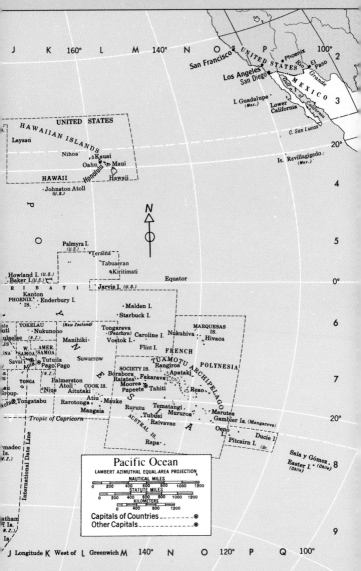

J K 160° L M 140° N O P 100° 2

San Francisco
Los Angeles
San Diego
UNITED STATES
Phoenix
El Paso
Rio Grande
MEXICO 3

I. Guadalupe (Mex.)
Lower California
GULF of California

C. San Lucas

UNITED STATES
H A W A I I A N   I S L A N D S

Laysan 20°

Nihoa
Kauai
Oahu Maui
Honolulu
HAWAII
Hawaii

Is. Revillagigedo (Mex.)

Johnston Atoll (U.S.)

4

P
O
C

N

Palmyra I. (U.S.) 5

Teraina

Tabuaeran
Kiritimati

Howland I. (U.S.)
Baker I. (U.S.)
Jarvis I. (U.S.)
Equator 0°
K I R I B A T I

Kanton
PHOENIX Enderbury I.
IS.

Malden I. 6

Starbuck I.

TOKELAU (New Zealand)
Nukunono (N.Z.)
Tongareva (Penrhyn)
Caroline I.
MARQUESAS IS.
Nukuhiva
Hivaoa
FRENCH
POLYNESIA

Fakaofo
Tuvalu (N.Z.)
AMER. SAMOA
W. SAMOA
Savaii
Apia
Tutuila
Pago Pago
Manihiki
Vostok I.
Flint I.
Suwarrow
TUAMOTU ARCHIPELAGO
SOCIETY IS.
Rangiroa
Apataki
Borabora
Raiatea Fakarava
Moorea
Papeete Tahiti
Reao
Niue
TONGA
Palmerston Atoll
COOK IS.
Aitutaki
Atiu Mauke
Rarotonga
Mangaia
Rurutu
Tubuai
Tematangi
Mururoa
Marutea
Gambier Is. (Mangareva)

7

Tropic of Capricorn 20°
AUSTRAL IS.
Raivavae
Rapa
Oeno
Pitcairn I. (Br.)
Ducie I.

8

Kermadec Is. (N.Z.)
Sala y Gómez
Easter I. (Chile) (Chile)

International Date Line

Chatham Is. (N.Z.)
Is.

9

Pacific Ocean

LAMBERT AZIMUTHAL EQUAL-AREA PROJECTION

NAUTICAL MILES
0 200 400 600 800 1000 1200
STATUTE MILES
0 200 400 600 800 1000 1200
KILOMETERS
0 400 800 1200

Capitals of Countries .... ⊛
Other Capitals .... ⊚

J Longitude K West of L Greenwich M 140° N O 120° P Q 100°

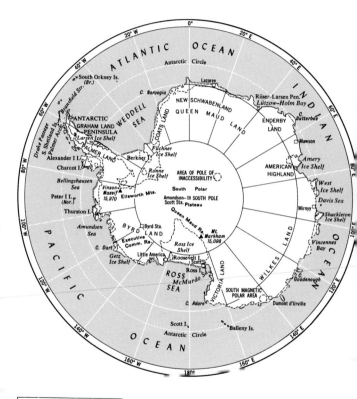

Antarctica

SCALE ON MERIDIANS

MILES
0 200 400 600 800 1000

KILOMETERS
0 200 400 600 800 1000

Some countries have more than one "national flag"; a few have several different designs serving as a national flag under different circumstances. The flags shown here are civil flags, those flown on land by private citizens.

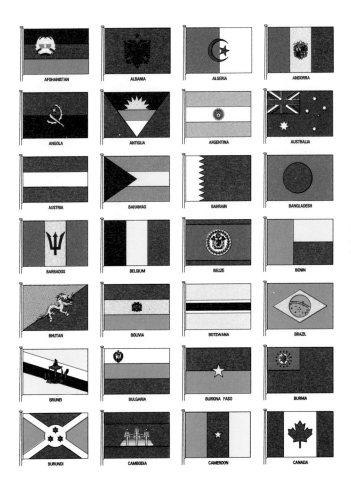

AFGHANISTAN

ALBANIA

ALGERIA

ANDORRA

ANGOLA

ANTIGUA

ARGENTINA

AUSTRALIA

AUSTRIA

BAHAMAS

BAHRAIN

BANGLADESH

BARBADOS

BELGIUM

BELIZE

BENIN

BHUTAN

BOLIVIA

BOTSWANA

BRAZIL

BRUNEI

BULGARIA

BURKINA FASO

BURMA

BURUNDI

CAMBODIA

CAMEROON

CANADA

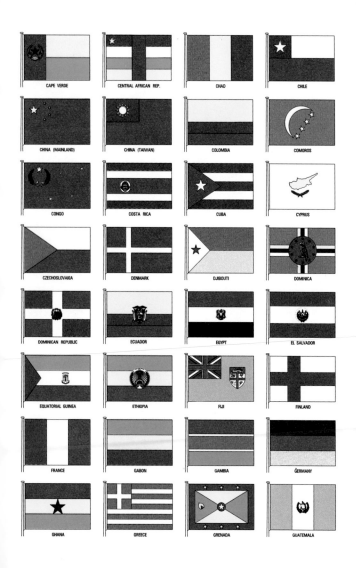

CAPE VERDE

CENTRAL AFRICAN REP.

CHAD

CHILE

CHINA (MAINLAND)

CHINA (TAIWAN)

COLOMBIA

COMOROS

CONGO

COSTA RICA

CUBA

CYPRUS

CZECHOSLOVAKIA

DENMARK

DJIBOUTI

DOMINICA

DOMINICAN REPUBLIC

ECUADOR

EGYPT

EL SALVADOR

EQUATORIAL GUINEA

ETHIOPIA

FIJI

FINLAND

FRANCE

GABON

GAMBIA

GERMANY

GHANA

GREECE

GRENADA

GUATEMALA

GUINEA

GUINEA–BISSAU

GUYANA

HAITI

HONDURAS

HUNGARY

ICELAND

INDIA

INDONESIA

IRAN

IRAQ

IRELAND

ISRAEL

ITALY

IVORY COAST

JAMAICA

JAPAN

JORDAN

KENYA

KIRIBATI

NORTH KOREA

SOUTH KOREA

KUWAIT

LAOS

LEBANON

LESOTHO

LIBERIA

LIBYA

LIECHTENSTEIN

LUXEMBOURG

MADAGASCAR

MALAWI

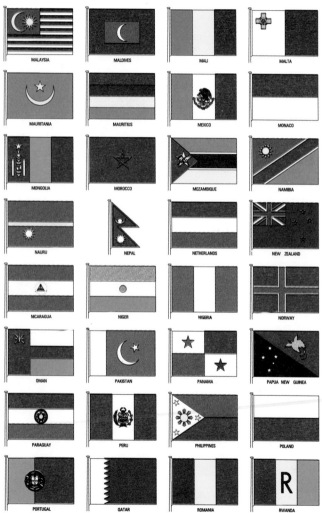

MALAYSIA	MALDIVES	MALI	MALTA
MAURITANIA	MAURITIUS	MEXICO	MONACO
MONGOLIA	MOROCCO	MOZAMBIQUE	NAMIBIA
NAURU	NEPAL	NETHERLANDS	NEW ZEALAND
NICARAGUA	NIGER	NIGERIA	NORWAY
OMAN	PAKISTAN	PANAMA	PAPUA NEW GUINEA
PARAGUAY	PERU	PHILIPPINES	POLAND
PORTUGAL	QATAR	ROMANIA	RWANDA

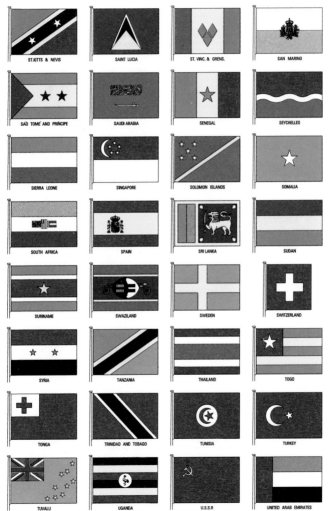

ST.KITTS & NEVIS	SAINT LUCIA	ST. VINC. & GRENS.	SAN MARINO
SAO TOME AND PRÍNCIPE	SAUDI ARABIA	SENEGAL	SEYCHELLES
SIERRA LEONE	SINGAPORE	SOLOMON ISLANDS	SOMALIA
SOUTH AFRICA	SPAIN	SRI LANKA	SUDAN
SURINAME	SWAZILAND	SWEDEN	SWITZERLAND
SYRIA	TANZANIA	THAILAND	TOGO
TONGA	TRINIDAD AND TOBAGO	TUNISIA	TURKEY
TUVALU	UGANDA	U.S.S.R	UNITED ARAB EMIRATES

Flags of the World

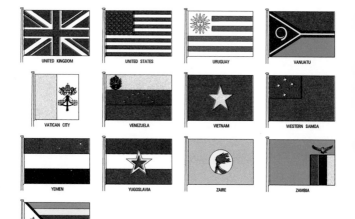

UNITED KINGDOM

UNITED STATES

URUGUAY

VANUATU

VATICAN CITY

VENEZUELA

VIETNAM

WESTERN SAMOA

YEMEN

YUGOSLAVIA

ZAIRE

ZAMBIA

ZIMBABWE

INTERNATIONAL FLAGS

UNITED NATIONS

RED CROSS

RED CRESCENT

OLYMPIC GAMES

NORTH ATLANTIC
TREATY ORGANIZATION

ORGANIZATION OF
AMERICAN STATES

ORGANIZATION OF
AFRICAN UNITY

UNITED STATES 126
Alabama 128
Alaska 129
Arizona 130
Arkansas 131
California 132
Colorado 134
Connecticut 136
Delaware 139
Florida 140
Georgia 142
Hawaii 129
Idaho 143
Illinois 144
Indiana 145
Iowa 146
Kansas 147
Kentucky 148
Louisiana 150
Maine 151
Maryland 139
Massachusetts 136
Michigan 152
Minnesota 153
Mississippi 154
Missouri 155
Montana 156
Nebraska 157
Nevada 132

New Hampshire 158
New Jersey 159
New Mexico 135
New York 160
North Carolina 162
North Dakota 164
Ohio 166
Oklahoma 168
Oregon 169
Pennsylvania 170
Rhode Island 137
South Carolina 162
South Dakota 165
Tennessee 148
Texas 172
Utah 174
Vermont 158
Virginia 139
Washington 175
West Virginia 138
Wisconsin 176
Wyoming 177
CANADA 126
Alberta 191
British Columbia 190
Manitoba 189
New Brunswick 182
Newfoundland 183
Nova Scotia 183

Ontario 186
Prince Edward
   Island 183
Québec 184
Saskatchewan 188
METROPOLITAN
   AREAS
Atlanta 142
Baltimore 139
Boston 137
Buffalo 160
Calgary 191
Charlotte 163
Chicago 178
Cincinnati 167
Cleveland 167
Dallas 172
Denver 178
Detroit 178
Edmonton 191
Fort Worth 172
Greensboro 163
Houston 173
Kansas City 155
Los Angeles 179
Louisville 149
Memphis 148
Miami 141
Milwaukee 176

Minneapolis 153
Montréal 184
Nashville 148
New Orleans 150
New York 180
Norfolk 138
Orlando 140
Ottawa 186
Philadelphia 171
Phoenix 130
Pittsburgh 170
Portland, Ore. 180
Rochester 160
Salt Lake City 174
St. Louis 155
St. Paul 153
St. Petersburg 140
San Diego 180
San Francisco 133
Seattle 175
Tampa 140
Toronto 187
Vancouver 190
Washington, D.C. 139
Winston-Salem 163
MEXICO 181
MILEAGE TABLE 192

SYMBOLS

═══════ Limited Access Highways	──────── Major Highways
▬▬▬▬▬ Toll Roads	──────── Other Important Roads
═══════ National Parkways	- - - - - - Ferries
▬▬▬▬▬ Selected Scenic Routes	⊬─ 32 ─⊬ Mileage Between Points
🛡90 U.S. Interstate Route Numbers	☐ ■ Points of Interest
(150) Federal Route Numbers	♣ State Parks, Recreation Areas
(15) State and Other Route Numbers	✈ Major Airports
🛡 Trans-Canada Highway	⊛ National Capitals
◀191 Adjoining Map Pages	⊛ State and Provincial Capitals

United States, Canada

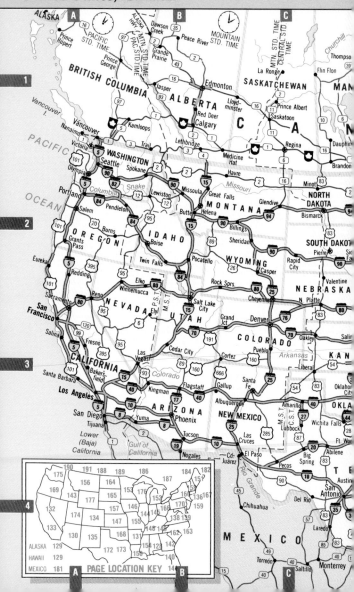

CENTRAL
STD. TIME

ATLANTIC
STD. TIME

James
Bay

EASTERN
STD. TIME

QUÉBEC

Sept-Îles

Baie-Comeau

Matane

BA

ake

Vinnipeg

CANADA

ONTARIO

EASTERN STD
CENTRAL STD
TIME
TIME

innipeg

Kenora

Kapuskasing

Chibougamau

Alma

N.B.

Ft. Frances
and Forks

Thunder Bay

Kirkland
Lake

Val-d'Or

Québec

MAINE

argo

Lake Superior

Sault Ste. Marie

North Bay

Sudbury

Montréal

Augusta

Duluth

MICHIGAN

Orillia

Ottawa

VT

N.H.

Portland

MINNESOTA

St. Paul

L. Michigan

L. Huron

Toronto

NEW
YORK

Albany

Boston
MASS.

Minneapolis

Green Bay

WISCONSIN

London

Lake Ontario

Buffalo

CT

R.I.

Albert Lea

La Crosse

Milwaukee

Lake Erie

Scranton

New York

Sioux City

Madison

Grand Rapids

Detroit

Cleveland

PENNSYLVANIA

Philadelphia

IOWA

Davenport

Chicago

OHIO

Pittsburgh

Atlantic City

Des Moines

INDIANA

Columbus

Baltimore

DEL.

ILLINOIS

Indianapolis

W. VA.

Washington

Kansas City

Springfield

Louisville

Cincinnati

Charleston

Richmond

peka

St. Louis

KENTUCKY

Lexington

VIRGINIA

Norfolk

MISSOURI

W. KY. PKWY

Roanoke

ATLANTIC

ita

Joplin

Nashville

Knoxville

Greensboro

Raleigh

C. Hatteras

Tulsa

ARKANSAS

TENNESSEE

N. CAROLINA

Charlotte

Ft. Smith

Memphis

Atlanta

Columbia

Wilmington

Little Rock

MISSISSIPPI

Birmingham

GEORGIA

S. CAROLINA

Charleston

Dallas

Shreveport

LOUISIANA

Jackson

ALABAMA

Macon

Savannah

Montgomery

Columbus

ston

Beaumont

Baton Rouge

Mobile

Tallahassee

Jacksonville

Galveston

Lafayette

New Orleans

Pensacola

FLORIDA

Daytona Beach

C.S.T.

E.S.T.

Orlando

C. Canaveral

pus Christi

Tampa

St. Petersburg

TPK

W. Palm Beach

nsville

GULF OF MEXICO

Ft. Myers

Miami

Key West

BAHAMAS

OCEAN

Alabama

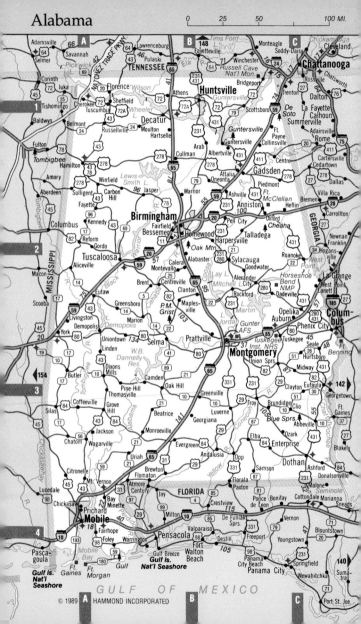

0   25   50   100 MI.

© 1989 HAMMOND INCORPORATED

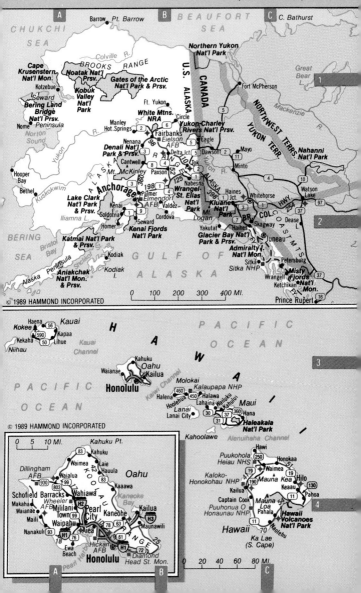

ALASKA

CHUKCHI SEA
Barrow • Pt. Barrow
BEAUFORT SEA
C. Bathurst

Colville R.
BROOKS RANGE
Cape Krusenstern Nat'l Mon.
Noatak Nat'l Prsv.
Gates of the Arctic Nat'l Park & Prsv.
Northern Yukon Nat'l Park
U.S. ALASKA
CANADA
Great Bear L.
Mackenzie R.
NORTHWEST TERRS.
Fort McPherson
Kotzebue
Kobuk Valley Nat'l Park
Ft. Yukon
White Mtns. NRA
Circle
Yukon-Charley Rivers Nat'l Prsv.
Eagle
Dawson
Mayo
Minto
Nahanni Nat'l Park
Bering Land Bridge Nat'l Prsv.
Nome
Seward Peninsula
Manley Hot Springs
Fairbanks
Eielson AFB
Delta Jct.
Tok
YUKON TERR.
Watson Lake
Hooper Bay
Bethel
Nenana
Denali Nat'l Park & Prsv.
Mt. McKinley
Cantwell
Paxson
Nabesna
Wrangell-St. Elias Nat'l Park
Whitehorse
Dease L.
Kuskokwim R.
Yukon R.
Anchorage
Palmer
Elmendorf AFB
Valdez
Mt. Logan
Kluane Nat'l Park
Haines Jct.
Haines
Skagway
Juneau
NORTHERN COAST MTS.
Lake Clark Nat'l Park & Prsv.
Iliamna L.
Kenai
Soldotna
Homer
Cordova
Kenai Fjords Nat'l Park
Yakutat
Glacier Bay Nat'l Park & Prsv.
Admiralty Nat'l Mon.
Sitka
Sitka NHP
Petersburg
BERING SEA
Bristol Bay
Katmai Nat'l Park & Prsv.
Aniakchak Nat'l Mon. & Prsv.
Alaska Peninsula
Kodiak
Kodiak I.
GULF OF ALASKA
Wrangell
Ketchikan
Misty Fjords Nat'l Mon.
Prince Rupert

0 100 200 300 400 MI.

© 1989 HAMMOND INCORPORATED

HAWAII

Haena
Kokee
Kekaha
Niihau
Kauai
Kapaa
Lihue
Kauai Channel
PACIFIC OCEAN
Kahuku
Oahu
Kailua
Waianae
Honolulu
Molokai
Kalaupapa NHP
Halena
Hoolehua
Halawa
Lahaina
Wailuku
Maui
Hana
Haleakala Nat'l Park
Lanai
Lanai City
Kahoolawe
Alenuihaha Channel
Kailua
Maui Channel

© 1989 HAMMOND INCORPORATED

Hawi
Puukohola Heiau NHS
Honokaa
Waimea
Mauna Kea
Hilo
Kaloko-Honokohau NHP
Captain Cook
Kailua
Mauna Loa
Keaau
Pahoa
Puuhonua O Honaunau NHP
Pahala
Hawaii
Hawaii Volcanoes Nat'l Park
Naalehu
Ka Lae (S. Cape)

Oahu (inset)

0 5 10 MI.

Kahuku Pt.
Dillingham AFB
Kahuku
Laie
Waialua
Haula
Waimea
Schofield Barracks
Wheeler AFB
Wahiawa
KOOLAU RANGE
Kaaawa
Makaha
Mililani Town
Pearl City
Kaneohe
Kailua
Maunawili
Waianae
Waipahu
Aiea
WAIANAE RANGE
Maili
Nanakuli
Hickam AFB
Diamond Head St. Mon.
Ewa Beach
Honolulu
Pearl Harbor

0 20 40 60 80 MI.

Arizona

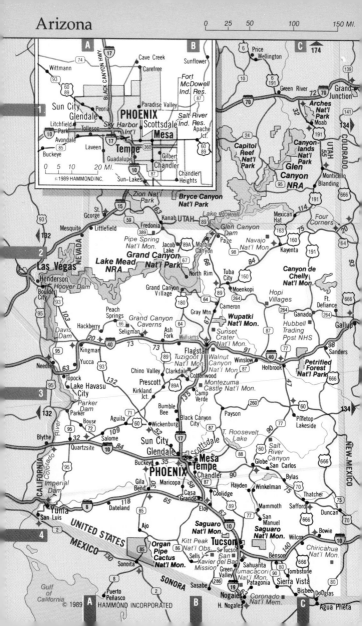

0   25   50   100   150 MI.

Inset Map (Phoenix area)

Wittmann • 74 • Black Canyon Hwy • 17 • Cave Creek • Carefree • Sunflower

Sun City • 60 89 • Peoria • Guadalupe • PHOENIX • Paradise Valley • Fort McDowell Ind. Res.

Glendale • Litchfield Park • Tolleson • Sky Harbor Int'l • Scottsdale • Salt River Ind. Res. • Apache Jct.

Avondale • 85 • Laveen • 17 • Tempe • Mesa • 60 89

Buckeye • 10 • Guadalupe • 360 • Gilbert • Chandler • 87

Sun Lakes • Chandler Heights

© 1989 HAMMOND INC.

0   5   10   20 MI.

Main Map

Price • Wellington • 174 • 6

10 • 191 • Green River • Grand Junction • 139 • 72 70

Zion Nat'l Park • 163 • Bryce Canyon Nat'l Park • Lake Powell • Arches Nat'l Park • Moab • 141 • 134

St. George • 15 • 59 • Fredonia • 389 • Kanab • UTAH • 89 • Glen Canyon NRA • Capitol Reef Nat'l Park • Canyonlands Nat'l Park • UTAH 55 • Monticello • Blanding • 666

Mesquite • Littlefield • Pipe Spring Nat'l Mon. • Jacob Lake • Marble Canyon • Glen Canyon Dam • Page • Mexican Hat • Four Corners • 114 • 191

NEVADA • Lake Mead NRA • 67 • Grand Canyon Nat'l Park • 89A • Navajo Nat'l Mon. • 98 • Kayenta • 163 • 75 • 64 • 70

Las Vegas • North Rim • Tuba City • 160 • 84 • Canyon de Chelly Nat'l Mon. • Ft. Defiance

Henderson • Boulder City • Hoover Dam • 93 • Grand Canyon Village • 89 • Moenkopi • Hopi Villages • 264 • Ganado • 264 • Gallup

Davis Dam • 95 • Peach Springs • Grand Canyon Caverns • 180 • 64 • Gray Mtn. • Cameron • Wupatki Nat'l Mon. • Hubbell Trading Post NHS • 666

Needles • 63 • Hackberry • 66 • Seligman • Ash Fork • 64 • Sunset Crater Nat'l Mon. • 89 • 91 • Winslow • 40 • Holbrook • 98 • Sanders

Topock • Kingman • Yucca • 93 • 40 • 73 • 73 • Williams • Flagstaff • Tuzigoot Nat'l Mon. • Walnut Canyon Nat'l Mon. • 87 • Petrified Forest Nat'l Park • 666

Lake Havasu City • Chino Valley • Clarkdale • Cottonwood • 47

Parker Dam • Parker • 72 • 95 • Aguila • 71 • Prescott • Kirkland Jct. • 89A • Montezuma Castle Nat'l Mon. • Camp Verde • 260 • Pinetop-Lakeside • 134

Bouse • 60 • Bumble Bee • 135 • Payson • 60 • NEW MEXICO

Blythe • Salome • 84 • Wickenburg • 52 • Black Canyon City • T. Roosevelt Lake • 88 • Salt River Canyon • 666

Quartzsite • 10 • 109 • Sun City • Glendale • 87 • Scottsdale • 90 • 77 • Globe • San Carlos • Bylas • 70

CALIFORNIA • 95 • Buckeye • 35 • Mesa • Tempe • Chandler • 90 • Hayden • Winkelman • Mammoth • Safford • Thatcher • Duncan • 75

Imperial Dam • Gila Bend • PHOENIX • Maricopa • 87 • Coolidge • 89 • San Manuel • 70

Yuma • 8 • 118 • Dateland • 85 • Casa Grande • Eloy • 77 • 666 • Bowie • 10

San Luis • UNITED STATES • Ajo • Saguaro Nat'l Mon. • 10 • Tucson • Saguaro Nat'l Mon. • Benson • Wilcox • Chiricahua Nat'l Mon.

MEXICO • 2 • Organ Pipe Cactus Nat'l Mon. • 85 • Kitt Peak Nat'l Obs. • Sells • Xavier del Bac Mission • San Xavier • Sahuarita • Green Valley • 140 • 80

SONORA • 2 • Sonoita • Sasabe • 286 • Tumacácori Nat'l Mon. • Patagonia • Sierra Vista • Tombstone • Bisbee • Douglas

Gulf of California • Puerto Peñasco • 8 • Nogales • H. Nogales • Coronado Nat'l Mem. • Agua Prieta

© 1989 HAMMOND INCORPORATED

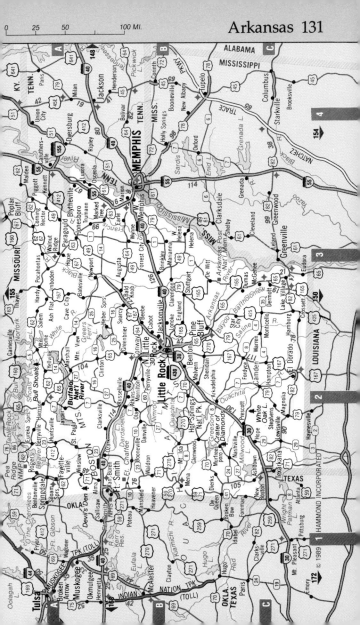

0   25   50   100 MI.

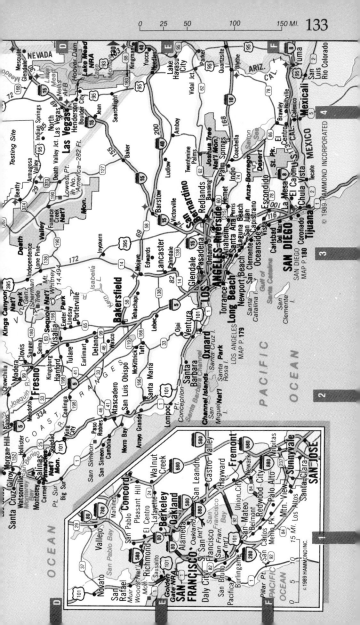

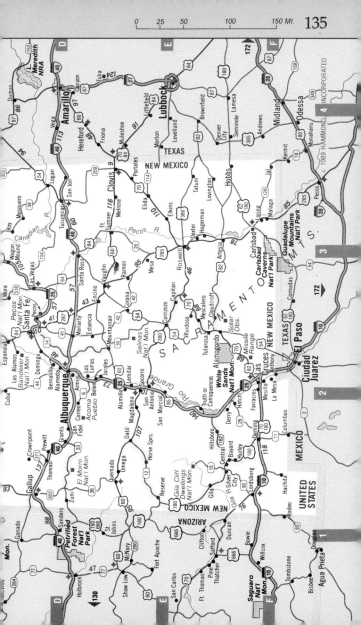

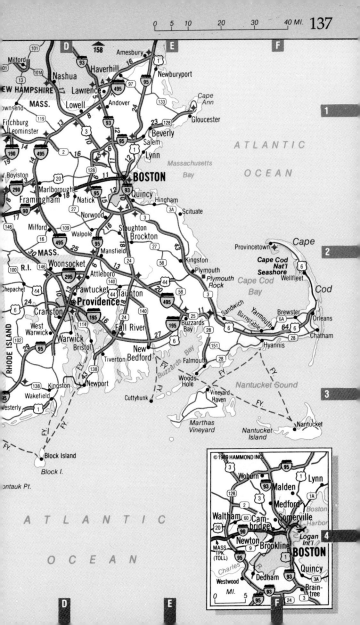

D
© 1989 HAMMOND INC.
5 MI.
Bethesda
Silver Spring
Takoma Pk.
College Pk.
Greenbelt
495
CAPITAL
BELTWAY
95
C.&O. Canal NHP
MD.
VA.
Chevy Chase
29
Hyattsville
G. WASH. MEM. PKWY
123
McLean
267
7
WASHINGTON
White House
Capitol
Arlington
Falls Church
66
50
Washington D.C.
ANACOSTIA FRW'Y
214
50
Annandale
236
395
395
295
Hillcrest-Hts.
495
CAPITAL
Alexandria
5
Andrews AFB
95
BELTWAY
1

E
96
BELTWAY
495
BALTO WASH. PKWY
95
1

F
© 1989 HAMMOND INC.
5 MI.
83
695
Towson
Parkville
695
1
Pikesville
140
NORTH
83
45
147
Overlea
1
Pimlico Race Tr.
Mem. Sta.
695
BALTIMORE
895
40
150
70
40
Ft. McHenry Nat'l Mon.
HARBOR TUNNEL (TOLL)
Essex
Catonsville
Dundalk
Arbutus
895
2
KEY BR. (TOLL)
695
Elkridge
BALTO. WASH. PKWY
B-W. Int'l.
Sparrows Pt.
Patapsco R.

PENNSYLVANIA
230
70
170
81
S.
Gettysburg
83
SUSQUEHANNA R.
Wilmington
DEL. TPK. (TOLL)
N. J. TPK. (TOLL)
159
A.C. EXPWY (TOLL)
NEW JERSEY
Frostburg
110
Cumberland
Hancock
97
MARYLAND
66
Elkton
95
40
G. ST. PKWY (TOLL)
Keyser
522
Martinsburg
Hagerstown
15 Westminster
Frederick
Reisterstown
Bel Air
Havre de Grace
Aberdeen
Odessa
DELAWARE
kland
Potomac R.
50
Harpers Ferry
Harpers Ferry NHP
45
Towson
Smyrna
DEL. BAY
Cape May
143
Charles Town
MD.
70
270
BALTIMORE
300
Dover
FY.
Lewes
neca Rocks RA
Winchester
Leesburg
Gaithersburg
Rockville
Laurel
BW TW PKWY
95
Ft. Meade
301
404
Milford
13
Georgetown
Rehoboth Beach
WEST VIRGINIA
Strasburg
Berryville
50
7
58
Annapolis
65
Seaford
9
113
1
Woodstock
Front Royal
Marshall
19
WASHINGTON
Arlington
Alexandria
CHESAPEAKE
Cambridge
50
Laurel
DEL.
Berlin
VIRGINIA
211
66
Manassas
Ft. Belvoir
MD.
Salisbury
Ocean City
New Market
17
Luray
Warrenton
Quantico
La Plata
Waldorf
5
Lexington
Snow Hill
Pocomoke City
rrisonburg
G
Culpeper
3
301
G. Wash. Birthpl. Nat'l Mon.
Warsaw
Crisfield
Chincoteague
VA.
aunton
SKYLINE DRIVE
Shenandoah Nat'l Park
Orange
Gordonsville
Fredericksburg
Camp A.P. Hill
Assateague Island Nat'l Seashore
ynesboro
PKWY
29
112
Tappahannock
360
BAY
Exmore
13
Charlottesville
33
Ashland
295
Kilmarnock
a Vista
64
66
Richmond NBP
3
ATLANTIC
herst
15
James R.
Sprouses
Richmond
RICH. NBP
Kilmarnock
17
Cape Charles
Lynchburg
63
Appomattox C. H. NHP
51
RICH-PETERSBG. TPK. (TOLL)
23
Williamsburg
Colonial NHP
Yorktown
Langley AFB
Appomattox
Farmville
Petersburg
Hopewell
10
Newport News
Hampton
CHESAPEAKE BAY BR.-TUN. (TOLL)
Roanoke R.
Brookneal
40
Blackstone
McKenney
51
460
Wakefield
Smithfield
Norfolk
Naval Base
Ft. Story
tavista
na
501
Keysville
15
South Hill
36
58
Emporia
Franklin
Portsmouth
Suffolk
21
44
Virginia Beach
58
Boggs Island Lake
L. Gaston
Chesapeake
OCEAN
Roxboro
501
Oxford
85
Henderson
75
95
Roanoke Rapids
Roanoke R.
13
17
168
Durham
162
64
Rocky Mount
Ahoskie
Elizabeth City
158
Kitty Hawk
Edenton
Windsor
Albemarle Sd.

D   E   F

Florida

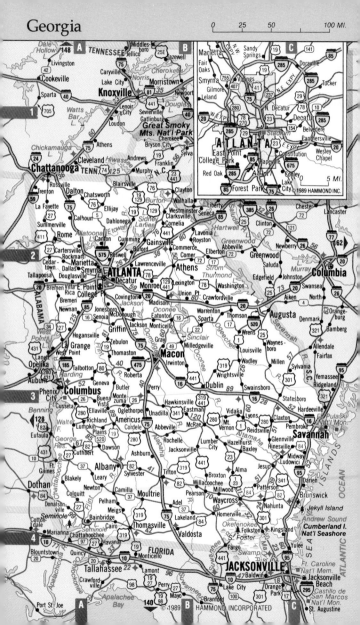

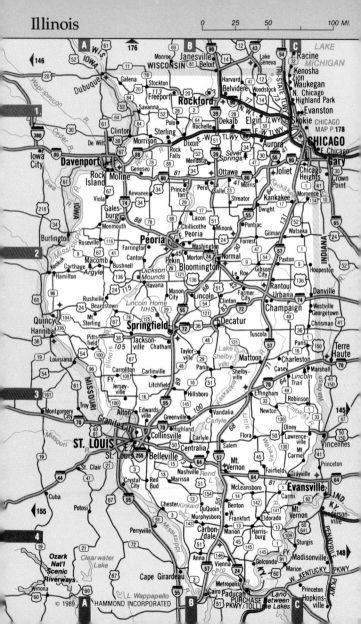

Illinois

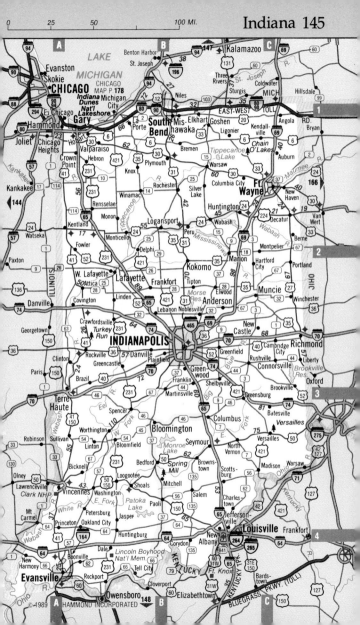

Iowa

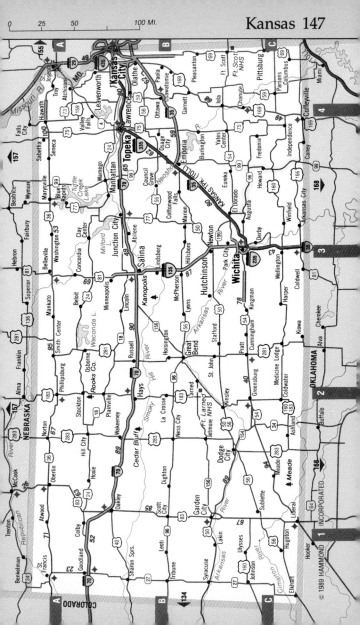

100 MI.

© 1989 HAMMOND INCORPORATED

Kentucky, Tennessee

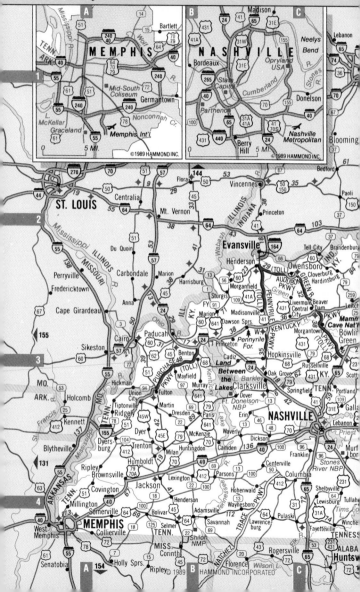

MEMPHIS

Bartlett
Mid-South Coliseum
Germantown
Nonconnah Cr.
McKellar
Graceland
Memphis Int'l.
5 MI.
©1989 HAMMOND INC.

NASHVILLE

Madison
Neelys Bend
Bordeaux
Opryland USA
State Capitol
Cumberland
Donelson
Parthenon
Berry Hill
Nashville Metropolitan
5 MI.
©1989 HAMMOND INC.

Lebanon
Blooming
Bedford
Flora
Vincennes
Paoli

ST. LOUIS
Centralia
Mt. Vernon
ILLINOIS
INDIANA
Princeton

Du Quoin
Evansville
Tell City
Brandenbur
Henderson
Owensboro
IND.
Perryville
Carbondale
Marion
Cloverburg
Hardinsburg
Fredericktown
Harrisburg
Morganfield
AUDUBON PKWY
Livermore
Beaver Dam
Sturgis
Anna
Mamm
Cave Nat'l
Cape Girardeau
Madisonville
Morgantown
Bowling
Green
Paducah
Marion
Dawson Sprs.
Hopkinsville
Russellville
Cairo
Benton
Princeton
Pennyrile For.
Oak Grove
KY.
Sikeston
Cadiz
Land
Between
the Lakes
Portland
MO.
Hickman
Mayfield
Clarksville
Springfield
Gallal
ARK.
Union City
Murray
Ft. Donelson NBP
Dover
TENN.
Lebanon
Holcomb
Tiptonville
Martin
Paris
Erin
NASHVILLE
Priest
Kennett
Ridgely
Dresden
Waverly
Dickson
Murf
bor
Dyer
McKenzie
Camden
Stones
River NBP
Blytheville
Trenton
Milan
Huntingdon
Franklin
Dyersburg
Humboldt
Centerville
Columbia
Shelbyville
Ripley
Brownsville
Jackson
Lexington
Parsons
Tullahi
Covington
Henderson
Hohenwald
Lewisburg
Tims Fo
Millington
Somerville
Adamsville
Waynesboro
TRACE PKWY
Pulaski
Fayetteville
Winche
West
Memphis
MEMPHIS
Bolivar
Selmer
Savannah
Lawrenceburg
TENNES
Collierville
TENN.
Shiloh NMP
ALABA
Senatobia
Holly Sprs.
MISS.
Corinth
NATCHEZ
Rogersville
Huntsv
Ripley
©1989
Florence
Wilson L.
HAMMOND INCORPORATED

Louisiana

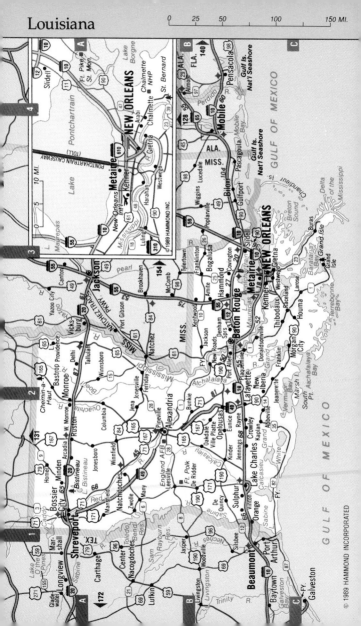

© 1989 HAMMOND INCORPORATED

Maine 151

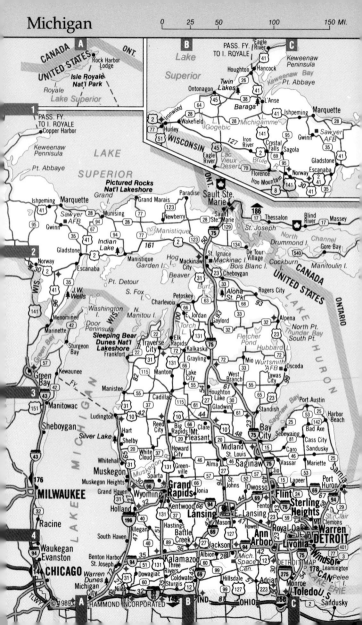

Michigan

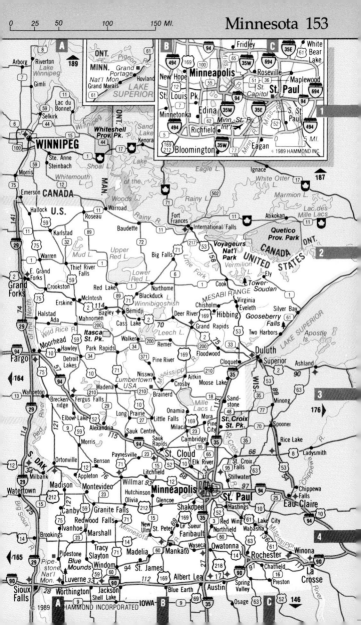

Mississippi

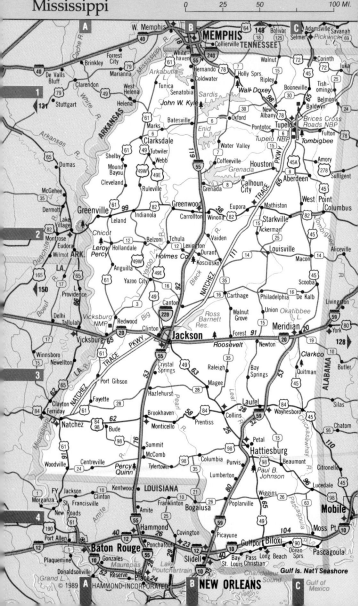

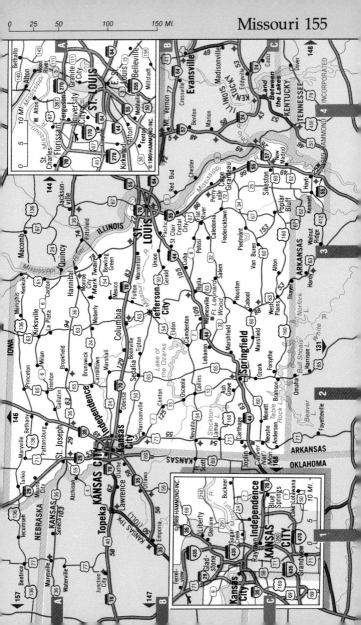

Montana

0 25 50 100 150 MI.

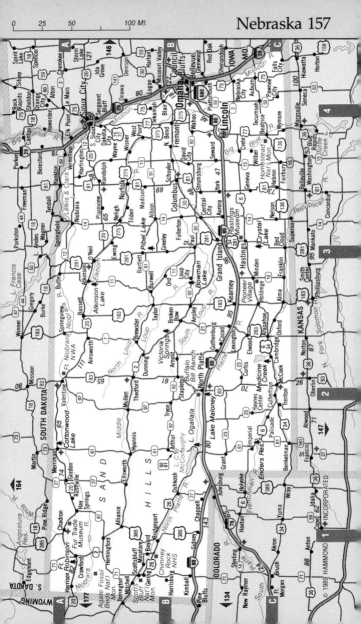

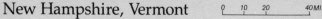

New Hampshire, Vermont

0   10   20   40 MI.

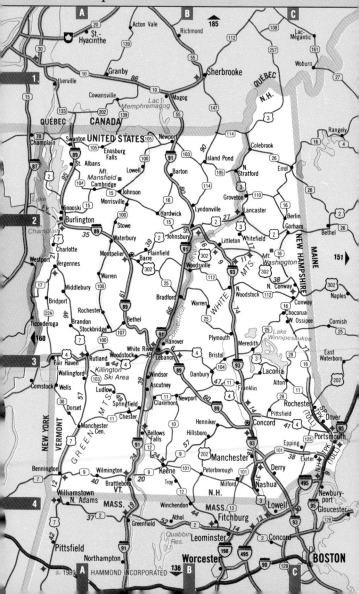

© 1989 HAMMOND INCORPORATED

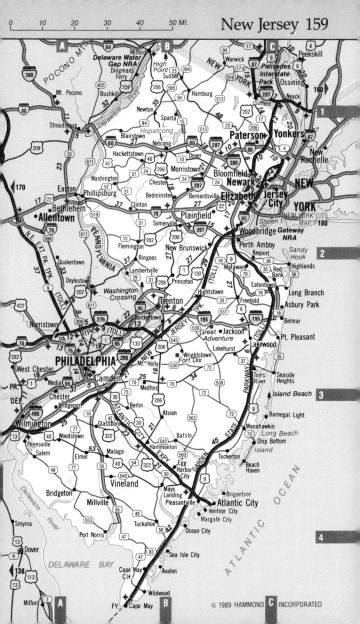

New Jersey 159

© 1989 HAMMOND INCORPORATED

New York

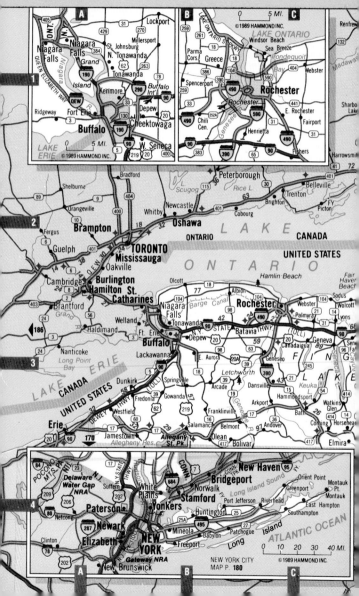

NEW YORK CITY
MAP P. **180**

© 1989 HAMMOND INC.

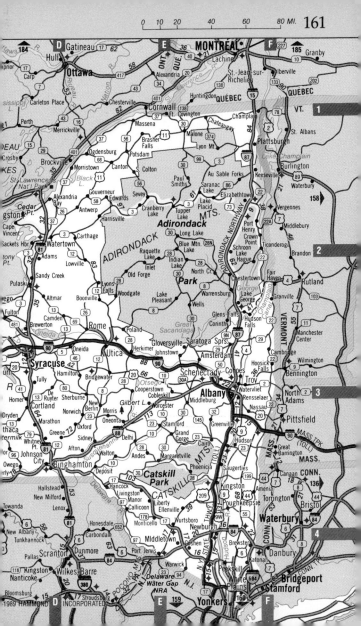

North Dakota, South Dakota

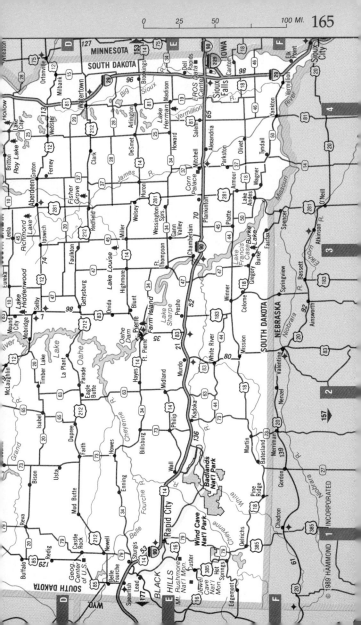

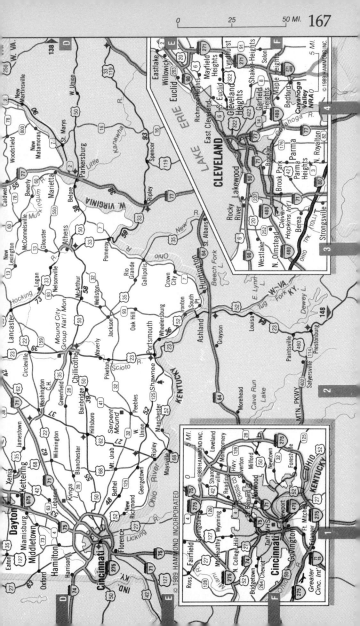

W. VA.

138 D

258 | 2 New Martinsville

7 New Matamoras

78 | 860 | 90

Woodsfield

St. Marys

Little Kanawha R.

2 Marietta

Parkersburg

16

Spencer 119

Beverly 77 550

Belpre

Ripley

33

16

Kanawha 33

ERIE LAKE

CLEVELAND

East Cleveland

Lakewood

90

Rocky River

Westlake

N. Olmstead

W. VIRGINIA

Caldwell 78 555

Beverly

Marietta

Belpre

Muskingum R.

New Lexington 13

McConnelsville 60

Glouster 13

Athens 33

Pomeroy

7

Ohio R.

Logan 33

Nelsonville 78

Hocking R. 93

Rio Grande

Gallipolis

New R.

Beech Fork

St. Albans

Huntington 64

Louisa

E. Lynn

Tug Fork

W-VA. KY.

Dewey L.

148

Lancaster 22

Circleville 23

Washington C.H. 22 62

Greenfield 35

Bainbridge 50

Hillsboro 41

Wilmington

Jamestown 35

Xenia 42

Kettering 675

Lebanon

Kings

Blanchester 68

Mt. Orab 62

Ripley

68

Maysville

Morehead 64

Cave Run Lake

Grayson

Ashland

Ironton 52

Wheelersburg 52

Portsmouth

Shawnee

Scioto R.

Piketon 23

Waverly

Chillicothe 35

Serpent Mound

Peebles 32

W. Union 52

Mound City Group Nat'l Mon

McArthur 50 327

Jackson 93

Oak Hill 35

Wellston

Crown City

South Pt.

KENTUCKY

Paintsville 460

Salyersville

Prestonburg

MTN. PKWY.

23

52

Dayton

Miamisburg 725

Middletown 73

Hamilton 127

Oxford 27

Eaton 35 127

Harrison

IND. KY.

74

50

Florence

Covington

75

71

275

Cincinnati

CLEVELAND INSET:

Eastlake 2

Willowick

Willoughby 90

Euclid 6 20

Mayfield Heights

Lyndhurst

Highland Heights

Richmond Heights 283

Mayfield Heights 322

Cleveland Heights

Solon 91

Shaker Heights

Maple Heights

Bedford 271 43

Cuyahoga Valley NRA

Garfield Heights 422

Brooklyn

Parma 176

Parma Heights 42

Brook Park

Berea

N. Royalton 82

Strongsville

Cuyahoga R.

480

90 237

Clev. Hopkins Int'l

252

480

Ohio Tpk. (TOLL)

90 20

5 MI.

CINCINNATI INSET:

© 1989 HAMMOND INCORPORATED

5 MI.

Loveland 48

Montgomery 126

Milford 28

Newtown 275

Foresthille 125

Sharonville

Silverton 50

Reading 42

Norwood

CROSS CO. HWY.

Bond Hill

Forestville

Springdale 4

Wyoming 126

Mt. Healthy 127

N. College Hill

Cheviot 74

Ross Fairfield 128

Bridgetown 50

Newport 52

Ft. Mitchell

Ft. Thomas

Covington 75

Greater Cinc. Int'l 275

Licking R.

KENTUCKY

OHIO

Cincinnati

© 1989 HAMMOND INC.

Oklahoma

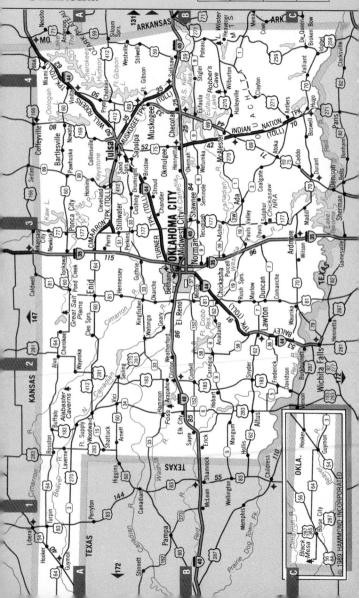

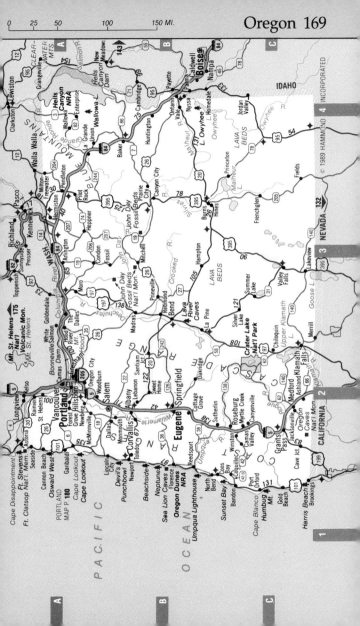

Texas

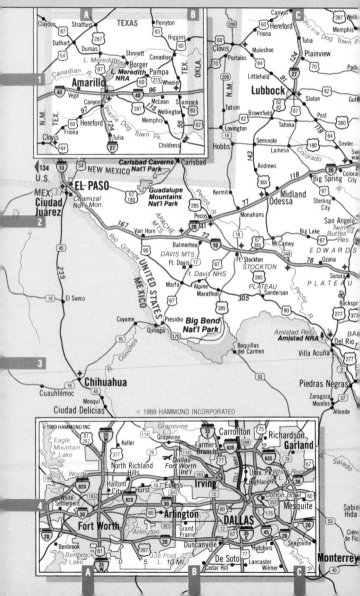

Utah

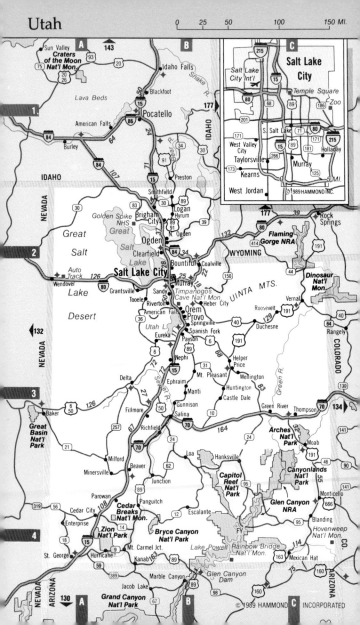

0 25 50 100 150 MI.

A **B** **C**

Salt Lake City

Salt Lake City Int'l

Temple Square
Zoo

S. Salt Lake
West Valley City
Taylorsville
Kearns
West Jordan
Murray
Holladay

© 1989 HAMMOND INC.

Sun Valley
Craters of the Moon Nat'l Mon.
143

Idaho Falls
Snake R.
Blackfoot
Lava Beds
Pocatello
American Falls
Burley

IDAHO

177

Rock Springs

Smithfield
Logan
Hyrum
Golden Spike NHS
Brigham City
N. Ogden
Ogden
Clearfield
Bountiful Coalville
Salt Lake City
Great Salt Lake
Auto Track
Wendover
Grantsville
Tooele
Riverton
Sandy
American Falls
Timpanogos Cave Nat'l Mon.
Heber City
Orem
Provo
Springville
Utah L.
Eureka
Payson
Spanish Fork
Nephi
Helper
Price

WYOMING
Flaming Gorge NRA
Dinosaur Nat'l Mon.
UINTA MTS.
Roosevelt Vernal
Duchesne
Rangely

COLORADO

Great Salt Lake Desert

NEVADA

132

Great Basin Nat'l Park
Baker
Delta
Fillmore
Richfield
Milford
Minersville
Beaver
Parowan
Cedar City
Enterprise
Zion Nat'l Park
St. George
Hurricane
Cedar Breaks Nat'l Mon.
Panguitch
Junction
Loa
Bryce Canyon Nat'l Park
Escalante
Mt. Carmel Jct.
Kanab

Ephraim
Manti
Gunnison
Salina
Mt. Pleasant
Wellington
Huntington
Castle Dale
Green River
Thompson

Hanksville
Capitol Reef Nat'l Park
Canyonlands Nat'l Park
Arches Nat'l Park
Moab
Monticello
Blanding
Glen Canyon NRA
Hovenweep Nat'l Mon.
Lake Powell
Rainbow Bridge Nat'l Mon.
Glen Canyon Dam
Mexican Hat

Marble Canyon
Jacob Lake
Grand Canyon Nat'l Park

NEVADA
ARIZONA

130

© 1989 HAMMOND INCORPORATED

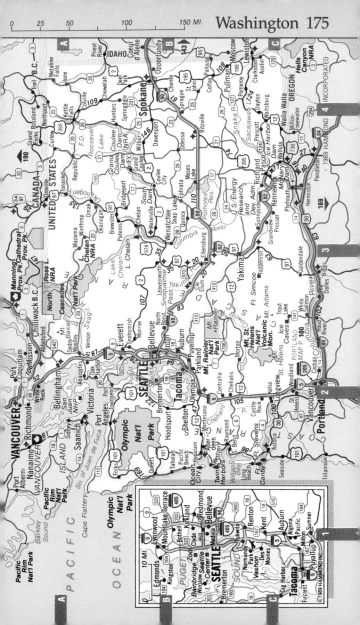

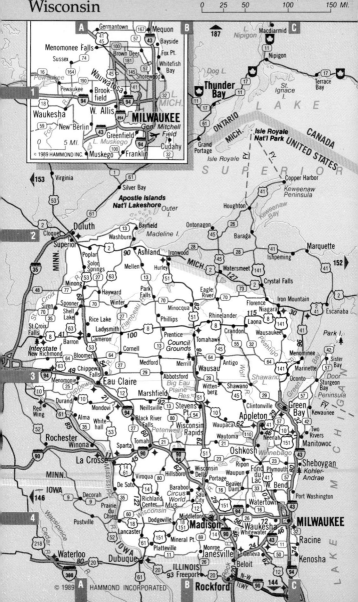

Wisconsin

0 25 50 100 150 MI.

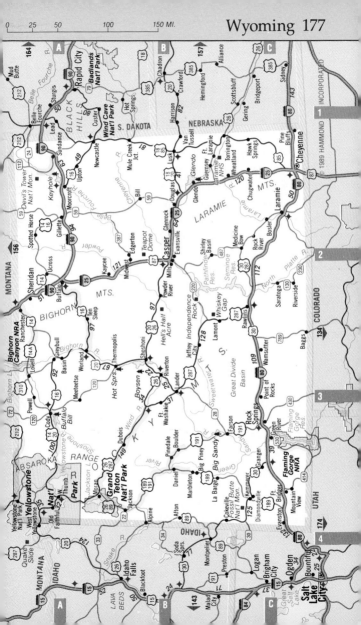

Chicago, Denver, Detroit

Chicago map (top):

Fox Lake · McHenry · Grayslake · Illinois Beach · Waukegan · North Chicago · Lake Bluff · Lake Forest · Highwood · Highland Park · Crystal Lake · Mondelein · Wauconda · Lake Zurich · Deerfield · Glencoe · Winnetka · Wilmette · Algonquin · Barrington · Wheeling · Arlington Hts. · Carpentersville · Palatine · N–W. TOLLWAY · Evanston · Elgin · Streamwood · Des Plaines · Morton Grove · Park Ridge · Skokie · S. Elgin · Chicago Int'l · Norridge · Wrigley Field · St. Charles · Bloomingdale · Villa Park · Elmwood Park · **CHICAGO** · Lombard · Elmhurst · Oak Park · The Loop · W. Chicago · Glen Ellyn · Berwyn · Cicero · Soldier Field · E–W. TOLLWAY · Brookfield · Comiskey Pk. · Aurora · Lisle · Downers Grove · Midway · Naperville · Oaklawn · SKYWAY · Palos Park · Blue Island · Whiting · E. Chicago · **Gary** · Ogden Dunes · Plainfield · Orland Pk. · Calumet City · Hammond · Highland · Hobart · Lockport · Tinley Pk. · Shorewood · Joliet · Lansing · Schererville · New Lenox · Chicago Hts. · Frankfort · Park Forest · Plainfield

LAKE MICHIGAN

© 1989 HAMMOND INC.

ILL. / IND.

0 5 10 15 20 MI.

Denver map (bottom left):

Boulder · Lafayette · Brighton · Marshall · Broomfield · Northglenn · Thornton · Westminster · Arvada · Golden · Wheat Ridge · **DENVER** · Lakewood · Stapleton Int'l · Aurora · Morrison · Englewood · Littleton · Fenders · Parker

0 5 MI.

© 1989 HAMMOND INC.

Detroit map (bottom right):

Pontiac · Utica · Keego Hbr. · Sterling Hts. · Mt. Clemens · Bloomfield Hills · Warren · Franklin · St. Clair Shores · Royal Oak · E. Detroit · Southfield · Lake St. Clair · Livonia · **DETROIT** · U.S. · Garden City · Westland · Dearborn · Windsor · CANADA · Allen Pk. · Lincoln Park · Tecumseh · Detroit Metro. · MICH. / ONT.

0 5 MI.

© 1989 HAMMOND INC.

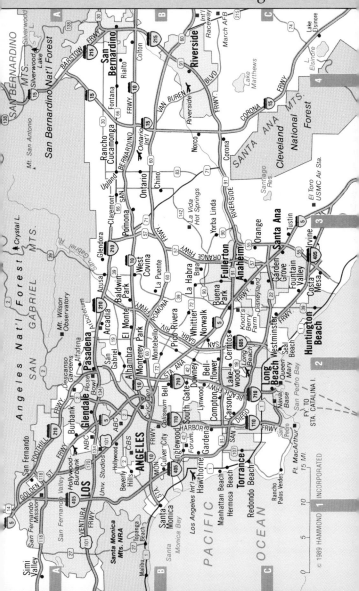

New York City, Portland, San Diego

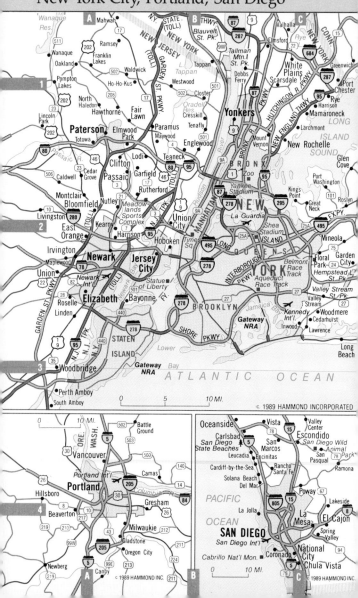

© 1989 HAMMOND INCORPORATED

© 1989 HAMMOND INC.

© 1989 HAMMOND INC.

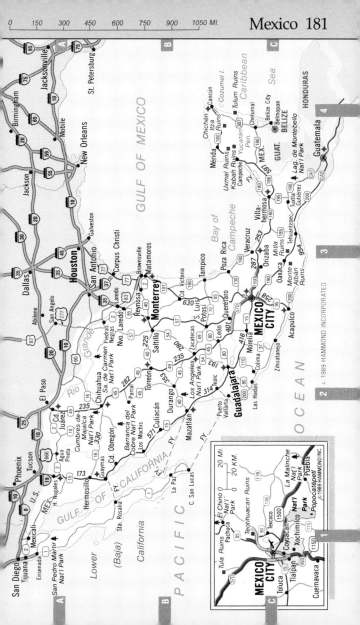

0   25   50   100 MI.

Inset map (Newfoundland)

QUEBEC 184

GULF OF ST. LAWRENCE

Blanc Sablon
430
St. Anthony
St. Barbe
430
Gros Morne Nat'l Pk.
217
349
Corner Brook
340
Lewisporte
330
Gander
Gambo
Terra Nova Nat'l Pk.
460
Cape St. George
Stephenville
135
1
NEWFOUNDLAND
Goobies
Bay Roberts
St. John's
70
Rose Blanche
Channel-Port aux Basques
Fortune
210
Argentia
100
Mt. Pearl
10

ATLANTIC OCEAN

CABOT STRAIT

© 1989 HAMMOND INC

Main map

GULF OF ST. LAWRENCE

Tignish
Mill River
2
PRINCE EDWARD ISLAND
142
88
Kensington
Prince Edward I. Nat'l Pk.
48
2
Summerside
Borden
Souris
34
77
Charlottetown
1
32
Georgetown
C. Tormentine
Wood Is.
16
26
Amherst
96
Tata-magouche
79
Pictou I.
New Glasgow
104
Glen holme
Earltown
104
Pictou
106
245
Antigonish
104
Westville
245
75
Monastery
Truro
121
Brookfield
289
Aspen
7
Guys-borough
16
316
Canso
Noel
215
215
224
Upper Musquodoboit
Sheet Harbour
New Harbour
101
354
357
224
Musquodoboit Harbour
Ecum Secum
103
118
107
7
Fall River
333
Halifax
Dartmouth
Chester
Terence Bay
Have

CAPE BRETON ISLAND

Cape North
Cape Breton Highlands Nat'l Pk.
CABOT STRAIT
Margaree Harbour
19
St. Ann's
N. Sydney
105
Glace Bay
Mabou
118
Iona
223
4
Sydney
19
L. Ainslie
Bras d'Or Lake
Fourchu
Louisbourg
22
Fortress of Louisbourg Nat'l Hist. Pk.
St. George's Bay
Port Hastings
20
104
St. Peters
Port Hawkesbury
Chedabucto Bay

ATLANTIC OCEAN

Québec

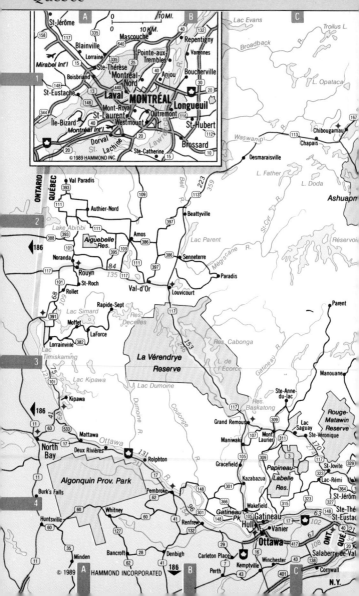

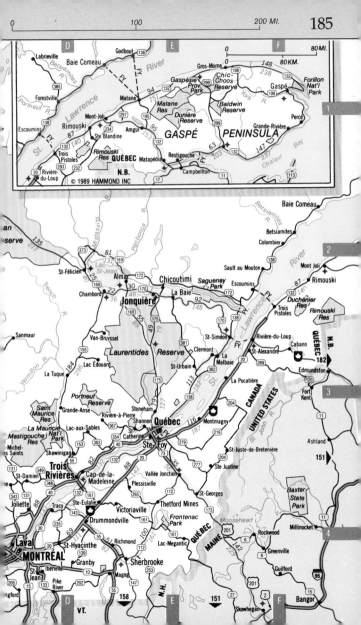

Ontario

© 1989 HAMMOND INCORPORATED

Inset map:
QUE.
Gatineau Park
Gatineau
Vanier
Hull
Kanata
OTTAWA
Ottawa Int'l.
Ottawa R.
0 5 MI.
0 5 KM.
© 1989 HAMMOND INCORPORATED
148
5
148
17
417
417
31

Echo Bay
Mississagi
Elliot Lake
Blind River
St. Joseph I.
Thessalon
Gogoma
Elk Lake
New Liskeard
Latchford
Ville-Marie
Témis-
Lady Evelyn L.
Temagami Lake
L. Timiskaming
184
Halfway Lakes
Wanapitei
Chelmsford
Sudbury
Espanola
Killarney Prov. Park
Estaire
Marten River
Sturgeon Falls
North Bay
Powassan
South River
Huntsville
Drummond I.
Cockburn I.
Gore Bay
Little Current
Killarney
French R.
Lake Nipissing
Manitoulin Island
South Baymouth
Fitzwilliam I.
Grundy Lake
Parry Sound
Mac Tier
Rosseau
Port Carling
L. Muskoka
Gravenhurst
Rogers City
Alpena
South Pt.
Tobermory
Bruce Peninsula Nat'l Park
Lion's Head
C. Croker
GEORGIAN BAY
Georgian Bay Is. Nat'l Park
Midland
Coldwater
Orillia
L. Simcoe
152
LAKE HURON
Oscoda
Southampton
MacGregor Point
Port Elgin
Owen Sound
Nottawasaga Bay
Collingwood
Barrie
Cookstown
Newmarket
Oshawa
Port Austin
Kincardine
Walkerton
Durham
Shelburne
Orangeville
Brampton
Mississauga
TORON
Bay City
Saginaw
Bad Axe
Goderich
Wingham
Listowel
Guelph
Waterloo
Kitchener
Cambridge
Burlington
Hamilton
St. Catharines
Buffalo
Flint
Port Huron
Sarnia
The Pinery
Parkhill
London
Woodstock
Stratford
Brantford
Niag
N.Y.
Pontiac
DETROIT
Ann Arbor
Windsor
Wallaceburg
Chatham
Blenheim
St. Thomas
Simcoe
Nanticoke
Long Pt. Bay
Dunkirk
Erie
Jamestown
Toledo
Tilbury
Rondeau
Leamington
Point Pelee Nat'l. Pk.
Pelee I.
LAKE ERIE
CANADA
UNITED STATES

North Channel
MICHIGAN
U.S.
CANADA
Saginaw Bay
St. Clair
Thames R.
166

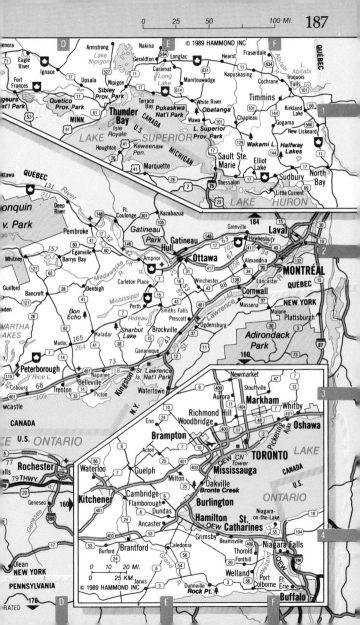

955 La Loche

155

Peter Pond Lake

191

Buffalo Narrows
155

Cole Bay 965 Beauval

Primrose L.

Medley 55
28 Pierceland
41

Meadow Lake Prov. Pk.
904
224 903
55 4

Green Lake
155
Meadow Lake
4
55

Doré L.

165 La Ronge Lac la Ronge

Brabant Lake Southend
905
102

Lac La Ronge Prov. Pk.
2
135

106
165
146 235

Montreal Lake

Prince Albert Nat'l Pk.

Nipawin Prov. Pk.
Cumberland

106

Tobin L. 122 Hou

Carrot 55

16 17 Glaslyn 110 Shell Lake
Lloydminster 21 156 177
85 The Battlefords 169
Maidstone 26 433
16 North Battleford
Battleford 40
21 4 86
Unity 139 16
14
13 Provost 14 Macklin 93
Altario 51 Kerrobert 51
12 21

Smeaton 55
Choiceland
Nipawin Wildcat Hi Wilderness A
Shellbrook 6
Prince Albert 3 59 97 Hudson
Blaine Lake 12 40 Melfort 35 156 Red
87 Tisdale
11
Wakaw 6 Greenwater Prov. Pk.
20 Endeavou
Saskatoon Humboldt Kelvington 49
14 Watson Wadena
7 16 Viscount 174 Quill Sheho
Colonsay Lanigan 16 Lakes 259 47
Delisle Dundurn Foam 161 16
Harris Nokomis Lake Springside
Rosetown 90 Hanley Simpson Raymore 15
145 45 Watrous 6
Kindersley 7 Kenaston 35 Melville
Alsask 44 Dinsmore Davidson 20 15 116 187
Eatonia Elrose 44 Danielson 360 Ft. 48
9 42 Qu'Appelle Qu'
41 Glidden Douglas Holdfast Qu'Appelle
Leader 21 342 Chamberlain 2 Lumsden White 10
Saskatchewan Tuxford City Montmartre
Landing Prov. Pk. 107 Regina 47 Mo
Gull 94 1 Moose Jaw 44 Pr
Lake 105 Webb Swift Current Old Wives L. 71 6
169 37 Notukeu Cr. 339 39 Corinne Francis
Walsh Cadillac 2 Avonlea 334 Milestone 146 35 33
1 Cypress Hills Prov. Pk. Shaunavon 13 Pangman 235 Weyburn 13 Stou
Maple Creek 37 Lafleche Assiniboia 13 73 39
21 13 18 Wood 130 34 Minton 18 Estevan
41 501 Climax Val Marie Rockglen Big 35 Souris
21 18 Grasslands Nat'l Pk. Killdeer Beaver Noonan
232 233 2 209 Upheim 18
242 156 24 248 511 16

ALBERTA SASKATCHEWAN CANADA UNITED STATES N.D.

© 1989 HAMMOND INC.

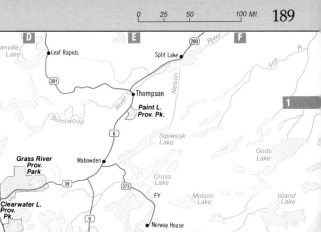

Alberta, British Columbia

Highway Mileage Table

HIGHWAY DISTANCES BETWEEN MAJOR CITIES	Atlanta	Birmingham	Boston	Buffalo	Chicago	Cincinnati	Cleveland	Dallas	Denver	Detroit	Houston	Kansas City, Mo.	Los Angeles	Mexico City	Miami	Minneapolis	Montréal	Nashville	New Orleans	New York City	Oklahoma City	Philadelphia	Phoenix	Pittsburgh	Portland, Ore.	St. Louis	Salt Lake City	San Francisco	Seattle	Washington, D.C.
Atlanta		152	1068	877	695	461	686	805	1401	726	814	810	2197	1775	665	1105	1230	256	493	855	865	766	1810	697	2736	558	1900	2523	2756	630
Birmingham	152		1185	902	636	476	716	653	1282	741	662	706	2056	1623	765	1066	1289	205	351	974	722	884	1658	742	2599	476	1781	2393	2575	748
Boston	1068	1185		449	975	876	632	1819	1989	699	1916	1456	3052	2877	1539	1385	324	1165	1536	216	1701	304	2682	598	3114	1178	2405	3163	3036	437
Buffalo	877	902	449		529	430	186	1373	1543	252	1470	1010	2606	2431	1431	939	393	719	1253	445	1250	365	2236	217	2660	802	1958	2716	2590	359
Chicago	695	656	975	529		295	343	936	1016	275	1085	499	2095	2046	1377	412	848	451	929	843	797	762	1722	461	2157	291	1431	2189	2063	687
Cincinnati	461	476	876	430	295		244	943	1169	265	1040	590	2186	2001	1133	705	820	290	820	659	880	578	1816	284	2421	338	1644	2402	2356	492
Cleveland	686	716	632	186	343	244		1187	1357	167	1284	824	2420	2245	1322	753	576	533	1063	507	1062	426	2050	125	2460	546	1772	2530	2404	351
Dallas	805	653	1819	1373	936	943	1187		784	1188	242	499	1403	1188	1327	956	1763	686	498	1607	209	1526	1005	1232	2064	645	1241	1806	2112	1372
Denver	894	1282	1989	1543	1016	1169	1357	784		1284	1026	604	1134	2001	2100	841	1862	1158	1282	1851	628	1770	818	1482	1278	856	512	1270	1347	1696
Detroit	726	741	699	252	275	265	167	1188	1284		1337	751	2347	2298	1387	685	573	555	1085	667	1043	586	1977	285	2394	543	1700	2458	2336	511
Houston	814	662	1916	1470	1085	1040	1284	242	946	1337		741	1553	961	1242	1198	1860	783	359	1636	455	1546	1153	1319	2295	794	1431	1955	2302	1410
Kansas City, Mo.	810	706	1456	1010	499	590	824	499	213	751	741		1596	1687	1491	457	1324	554	821	1319	354	1238	1226	937	1866	252	1116	1874	1872	1048
Los Angeles	2197	2056	3052	2606	2095	2186	2420	1403	1801	2347	1553	1596		2020	2737	1940	2920	2058	1901	2915	1358	2721	398	2533	988	1848	734	403	1145	2644
Mexico City	1800	1648	2902	2456	2071	2026	2270	1149	1852	2337	986	1647	2017		2177	2104	2846	1769	1345	2622	1555	2532	1625	2305	3320	1794	2100	2419	2948	2396
Miami	665	765	1542	1418	1360	1126	1303	1309	1559	1347	1216	1470	2712	2177		1770	1705	921	875	1330	1537	1241	2314	1216	3337	1223	2545	3075	3421	1105
Minneapolis	1105	1066	1385	939	412	705	753	956	252	685	1198	457	1940	2144	1771		1258	861	1241	1253	791	1172	1630	871	1750	546	1239	1997	1641	1097
Montréal	1230	1289	324	393	848	820	576	1763	1184	573	1860	1324	2920	2821	1403	1258		1109	1640	388	1638	467	2550	611	2891	1116	2273	3031	2697	600
Nashville	256	205	1165	719	451	290	533	686	638	555	783	554	2058	1744	909	861	1109		530	949	676	868	1725	559	2435	302	1670	2410	2512	686
New Orleans	493	351	1536	1253	925	820	1063	498	989	1085	359	821	1901	1320	878	1241	1640	530		1325	704	1235	1503	1093	2568	695	1739	2303	2610	1099
New York City	855	974	216	445	843	659	507	1607	1173	667	1636	1319	2915	2597	1327	1253	388	949	1325		1486	92	2459	386	2932	966	2267	3025	2904	225
Oklahoma City	845	726	1684	1308	797	844	1052	215	560	1049	457	347	1357	1403	1518	813	1671	738	678	1472		1391	987	1097	1941	506	1108	1678	1962	1307
Philadelphia	766	884	304	365	762	578	426	1526	1092	586	1546	1238	2721	2507	1230	1172	467	868	1235	92	1406		2464	305	2872	885	2186	2944	2823	136
Phoenix	1810	1658	2682	2236	1722	1816	2050	1005	1430	1977	1155	1226	398	1680	2388	1630	2550	1725	1503	2459	993	2464		2163	1315	1478	653	800	1541	2274
Pittsburgh	697	742	598	217	461	284	125	1232	804	285	1319	937	2533	2280	1237	871	611	559	1093	386	1117	305	1366		2577	591	1890	2648	2522	230
Portland, Ore.	2654	2552	3085	2639	2112	2405	2453	2043	1819	2385	2233	1846	970	2990	3414	1690	2746	2398	2541	2953	1941	2872	1478	2571		2096	802	652	175	2797
St. Louis	558	476	1178	802	291	338	546	645	336	543	794	252	1848	1755	1222	546	1116	302	695	966	496	885	653	591	2123		1368	2126	2109	801
Salt Lake City	1900	1781	2405	1958	1431	1644	1772	1241	1094	1700	1431	1116	734	2480	2603	1239	2273	1670	1739	2267	1115	2186	800	1890	762	1368		759	871	2111
San Francisco	2523	2393	3163	2716	2189	2402	2530	1806	1852	2458	1955	1874	403	2423	3193	1997	3031	2410	2303	3025	1674	2944	1541	2648	643	2126	759		827	2869
Seattle	2756	2575	3036	2590	2063	2356	2404	2112	1773	2336	2302	1872	1145	3165	3451	1641	2697	2512	2610	2904	2063	2823	1541	2522	172	2109	871	827		2748
Washington, D.C.	630	748	437	359	687	492	351	1372	1018	511	1410	1048	2644	2371	1105	1097	600	686	1099	225	1344	136	2274	230	2809	801	2111	2869	2748	

A

Aachen, Ger. 71/B3
Aalborg, Den. 69/B3
Aalst, Belg. 73/C6
Aarau, Switz. 80/D1
Aare (riv.), Switz. 80/C1
Aba, Nigeria 60/C4
Abadan, Iran 100/F5
Abakan, U.S.S.R. 91/E3
Abbotsford, Br. Col. 190/C4
Abéché, Chad 61/E3
Abeokuta, Nigeria 60/C4
Aberdeen, Md. 139/F2
Aberdeen, S. Dak. 165/D3
Aberdeen, Scot. 66/F2
Aberdeen, Wash. 175/B2
Abidjan, Iv. Coast 60/B4
Abilene, Kans. 147/B3
Abilene, Texas 173/D2
Abington, Pa. 171/F1
Abitibi (riv.), Ont. 187/F1
Abraham Lincoln Birthplace Nat'l
  Hist. Site, Ky. 149/D3
Abruzzi (reg.), Italy 78/D3
Absaroka (range), Wyo. 177/A3
Abu Dhabi (cap.), U.A.E. 95/G5
Abuja, Nigeria 60/C4
Acadia Nat'l Pk., Maine 151/C3
Acapulco, Mex. 47/E5
Accra (cap.), Ghana 60/C4
Achill (isl.), Ire. 67/A4
Achinsk, U.S.S.R. 91/E3
Acoma Pueblo, N. Mex. 135/D2
Aconcagua (mt.), Arg. 58/C6
Acre, Isr. 98/C2
Ada, Okla. 168/C3
Adalia (gulf), Turkey 96/C4
Adams (mt.), Wash. 175/C3
Adana, Turkey 96/F4
Adapazari, Turkey 96/D2
Addis Ababa (cap.), Eth. 61/F4
Adelaide, Austr. 114/C4
Aden, Yemen 94/F7
Aden (gulf) 94/F7
Adige (riv.), Italy 78/C2
Adirondack (mts.), N.Y. 161/E2
Admiralty (isls.), Papua N.G.
  116/E4
Admiralty Island Nat'l Mon.,
  Alaska 129/C4
Adrian, Mich. 152/C4
Adriatic (sea), Europe 64/F4
Aegean (sea) 65/G5
Afghanistan 102/A1
Africa 60-63
Agadir, Morocco 60/A1
Agaña (cap.), Guam 116/E4
Agate Fossil Beds Natl Mon.,
  Nebr. 157/A1
Agra, India 102/C2
Agrigento, Italy 79/D6
Aguascalientes, Mex. 46/D4
Agulhas (cape), S. Africa 63/D8
Ahaggar (mts.), Alg. 60/C2
Ahmadabad, India 102/C2
Ahvaz (Ahwaz), Iran 100/F5
Ahvenanmaa (Aland) (isls.), Fin.
  69/D2
Aiea, Hawaii 129/A4
Aiken, S.C. 162/B3
Ainsworth, Nebr. 157/A3
Airdrie, Alta. 191/E3
Airdrie, Scot. 66/B1
Aire (riv.), Eng. 67/F4
Air Force Acad., Colo. 134/B3
Aisne (riv.), France 74/F3
Aitape, Papua N.G. 112/B6
Aix-en-Provence, France 75/F6
Ajaccio, France 75/B7
Ajanta, India 102/C2

Ajax, Ont. 187/F3
'Ajlun, Jordan 98/D3
Ajmer, India 102/C2
Akita, Japan 107/E3
Akola, India 102/C2
Akron, Ohio 166/B3
Aktyubinsk, U.S.S.R. 90/C3
Akureyri, Ice. 64/C2
Akyab, Burma, see Sittwe
Alabama (riv.), Ala. 128/A3
Alabama (state), U.S. 128
Alajuela, C. Rica 48/C3
Alameda, Calif. 133/E1
Alamogordo, N. Mex. 135/E3
Alamosa, Colo. 134/C2
Alaska (gulf), Alaska 129/B2
Alaska (state), U.S. 129
Albacete, Spain 77/E3
Albania 85/C3
Albany (cap.), N.Y. 161/F3
Albany, Ga. 142/A4
Albany, Oreg. 169/B3
Albemarle, N.C. 162/C2
Albemarle (sound), N.C. 163/F1
Albert (lake), Africa, see Mobutu
  Sese Seko
Albert Lea, Minn. 153/B4
Albertville, Ala. 128/B1
Albuquerque, N. Mex. 135/D2
Albury, Austr. 115/H7
Aldabra (isls.), Seychelles 63/G5
Aldan (riv.), U.S.S.R. 91/G3
Alderney (isl.), Chan. Is. 67/E6
Aleppo, Syria 97/G3
Alessandria, Italy 78/B2
Alesund, Nor. 68/A2
Aleutian (isls.), Alaska 44/C6
Alexander I (isl.), Antarc. 118
Alexander City, Ala. 128/C2
Alexandretta (gulf), Turkey 97/F4
Alexandria (cap.) Egt 61/E1
Alexandria, La. 150/B2
Alexandria, Minn. 153/A3
Alexandria, Va. 139/D1
Algarve (reg.), Port. 76/B4
Algeciras, Spain 76/D4
Algeria 60/C2
Algiers (cap.), Alg. 60/C1
Alhambra, Calif. 179/B2
Alicante, Spain 77/F3
Alice Springs, Austr. 114/C3
Alice, Texas 173/D4
Aligarh, India 102/C2
Aliquippa, Pa. 170/A3
Alkmaar, Neth. 72/E2
Al Kuwait (cap.), Kuwait 94/F4
Allahabad, India 102/D2
Allegheny (res.), U.S. 160/B4,
  170/B2
Allegheny (riv.), Pa. 170/B2
Allen Park, Mich. 178/B4
Allentown, Pa. 171/F3
Allepey, India 102/C4
Aller (riv.), Ger. 70/C2
Alliance, Nebr. 157/B1
Alliance, Ohio 166/B4
Alma, Que. 185/E2
Alma-Ata, U.S.S.R. 102/D3
Almeria, Spain 77/E4
Alor Setar, Malaysia 111/B6
Alpena, Mich. 152/C2
Alpine, Texas 172/B2
Alps (mts.), Europe 80-81/C-F2
Alsace (prov.), France 74/G3
Altadena, Calif. 179/A2
Altai (mts.), Asia 104/B1
Alton, Ill. 144/A3
Alton, N.H. 158/C3
Altoona, Pa. 170/C4

Altun Shan (Altyn Tagh) (mts.),
  China 104/B2
Altus, Okla. 168/C2
Amagasaki, Japan 107/E4
Amalfi, Italy 79/E4
Amami-O-Shima (isl.), Japan
  107/H3
Amara, Iraq 100/E5
Amarillo, Texas 172/A1
Amazon (riv.), S. Amer. 57/D3
Ambato, Ecuador 56/B3
Amber (cape), Madag., see
  Bobaomby
Ambergris (cay), Belize 48/C1
Ambon, Indon. 113/H6
Amelia (isl.), Fla. 140/E3
American Falls, Idaho 143/B4
American Fork, Utah 174/B2
American Samoa 117/J7
Americus, Ga. 142/A3
Ames, Iowa 146/B2
Amherst, Mass. 136/C1
Amherst, N.S. 183/D3
Amiens, France 74/D3
Amman (cap.), Jordan 99/D4
Ammassalik, Greenl. 40/Q3
Amol, Iran 101/H2
Amos, Que. 184/A2
Amoy, China, see Xiamen
Amravati, India 102/C2
Amritsar, India 102/C1
Amsterdam (isl.), Fr. 35/M7
Amsterdam (cap.), Neth. 72/E3
Amsterdam, N.Y. 161/E3
Amudar'ya (riv.), Asia 92/F3
Amur (riv.), Asia 92/J3
Anaconda, Mont. 156/B1
Anacortes, Wash. 175/A2
Anadarko, Okla. 168/B2
Anadyr', U.S.S.R. 91/J2
Anaheim, Calif. 179/C3
Anatolia (reg.), Turkey 96/CF3
Ancaster, Ont. 187/E4
Anchorage, Alaska 129/B2
Ancona, Italy 78/D3
Andalusia (reg.), Spain 76/C4
Andalusia, Ala. 128/B3
Andaman (isls.), India 103/E3
Anderson, Ind. 145/C2
Anderson, S.C. 162/B2
Andes (mts.), S. Amer. 56/B3,
  C5/58
Andizhan, U.S.S.R. 90/D3
Andorra 77/G1
Andorra la Vella (cap.), Andorra
  77/G1
Andover, Mass. 137/D1
Andrews A.F.B., Md. 139/E1
Andros (isl.), Bah. 50/B1
Androscoggin (riv.), U.S. 151/A3
Anegada (isl.), U.K. 51/F3
Angara (riv.), U.S.S.R. 91/E3
Angarsk, U.S.S.R. 91/F3
Angel (falls), Ven. 56/C2
Angers, France 74/C4
Angkor Wat (ruins), Camb.
  111/D4
Anglesey (isl.), Wales 67/D4
Angola 62-63/D6
Angoulême, France 75/C5
Anguilla (isl.) 51/F3
Anhui (Anhwei) (prov.), China
  105/E2
Aniakchak Nat'l Mon., Alaska
  129/A2
Anjou, Que. 184/B1
Ankara (cap.), Turkey 96/E3
Ankeny, Iowa 146/B2
Ann (cape), Mass. 137/E1
Annaba, Alg. 60/C1

Index

An Najaf, Iraq 100/D4
Annandale, Va. 139/D1
Annapolis (cap.), Md. 139/C2
Annapolis Royal, N.S. 182/C4
Ann Arbor, Mich. 152/C4
An Nasiriya, Iraq 100/D4
Annecy, France 75/G5
Anniston, Ala. 128/C2
Annobón (isl.), Equat. Guinea 62/C5
Anshan, China 105/F1
Antakya, Turkey 97/G4
Antalya, Turkey 96/D4
Antananarivo (cap.), Madag. 63/G4
Antarctica 118
Antibes, France 75/G6
Anticosti (isl.), Que. 43/K6
Antigonish, N.S. 183/E3
Antigua (isl.), 55/V
Antigua and Barbuda 51/G3
Antigua, Guat. 48/B2
Antilles (isls.), W. Indies 50-51/B-F2-4
Antofagasta, Chile 58/B5
Antsiranana, Madag. 63/G6
Antwerp, Belg. 73/D5
Anuradhapura, Sri Lanka 102/D4
Anyang, China 105/F3
Anzio, Italy 79/D4
Aomori, Japan 107/F2
Aosta, Italy 78/A2
Apache (mts.), Texas 172/B2
Apalachee (bay), Fla. 136/B2
Apalachicola, Fla. 140/B1
Apataki (isl.), Fr. Poly. 117/M7
Apeldoorn, Neth. 72/G3
Apennines (mts.), Italy 78-79/C-E3-4
Apia (cap.), W. Samoa 117/J7
Apo (vol.), Phil. 109/E7
Appalachian (mts.), U.S. 45/K-L3-4
Appenzell, Switz. 81/E1
Appleton, Wis. 176/C3
Appomattox Court House Nat'l Hist. Pk., Va. 139/D4
Apulia (reg.), Italy 79/F4
Apurimac (riv.), Peru 56/B4
Aqaba (gulf), Asia 94/D4
'Aqaba, Jordan 99/D6
Araba, Wadi (valley), Asia 99/D5
Arabian (des.), Egypt 94/C4
Arabian (sea), Asia 93/F5
Aracaju, Braz. 57/F4
Arad, Rom. 84/C2
Arafura (sea) 116/E2
Aragón (reg.), Spain 77/F2
Araguaia (riv.), Braz. 57/E3
Arak, Iran 100/F3
Arakan Yoma (mts.), Burma 110/A3
Araks (riv.), Asia 89/G7
Aral (sea), U.S.S.R. 90/C3
Aran (isls.), Ire. 67/A4
Aranjuez, Spain 77/E3
Aransas Pass, Texas 173/E3
Ararat, Mt., Turkey 97/L3
Arauca (riv.), S. Amer. 56/C2
Arbutus, Md. 139/E1
Arcadia, Calif. 179/B2
Archangel (Arkhangel'sk), U.S.S.R. 88/F2
Arches Nat'l Pk., Utah 174/C3
Arco, Idaho 143/B3
Arctic Ocean 33
Ardabil, Iran 100/F1
Ardmore, Okla. 168/D3
Ardmore, Pa. 171/E1
Arecibo, P. Rico 54/G1
Arequipa, Peru 56/B4

Argenteuil, France 74/A1
Argentia, Newf. 183/F2
Argentina 58-59/B-D5-8
Argos, Greece 85/C4
Arhus, Den. 69/B3
Arima, Trin. & Tob. 55/T
Aripuanã (riv.), Braz. 56/C3
Arizona (state), U.S. 130
Arkadelphia, Ark. 131/C2
Arkansas (riv.), U.S. 44/F3
Arkansas (state), U.S. 131
Arkansas City, Kans. 147/C3
Arkansas Post Nat'l Mem., Ark. 131/C3
Arles, France 75/F6
Arlington Hts., Ill. 178/A1
Arlington, Texas 172/B4
Arlington, Va. 139/D1
Arlon, Belg. 73/G8
Armavir, U.S.S.R. 89/F6
Armenia, Col. 56/B2
Armenian S.S.R., U.S.S.R. 89/F6
Arnhem, Neth. 72/G4
Arno (riv.), Italy 78/C3
Arnprior, Ont. 187/E2
Arosa, Switz. 81/E2
Arran (isl.), Scot. 66/D3
Arras, France 74/E2
Artesia, N. Mex. 135/E3
Aru (isls.), Indon. 113/J7
Aruba (isl.) 50/D4, 55/O
Arusha, Tanz. 63/F5
Arvada, Colo. 178/A4
Arzamas, U.S.S.R. 89/F3
Asahikawa, Japan 107/F2
Asansol, India 103/D2
Asbury Park, N.J. 159/C2
Ascension (isl.), St. Helena 62/A5
Ashdod, Isr. 99/B4
Asheboro, N.C. 163/D2
Asheville, N.C. 162/B2
Ashkhabad, U.S.S.R. 90/C4
Ashland, Ky. 149/F2
Ashland, Oreg. 169/C2
Ashland, Wis. 176/B2
Ashqelon, Isr. 99/B4
Ashtabula, Ohio 166/A4
Asia 92-93
Asmara, Eth. 61/F3
Aspen, Colo. 134/B2
Assiniboine (riv.), Man. 189/D4
Assisi, Italy 78/D3
Astoria, Oreg. 169/A2
Astrakhan', U.S.S.R. 89/G5
Asturias (reg.), Spain 76/C1
Asunción (cap.), Par. 59/D5
Aswân, Egypt 61/F2
Asyût, Egypt 61/F2
Atacama (des.), Chile 58/B5
Atar, Maur. 60/A2
Atbara, Sudan 61/F3
Atchafalaya (riv.), La. 150/B2
Atchison, Kans. 147/A4
Athabasca (lake), Can. 42/E4
Athabasca (riv.), Alta. 42/E4
Athens, Ala. 128/B1
Athens, Ga. 142/B2
Athens (cap.), Greece 85/C4
Athens, Ohio 167/D3
Athlone, Ire. 67/C4
Áthos (mt.), Greece 85/D3
Atitlán (lake), Guat. 48/B2
Atka (isl.), Alaska 130/M4
Atlanta (cap.), Ga. 142/B1
Atlantic Beach, Fla. 140/A3
Atlantic City, N.J. 159/B4
Atlantic Ocean, see North Atlantic, South Atlantic
Atlas (mts.), Africa 60/B1
Atrak (riv.), Iran 101/J2

Attleboro, Mass. 137/D2
Au Sable Forks, N.Y. 161/F1
Auburn, Ala. 128/C2
Auburn, Maine 151/A4
Auburn, N.Y. 161/D3
Auburn, Wash. 175/C1
Auckland, N.Z. 115/D3
Augsburg, Ger. 71/D4
Augusta (cap.), Maine 151/B3
Augusta, Ga. 142/C2
Aurangabad, India 102/C3
Aurora, Colo. 178/B4
Aurora, Ill. 178/A2
Aurora, Ont. 187/F3
Auschwitz, Pol., see Oświęcim
Austin (cap.), Texas 173/D2
Austin, Minn. 153/C4
Austral (isls.), Fr. Poly. 117/M8
Australia 114-115
Australian Alps (mts.), Austr. 115/D4
Australian Cap. Terr., Austr. 115/D4
Austria 82/BC3
Auvergne (reg.), France 75/E5
Avignon, France 75/F6
Avila, Spain 76/D2
Avondale, Ariz. 130/A1
Ayacucho, Peru 56/B4
Ayr, Scot. 66/D3
Azerbaidzhan S.S.R., U.S.S.R. 89/G6
Azores (isls.), Port. 35/J4
Azov (sea), U.S.S.R. 89/E5
Aztec Ruins Nat'l Mon., N. Mex. 134/C2
Azuero (pen.), Panama 49/D4
Azusa, Calif. 179/A3

B

Ba'albek, Leb. 97/G5
Bab el Mandeb (str.) 94/E7
Babol, Iran 101/H2
Babuyan (isls.), Phil. 108/C1
Babylon (ruins), Iraq 100/D4
Bacâu, Rom. 84/D2
Bacolod, Phil. 109/E4
Badajos, Spain 76/C3
Badalona, Spain 77/H2
Baden, Switz. 81/D1
Baden-Baden, Ger. 71/C4
Baden-Württemberg (state), Ger. 71/C4
Badgastein, Austria 82/B3
Bad Kissingen, Ger. 71/D3
Badlands Nat'l Pk., S. Dak. 165/E1
Bad Nauheim, Ger. 71/C3
Baffin (isl.), N.W.T. 43/J3
Baghdad (cap.), Iraq 101/D4
Baguio, Phil. 108/C2
Bahamas 50/C1
Bahawalpur, Pak. 102/C2
Bahia, Braz., see Salvador
Bahia Blanca, Arg. 58/C6
Bahrain 95/G4
Baia Mare, Rom. 84/C2
Baie Comeau, Que. 185/D1
Bainbridge (isl.), Wash. 175/B1
Bairiki (cap.), Kiribati 117/H5
Baker (isl.), U.S. 117/J5
Baker, Oreg. 169/B4
Bakersfield, Calif. 133/E3
Bakhtaran, Iran 100/E3
Balashov, U.S.S.R. 89/F4
Balaton (lake), Hung. 83/D3
Balcones Escarpment (plat.), Texas 173/D3
Baldwin, Pa. 170/A1

Baldwin Park, Calif. 179/B2
Balearic (isls.), Spain 77/G3
Bali (isl.), Indon. 112/E7
Balikesir, Turkey 96/D3
Balikpapan, Indon. 112/F6
Balkan (mts.), Bulg. 84/D3
Balkhash (lake), U.S.S.R. 90/D3
Balkhash, U.S.S.R. 90/D3
Ballarat, Austr. 115/D4
Balleny (isls.), Antarc. 118
Ballymena, N. Ire. 66/C3
Balmorhea, Texas 172/B2
Baltic (sea), Europe 64/F3
Baltimore, Md. 139/F1
Bamako (cap.), Mali 60/B3
Bambari, Cent. Afr. Rep. 61/E4
Bamberg, Ger. 71/D4
Banaba (isl.), Kiribati 116/G7
Banda (sea), Indon. 113/H6
Bandar, India, see Machilipatnam
Bandar 'Abbas, Iran 101/K7
Bandar-e Anzali, Iran 100/C3
Bandar Seri Begawan, (cap.),
  Brunei 112/E4
Bandelier Nat'l Mon., N. Mex.
  135/D2
Bandundu, Zaire 63/D5
Bandung, Indon. 113/H2
Banff Nat'l Pk., Alta. 191/D3
Bangalore, India 102/C3
Bangkok (cap.), Thai. 111/C4
Bangladesh 103/E2
Bangor, Maine 151/B3
Bangor, Wales 67/D4
Bangui (cap.), Cent. Afr. Rep.
  60/D4
Banja Luka, Yugo. 84/B2
Banjarmasin, Indon. 112/E6
Banjul (cap.), Gambia 60/A3
Banks (isl.), N.W.T. 42/D1
Ban Me Thuot, Viet. 111/E4
Banngka (isl.), Indon. 112/D6
Baoding, China 105/E2
Baotou, China 104/D3
Baraboo, Wis. 176/B4
Barahona, Dom. Rep. 52/R7
Baranovichi, U.S.S.R. 89/B4
Barataria (bay), La. 150/C3
Barbados 51/G4, 55/S
Barberton, Ohio 166/B3
Barbuda (isl.), Ant. & Barb. 51/G3
Barcelona, Spain 77/H2
Barcelona, Ven. 56/C2
Bardstown, Ky. 149/D2
Bareilly, India 102/D2
Barents (sea), Europe 90/BC2
Bar Harbor, Maine 151/C3
Bari, Italy 79/F4
Barisol, Bang. 103/D2
Barkley (lake), U.S. 148/B3
Barnaul, U.S.S.R. 90/E3
Barnegat Light, N.J. 159/C3
Barnet, Eng. 67/B5
Barnstable, Mass. 137/F3
Baroda, India 102/C2
Barquisimeto, Ven. 56/C1
Barranquilla, Col. 56/B1
Barre, Vt. 158/B2
Barrie, Ont. 186/C3
Barrow, Alaska 129/A1
Barrow (pt.), Alaska 129/B1
Barrow (riv.), Ire. 67/C4
Barrow-in-Furness, Eng. 67/E3
Barstow, Calif. 133/E3
Bartlesville, Okla. 168/A4
Basel, Switz. 80/C1
Basilan (isl.), Phil. 109/D7
Basilicata (reg.), Italy 79/F4
Basra, Iraq 100/F5
Bass (str.), Austr. 115/D5
Bassas da India, Réunion 63/F7

Bassein, Burma 110/A3
Basse-Terre (cap.), Guad. 51/F4,
  55/H
Basseterre (cap.), St. Kitts &
  Nevis 51/F3, 55/W
Bastogne, Belg. 73/G7
Bastrop, La. 150/A2
Bata, Equat. Guinea 60/C4
Bataan (pen.), Phil. 108/C3
Batangas, Phil. 108/C4
Batavia, N.Y. 160/B3
Bath, Eng. 67/E5
Bath, Maine 151/A4
Bathurst, Gambia, see Banjul
Bathurst, N. Br. 182/C1
Bathurst (isl.), N.W.T. 42/F1
Batna, Alg. 60/C1
Baton Rouge (cap.), La. 150/B2
Batsto, N.J. 159/B3
Battambang, Camb. 111/C4
Battle (riv.), Can. 191/F3
Battle Creek, Mich. 152/C4
Battleford, Sask. 188/A4
Battle Mountain, Nev. 132/B3
Batumi, U.S.S.R. 89/F6
Bat Yam, Isr. 99/B3
Bavaria (state), Ger. 71/D4
Bayamo, Cuba 53/J4
Bayamón, P. Rico 54/C1
Bay City, Mich. 152/C3
Bay City Texas 173/E3
Bayeux, France 74/C3
Baykal (lake), U.S.S.R. 91/F3
Bayonne, France 75/C6
Bayonne, N.J. 180/B3
Bayreuth, Ger. 71/D4
Bay Roberts, Newf. 183/F1
Bay St. Louis, Miss. 154/B4
Baytown, Texas 173/F4
Beach Haven, N.J. 159/C3
Bear (isl.), Nor. 33
Beardstown, Ill. 144/A2
Beatrice, Nebr. 157/C3
Beaufort (sea), N. Amer. 40/CD2
Beaufort, S.C. 162/C4
Beaumont, Texas 173/F3
Beaver (isl.), Mich. 152/B2
Beaver Dam, Wis. 176/C4
Beaver Falls, Pa. 170/A3
Beaver Lodge, Alta. 190/C2
Beaverton, Oreg. 180/A4
Béchar, Alg. 60/B1
Beckley, W. Va. 138/B3
Bedford, Eng. 67/F4
Bedford, Ind. 145/B3
Bedford, Pa. 170/C4
Beersheba, Isr. 99/B5
Beeville, Texas 173/E3
Beihai, China 104/D3
Beijing (cap.), People's Rep. of
  China 105/E1
Beira, Moz. 63/F6
Beirut (cap.), Leb. 94/C3
Bejaïa, Alg. 60/C1
Békéscsaba, Hung. 83/F3
Belau, see Palau
Belém, Braz. 57/E3
Belfast, Maine 151/B3
Belfast (cap.), N. Ire. 67/D3
Belgaum, India 102/C3
Belgium 73
Belgorod, U.S.S.R. 89/E4
Belgrade (cap.), Yugo. 84/C2
Belize 48/B1
Belize City, Belize 48/B1
Bellary, India 102/C3
Belle Fourche, S. Dak. 165/D1
Belle Glade, Fla. 141/D4
Belleville, Ill. 144/B3
Belleville, Ont. 187/D3
Bellevue, Nebr. 157/B4

Bellevue, Wash. 175/B1
Bellflower, Calif. 179/C2
Bellingham, Wash. 175/A2
Bellingshausen (sea), Antarc. 118
Bellows Falls, Vt. 158/B4
Belmopan (cap.), Belize 48/B1
Belogorsk, U.S.S.R. 91/G3
Belo Horizonte, Braz. 57/F4
Beloit, Wis. 176/C4
Bel'tsy, U.S.S.R. 89/C5
Belvidere, Ill. 144/B1
Bemidji, Minn. 153/B2
Ben Nevis (mt.), Scot. 66/D2
Benares, see Varanasi
Bend, Oreg. 169/B2
Bendigo, Austr. 115/D4
Bene Beraq, Isr. 99/B3
Bengal (bay), Asia 93/G5
Bengbu, China 105/E2
Benghazi, Libya 61/D1
Benguela, Angola 62/D6
Beni (riv.), Bol. 56/C4
Beni Suef, Egypt 61/F2
Benin 60/C4
Benin City, Nigeria 60/C4
Bennington, Vt. 158/A4
Benton, Ark. 131/B2
Benton Harbor, Mich. 152/A4
Benue (riv.), Africa 60/C4
Benxi, China 105/F1
Beppu, Japan 106/C4
Berbera, Somalia 61/G3
Berberati, Cent. Afr. Rep. 60/D4
Berchtesgaden, Ger. 71/E5
Berea, Ky. 149/E2
Berea, Ohio 167/F3
Berezniki, U.S.S.R. 88/J3
Bergamo, Italy 78/B2
Bergen, Nor. 68/A2
Bergisch Gladbach, Ger. 71/B3
Bering (sea) 34/CD3
Bering (str.) 34/D2
Berkeley, Calif. 133/E1
Berlin (cap.), Ger. 70/E2
Berlin, N.H. 158/C2
Bermejo (riv.), Arg. 58/C5
Bermuda 41/M6, H3/51
Bern (cap.), Switz. 80/C2
Bernardsville, N.J. 159/B2
Berwick, Pa. 171/E3
Berwyn, Ill. 178/B3
Besançon, France 74/G4
Beskids (mts.), Europe 87/E4
Bessemer, Ala. 128/B2
Bethany, Okla. 168/B3
Bethel, Alaska 129/A2
Bethel, Conn. 136/A3
Bethesda, Md. 139/D1
Bethlehem, Pa. 171/F3
Bethlehem, West Bank 99/C4
Bettendorf, Iowa 146/B4
Beverly, Mass. 137/E1
Beverly Hills, Calif. 179/B1
Beyoğlu, Turkey 96/D6
Béziers, France 75/E6
Bhagalpur, India 102/D2
Bhatpara, India 102/D2
Bhavnagar, India 102/C2
Bhopal, India 102/C2
Bhutan 103/D2
Biak (isl.), Indon. 113/K6
Bialystok, Pol. 87/F2
Biarritz, France 75/C6
Biddeford, Maine 151/A4
Biel, Switz. 80/C1
Bielefeld, Ger. 70/C2
Bielsko-Biala, Poland 86/D4
Bien Hoa, Viet. 111/D5
Big Bend Nat'l Pk., Texas 172/B3
Biggar, Sask. 188/B3

Index

Bighorn (mts.), Wyo. 177/A2
Bighorn (riv.), U.S. 177/A3
Big Spring, Texas 172/C2
Big Sur, Calif. 133/D1
Bikaner, India 102/C2
Bikini (atoll), Marshall Is. 116/G4
Bilbao, Spain 77/E1
Billings, Mont. 156/C3
Billiton (isl.), Indon. 112/D6
Biloxi, Miss. 154/C4
Biminis, The (isls.), Bah. 50/B1
Binghamton, N.Y. 161/D2
Bioko (isl.), Equat. Guin. 60/C4
Birkenhead, Eng. 67/E4
Birmingham, Ala. 128/B2
Birmingham, Eng. 67/E4
Birobidzhan, U.S.S.R. 91/G3
Bisbee, Ariz. 130/C1
Biscay (bay), Europe 64/D4
Biscayne Nat'l Pk., Fla. 141/F4
Bisho, S. Africa 63/E6
Bismarck (cap.), N. Dak. 164/C2
Bismarck (arch.), Papua N.G. 116/E6
Bissau (cap.), Guinea-Bissau 60/A3
Bitola, Yugo. 85/C3
Bitterroot (range), U.S. 143/B2
Biysk, U.S.S.R. 90/E3
Bizerte, Tun. 60/C1
Black (for.), Ger. 71/B4
Black (sea) 65/H4
Blackburn, Eng. 66/G1
Black Canyon of the Gunnison Nat'l Mon., Colo. 134/B2
Blackfoot, Idaho 143/C4
Black Hills (mts.), U.S. 165/E1
Blackpool, Eng. 66/F1
Blacksburg, Va. 138/C4
Blackwater (riv.), Ire. 67/B4
Blagoveshchensk, U.S.S.R. 91/G3
Blainville, Que. 184/A1
Blanc (cape), Africa 60/A2
Blanc (mt.), Europe 80/B3
Blanco (cape), Oreg. 169/C4
Blanding, Utah 174/C4
Blantyre, Malawi 63/F6
Blida, Alg. 60/C1
Block (isl.), R.I. 137/D3
Bloemfontein, S. Africa 63/E7
Bloomfield, N.J. 180/A2
Bloomfield Hills, Mich. 178/A3
Bloomington, Ill. 144/B3
Bloomington, Ind. 145/B3
Bloomington, Minn. 153/B1
Bloomsburg, Pa. 171/D3
Blue (mts.), Jam. 53/W9
Blue (mts.), Oreg. 169/A4
Bluefield, W. Va. 138/B4
Blue Nile (riv.), Africa 61/F3
Blue Ridge (mts.), U.S. 162/A2, 138/C2
Blue Springs, Mo. 155/C1
Blytheville, Ark. 131/D4
Boa Vista, Braz. 56/C2
Bobaomby (cape), Madag. 63/G6
Bobo-Dioulasso, Burk. Faso 60/B3
Bobruysk, U.S.S.R. 89/C4
Boca Raton, Fla. 141/E4
Bochum, Ger. 70/B3
Bodélé (depr.), Chad 60-61/D3
Bodensee (lake), see Constance
Boerne, Texas 173/D3
Bogalusa, La. 150/B3
Bogor, Indon. 113/H2
Bogotá (cap.), Col. 56/B2
Bohemian (for.), Czech. 82/B2
Bohol (isl.), Phil. 109/E6
Bois Blanc (isl.), Mich. 152/B2

Boise (cap.), Idaho 143/A3
Bojador (cape), W. Sahara 60/A2
Bolivia 56/B2
Bologna, Italy 78/C2
Bolton, Eng. 66/G1
Bolzano, Italy 78/C1
Boma, Zaire 62/D5
Bombay, India 102/C3
Bomu (riv.), Africa 61/E4
Bon (cape), Tun. 60/D1
Bonaire (isl.), Neth. Ant. 51/E4, 55/M
Bonin (isls.), Japan 107/G2
Bonita Springs, Fla. 141/E3
Bonn, Ger. 71/B3
Bonneville (dam), U.S. 169/A2
Bonnyville, Alta. 191/F2
Bontoc, Phil. 108/C2
Boone, Iowa 146/B2
Boone, N.C. 162/B1
Boothbay Harbor, Maine 151/B4
Bootle, Eng. 66/F1
Bophuthatswana (aut. rep.), S. Africa 63/E7
Bora Bora (isl.), Fr. Poly. 117/L7
Borås, Swed. 69/C3
Bordeaux, France 75/C5
Borden, P.E.I. 183/D2
Bordentown, N.J. 159/B2
Borger, Texas 172/A1
Borisov, U.S.S.R. 89/C4
Borneo (isl.), Asia 112/E5
Bornholm (isl.), Den. 69/C3
Borujerd, Iran 100/F4
Bosporus (str.), Turkey 96/C2
Bossier City, La. 150/A1
Boston (cap.), Mass. 137/G4
Bothnia (gulf), Europe 65/G2
Botswana 63/E7
Bottineau, N. Dak. 164/A2
Bouaké, Iv. Coast 60/B4
Bouar, Cent. Afr. Rep. 60/D4
Boucherville, Que. 184/B1
Bougainville (isl.), Papua N.G. 116/F6
Boulder, Colo. 178/A3
Boulder City, Nev. 133/D3
Boulogne, France 74/D2
Bountiful, Utah 174/B2
Bourges, France 74/E4
Bournemouth, Eng. 67/F3
Douvet (isl.), Nor. 35/K8
Bow (riv.), Alta. 191/E3
Bowie, Texas 173/D1
Bowling Green, Ky. 148/C3
Bowling Green, Ohio 166/B2
Boynton Beach, Fla. 141/D4
Boyoma (Stanley) (falls), Zaire 63/E5
Bozeman, Mont. 156/C4
Bradenton, Fla. 141/D2
Bradford, Eng. 66/G1
Braga, Port. 76/B2
Brahmaputra (riv.), Asia 93/G4
Brăila, Rom. 84/D2
Brainerd, Minn. 153/B2
Braintree, Mass. 137/F4
Brampton, Ont. 187/E3
Branco (riv.), Braz. 56/C2
Brandenburg (state), Ger. 70/E2
Brandon, Man. 189/E4
Brantford, Ont. 187/E4
Bras d'Or (lake), N.S. 183/F3
Brasília (cap.), Braz. 57/E4
Braşov, Rom. 84/D2
Bratislava, Czech. 83/D2
Bratsk, U.S.S.R. 91/F3
Brattleboro, Vt. 158/A4
Bray, Ire. 67/C4
Brazil 56-57,59

Brazos (riv.), Texas 173/E2
Brazzaville (cap.), Congo 62/D5
Breda, Neth. 72/E4
Bregenz, Austria 82/A3
Bremen, Ger. 70/C2
Bremerhaven, Ger. 70/C2
Bremerton, Wash. 175/C1
Brescia, Italy 78/C2
Breslau, Pol., see Wroclaw
Brest, France 74/A3
Brest, U.S.S.R. 89/B4
Breton (sound), La. 150/C3
Brewer, Maine 151/B3
Bridgeport, Conn. 136/A3
Bridgeport, Nebr. 157/B1
Bridgeton, N.J. 159/A4
Bridgetown (cap.), Barbados 51/G4, 55/S
Bridgewater, N.S. 182/C4
Brigantine, N.J. 159/C4
Brigham City, Utah 174/B2
Brighton, Colo. 178/B3
Brighton, Eng. 67/F5
Brindisi, Italy 79/G4
Brisbane, Austr. 115/E3
Bristol (bay), Alaska 129/A2
Bristol, Conn. 136/B3
Bristol, Eng. 67/E5
Bristol, R.I. 137/D3
Bristol, Tenn. 149/F3
Bristol (chan.), U.K. 67/D5
Bristol, Va. 138/B4
British Columbia (prov.), Can. 190
British Indian Ocean Terr. 93/F6
Brittany (prov.), France 74/B3
Brno, Czech. 82/D2
Brockton, Mass. 137/E2
Brockville, Ont. 187/E3
Broken Bow, Nebr. 157/B3
Broken Hill, Austr. 115/D4
Bromley, Eng. 67/B6
Bronx (borough), N.Y. 180/B2
Brookfield, Wis. 176/A1
Brookhaven, Miss. 154/B3
Brookings, Oreg. 169/C1
Brookings, S. Dak. 165/E4
Brookline, Mass. 137/F4
Brooklyn (borough), N.Y. 180/B3
Brooks (range), Alaska 129/A1
Brooks, Alta. 191/F3
Broomfield, Colo. 178/A3
Brossard, Que. 184/B1
Brownfield, Texas 172/C1
Brownsville, Tenn. 148/A4
Brownsville, Texas 173/E4
Brownwood, Texas 173/D2
Bruges, Belg. 73/B5
Brunei 112/E5
Brunswick, Ga. 142/C4
Brunswick, Maine 151/A4
Brunswick, Ohio 166/A2
Brunswick (Braunschweig), Ger. 70/D2
Brussels (cap.), Belg. 73/E6
Bryan, Texas 173/E2
Bryansk, U.S.S.R. 89/D4
Bryce Canyon Nat'l Pk., Utah 174/B4
Bryn Mawr, Pa. 171/D1
Bubiyan (isl.), Kuwait 100/F6
Bucaramanga, Col. 56/B2
Bucharest (cap.), Rom. 84/D2
Buck Is. Reef Nat'l Mon., V.I. (U.S.) 54/G
Bucksport, Maine 151/B3
Budapest (cap.), Hung. 83/E3
Buena Park, Calif. 179/C2
Buenaventura, Col. 56/B2
Buenos Aires (cap.), Arg. 58/C6

Buenos Aires (lake), S. Amer. 58/B7
Buffalo, N.Y. 160/B3 •
Buffalo, Wyo. 177/A2
Bujumbura (cap.), Burundi 63/F5
Bukavu, Zaire 63/E5
Bukhara, U.S.S.R. 90/D4
Bulawayo, Zim. 63/E7
Bulgaria 84/D3
Bull Shoals (lake), U.S. 131/A2
Bunbury, Austr. 114/A4
Bundaberg, Austr. 115/E3
Buraida, S. Arabia 94/E4
Burbank, Calif. 179/A2
Burdwan, India 102/D2
Burgas, Bulg. 83/D3
Burgos, Spain 76/E1
Burkina Faso 60/B3
Burley, Idaho 143/B4
Burlingame, Calif. 133/F1
Burlington, Iowa 146/C4
Burlington, N.C. 163/D1
Burlington, Ont. 187/B4
Burlington, Vt. 158/A2
Burma 110/A2
Burnaby, Br. Col. 190/A1
Burnley, Eng. 66/G1
Burns, Oreg. 169/B3
Bursa, Turkey 96/C2
Buru (isl.), Indon. 113/H6
Burundi 63/F5
Bushehr (Bushire), Iran 100/G6
Busuanga (isl.), Phil. 108/B4
Butler, Pa. 170/A3
Butte, Mont. 156/C2
Butuan, Phil. 109/E6
Buzău, Rom. 84/D2
Buzzards (bay), Mass. 137/E3
Bydgoszcz, Pol. 86/C2
Byelorussian S.S.R., U.S.S.R. 89/C4
Bytom, Pol. 86/A3

C

Cabanatuan, Phil. 108/C3
Cabimas, Ven. 56/B1
Cabinda (dist.), Angola 62/D5
Cabot (str.), Can. 183/E2
Cabrillo Nat'l Mon., Calif. 180/B4
Cáceres, Spain 76/C3
Cache Creek, Br. Col. 190/C3
Caddo (lake), U.S. 150/C1
Cadiz, Phil. 109/D5
Cádiz, Spain 76/C4
Caen, France 74/C3
Caernarvon, Wales 67/D4
Cagayan de Oro, Phil. 109/E6
Cagliari, Italy 79/B5
Caguas, P. Rico 54/C1
Caicos (isls.), Turks & Caicos Is. 50/D2
Cairns, Austr. 115/D2
Cairo (cap.), Egypt 61/F1
Cairo, Ill. 144/B4
Cajamarca, Peru 56/B3
Calabar, Nigeria 60/D4
Calabria (reg.), Italy 79/F5
Calais, France 74/D3
Calais, Maine 151/C3
Calcasieu (lake), La. 150/C1
Calcutta, India 103/D2
Caldwell, Idaho 143/A4
Calgary, Alta. 191/E1
Cali, Col. 56/B2
Calicut, India, see Kozhikode
California (gulf), Mex. 46/B-C2-3
California (state), U.S. 132-133
Callao, Peru 56/B4
Calumet City, Ill. 178/B3

Camagüey, Cuba 50/B2, 53/G3
Cambodia 111/D4
Cambridge, Eng. 67/F4
Cambridge, Md. 139/F3
Cambridge, Mass. 137/F4
Cambridge, Ont. 187/E4
Camden, Ark. 131/C2
Camden, Maine 151/B3
Camden, N.J. 159/A3
Camden, S.C. 162/C3
Cameroon 60/D4
Cameroon (mt.), Cam. 60/C4
Campania (reg.), Italy 79/E4
Campbell River, Br. Col. 190/A4
Campbellsville, Ky. 149/D3
Campbellton, N. Br. 182/B1
Campeche (bay), Mex. 47/G4
Campina Grande, Braz. 57/F3
Campinas, Braz. 59/E5
Campo Grande, Braz. 57/D4
Campos, Braz. 59/E5
Cam Ranh (bay), Viet. 111/E5
Camrose, Alta. 191/E2
Canada 42-43
Canadian (riv.), U.S. 168/B3
Canandaigua, N.Y. 160/C3
Canary (isls.), Spain 76/B4, 35/J4
Canaveral (cape), Fla. 140/C4
Canberra (cap.), Austr. 115/E4
Cancún (isl.), Mex. 47/H4
Canmore, Alta. 191/D3
Cannanore (isls.), India 102/C3
Cannes, France 75/G6
Canon City, Colo. 134/B3
Canso, N.S. 183/F3
Cantabrian (mts.), Spain 76/CD1
Canterbury, Eng. 67/G5
Can Tho, Viet. 111/D5
Canton (Guangzhou), China 105/E3
Canton (Kanton) (isl.), Kiribati 117/J6
Canton, Miss. 154/B3
Canton, Ohio 166/B4
Canyon de Chelly Nat'l Mon., Ariz. 130/C2
Canyonlands Nat'l Pk., Utah 174/C4
Cap-de-la-Madeleine, Que. 185/D4
Cape (prov.), S. Africa 63/D8
Cape Breton (isl.), N.S. 183/E2
Cape Breton Highlands Nat'l Pk., N.S. 183/F1
Cape Charles, Va. 139/F4
Cape Coast, Ghana 60/B4
Cape Coral, Fla. 141/D3
Cape Fear (riv.), N.C. 163/D2
Cape Girardeau, Mo. 155/C4
Cape Krusenstern Nat'l Mon., Alaska 129/A1
Cape May, N.J. 159/B4
Cape Town (cap.), S. Africa 63/D8
Cape Verde 35/J5
Cape York (pen.), Austr. 115/D2
Cap-Haïtien, Haiti 52/P6
Capitol Reef Nat'l Pk., Utah 174/B4
Capri (isl.), Italy 79/E4
Caprivi Strip (reg.), Namibia 63/E6
Capulin Vol. Nat'l Mon., N. Mex. 134/C3
Caquetá (riv.), Col. 56/B2
Caracas (cap.), Ven. 56/C1
Caratasca (lag.), Hond. 49/D2
Carbondale, Ill. 144/B4
Carbondale, Pa. 171/E2
Carcassonne, France 75/D6
Cardiff (cap.), Wales 67/E5

Cardigan (bay), Wales 67/D4
Caribbean (sea) 50-51
Caribou, Maine 151/C1
Carleton Place, Ont. 187/E2
Carlisle, Eng. 66/E3
Carlisle, Pa. 171/D4
Carlow, Ire. 67/C4
Carlsbad, N. Mex. 135/F3
Carlsbad Caverns Nat'l Pk., N. Mex. 135/F3
Carman, Man. 189/E4
Carmel, Calif. 133/D1
Carmel (mt.), Isr. 98/C2
Carmichael, Calif. 132/C2
Caroline (isls.), Micronesia 116/EF5
Caroni (riv.), Ven. 56/C2
Carpentaria (gulf), Austr. 114/C2
Carrara, Italy 78/C2
Carrington, N. Dak. 164/B3
Carson, Calif. 179/C2
Carrollton, Texas 172/B4
Carson (sink), Nev. 132/B3
Carson City (cap.), Nev. 132/C2
Cartagena, Col. 56/B1
Cartagena, Spain 77/F4
Carúpano, Ven. 56/C1
Carver Nat'l Mon., Mo. 155/C2
Casablanca, Mor. 60/B1
Casa Grande, Ariz. 130/B3
Cascade (range), U.S. 44/B2
Casper, Wyo. 177/B2
Caspian (sea) 92/E3
Cassino, Italy 79/D4
Castellón de la Plana, Spain 77/G3
Castile (reg.), Spain 76-77/D-E2
Castillo de San Marcos Nat'l Mon., Fla. 140/A3
Castlegar, Br. Col. 191/D4
Castries (cap.), St. Lucia 51/G4, 55/L
Castro Valley, Calif. 133/E1
Catalonia (reg.), Spain 77/G2
Catamarca, Chile 58/C5
Catanduanes (isl.), Phil. 108/E4
Catania, Italy 79/E6
Cataño, P. Rico 54/C1
Catanzaro, Italy 79/F5
Catonsville, Md. 139/E1
Catskill (mts.), N.Y. 161/E4
Cauca (riv.), Col. 56/B2
Caucasus (mts.), U.S.S.R. 90/C3
Cavite, Phil. 108/C3
Cawnpore, India, see Kanpur
Caxias do Sul, Braz. 59/D5
Cayce, S.C. 162/C3
Cayenne (cap.), Fr. Guiana 57/D2
Cayey, P. Rico 54/C1
Cayman Islands 50/B3
Cayuga (lake), N.Y. 160/C3
Cebu, Phil. 109/E5
Cebu (isl.), Phil. 109/D5
Cedar Breaks Nat'l Mon., Utah 174/A4
Cedar City, Utah 174/A4
Cedar Falls, Iowa 146/B3
Cedar Key, Fla. 140/B2
Cedar Rapids, Iowa 146/B3
Celebes (sea), Asia 113/G5
Celebes (isl.), Indon. 113/G6
Celle, Ger. 70/D2
Central African Republic 61/DE4
Central America 48-49
Centralia, Ill. 144/B4
Centralia, Wash. 175/B2
Ceram (isl.), Indon. 113/H6
Cerritos, Calif. 179/C2
Cerro de Pasco, Peru 56/B4
České Budějovice, Czech. 82/C2
Ceuta, Spain 76/D5

Index

Ceylon, see Sri Lanka
Chaco, Gran (reg.), S. Amer. 58/C5
Chad 60-61/D3
Chad (lake), Africa 60/D3
Chadron, Nebr. 157/A1
Chamberlain, S. Dak. 165/E3
Chambersburg, Pa. 170/F4
Chambery, France 75/G5
Champaign, Ill. 144/C2
Champlain (lake), N. Amer. 158/A2
Chandigarh, India 102/C1
Chandler, Ariz. 130/D1
Chandleur (isls.), La. 150/C3
Changchun, China 105/F1
Chang Jiang (Yangtze) (riv.), China 104/D2
Changjin (res.), N. Korea 106/B2
Changsha, China 105/E3
Channel Islands 67/E6
Channel Isls. Nat'l Pk., Calif. 133/E2
Channel-Port-aux-Basques, Newf. 183/E1
Chapaevsk, U.S.S.R. 89/G4
Chapel Hill, N.C. 163/D1
Chardzhou, U.S.S.R. 90/D3
Charleroi, Belg. 73/D7
Charleston, S.C. 162/C4
Charleston, W. Va. 139/C3
Charles Town, W. Va. 139/D3
Charlevoix, Mich. 152/B2
Charlotte, N.C. 162/C2
Charlotte Amalie (cap.), V.I. (U.S.) 51/F3, 54/F
Charlottesville, Va. 139/D3
Charlottetown (cap.), P.E.I. 183/D2
Chartres, France 74/D3
Chateau-Thierry, France 74/E3
Chatham, Eng. 67/G5
Chatham, N. Br. 182/C2
Chatham (isls.), N.Z. 117/J9
Chatham, Ont. 186/A4
Chattahoochee, Fla. 140/A1
Chattahoochee (riv.), U.S. 142/A4
Chattanooga, Tenn. 149/D4
Cheboksary, U.S.S.R. 88/G3
Cheboygan, Mich. 152/B2
Chedabucto (bay), N.S. 183/F3
Cheektowaga, N.Y. 160/B1
Chefoo, China, see Yantai
Chehalis, Wash. 175/C2
Cheju, S. Korea 106/B4
Cheju (isl.), S. Korea 106/B4
Chekiang, China, see Zhejiang
Chelan (lake), Wash. 175/B3
Chelm, Pol. 87/F3
Cheltenham, Eng. 67/F5
Chelyabinsk, U.S.S.R. 90/D4
Chelyuskin (cape), U.S.S.R. 91/F2
Chemnitz, Ger. 71/E3
Cheney, Wash. 175/B4
Chengchow, China, see Zhengzhou
Chengde, China 105/E1
Chengdu (Chengtu), China 104/D2
Cherbourg, France 74/C3
Cherepovets, U.S.S.R. 88/E3
Cherkassy, U.S.S.R. 89/D5
Cherkessk, U.S.S.R. 89/F6
Chernigov, U.S.S.R. 89/D4
Chernobyl, U.S.S.R. 89/C4
Chernovtsy, U.S.S.R. 89/C5
Cherokee (lake), Tenn. 149/E3
Chesapeake (bay), U.S. 139/F3
Chesapeake, Va. 138/C3
Chester, Eng. 67/E4

Chester, Pa. 171/F4
Chesterfield, Pa. 67/F4
Chevy Chase, Md. 139/D1
Cheyenne (cap.), Wyo. 177/C1
Cheyenne (riv.), U.S. 165/E2
Chiang Mai, Thai. 110/B3
Chiba, Japan 107/F4
Chibougamau, Que. 184/C1
Chicago, Ill. 178/B2
Chicago Hts., Ill. 178/B3
Chichén-Itzá (ruins), Mex. 47/H4
Chickamauga (lake), Tenn. 149/D4
Chickasha, Okla. 168/B3
Chiclayo, Peru 56/B3
Chico, Calif. 132/B1
Chicopee, Mass. 136/B2
Chicoutimi, Que. 185/E2
Chiem See (lake), Ger. 71/E5
Chignecto (bay), Canada 182/C3
Chihuahua, Mex. 46/D2
Chile 56/B4, 58/B-C5-8
Chillicothe, Ohio 167/D2
Chiloé (isl.), Chile 58/B7
Chimborazo (mt.), Ecua. 56/B3
Chimbote, Peru 56/B3
Chimkent, U.S.S.R. 90/D3
Chin (hills), Burma 110/A2
China, People's Rep. of 104-105
China, Rep. of (Taiwan) 105/F3
Chinandega, Nic. 48/C2
Chincoteague, Va. 139/F3
Chindwin (riv.), Burma 110/A1
Chingola, Zambia 63/E6
Chinju, S. Korea 106/B4
Chino, Calif. 179/D2
Chippewa (riv.), Wis. 176/A3
Chiricahua Nat'l Mon., Ariz. 130/C4
Chiriquí (lag.), Pan. 49/D3
Chisholm, Minn. 153/B2
Chisimayu, Somalia 63/G5
Chita, U.S.S.R. 91/F3
Chittagong, Bang. 103/E2
Choluteca, Hond. 48/C2
Chŏngjin, N. Korea 106/C2
Ch'ŏngju, S. Korea 106/B3
Chongqing (Chungking), China 104/D2
Chŏnju, S. Korea 106/B4
Chonos (arch.), Chile 58/B7
Ch'ŏrwŏn, S. Korea 106/B3
Chorzów, Poland 86/B4
Christchurch, N.Z. 115/F4
Christiansburg, Va. 138/C4
Christiansted, V.I. (U.S.) 54/G
Christmas (isl.), Austr. 93/H6
Christmas (Kiritimati) (isl.), Kiribati 117/L5
Chubut (riv.), Arg. 58/C7
Chukchi (pen.), U.S.S.R. 91/K2
Chu Lai, Viet. 110/E4
Chula Vista, Calif. 180/C4
Ch'unch'ŏn, S. Korea 106/B3
Chur, Switz. 81/D2
Churchill, Man. 42/G4
Cicero, Ill. 178/B2
Cienfuegos, Cuba 52/E2
Cimarron (riv.), U.S. 168/A2
Cincinnati, Ohio 167/F1
Circleville, Ohio 167/D2
Cirebon, Indon. 113/H2
Ciskei (aut. rep.), S. Africa 63/E8
Citlaltépetl (mt.), Mex. 47/G2
Citrus Heights, Calif. 132/C2
Ciudad Bolívar, Ven. 57/C2
Ciudad Guayana, Ven. 56/C2
Ciudad Juárez, Mex. 46/C1
Ciudad Madero, Mex. 47/F3
Ciudad Obregón, Mex. 46/C2

Civitavecchia, Italy 78/C3
Claremont, Calif. 179/B3
Claremont, N.H. 158/B3
Clarion, Pa. 170/B3
Clarksburg, W. Va. 138/C2
Clarksdale, Miss. 154/B1
Clarksville, Tenn. 148/C3
Clayton, Mo. 155/A4
Clear (cape), Ire. 67/B5
Clear Lake, Iowa 146/A2
Clearfield, Pa. 170/C3
Clearfield, Utah 174/B2
Clearwater, Fla. 140/C1
Clearwater (mts.), Idaho 143/AB2
Clermont-Ferrand, France 75/E5
Cleveland, Miss. 154/A2
Cleveland, Ohio 167/F3
Cleveland, Tenn. 149/D4
Cleveland Hts., Ohio 167/F4
Clifton, N.J. 180/A2
Clinton, Iowa 146/B4
Clinton, Miss. 154/B2
Clinton, Okla. 168/B2
Clipperton (isl.), Fr. 41/H8
Clonmel, Ire. 67/C4
Clovis, Calif. 133/D2
Clovis, N. Mex. 135/D4
Cluj-Napoca, Rom. 84/C2
Clyde (riv.), Scot. 66/E3
Clydebank, Scot. 66/B1
Coast (mts.), Br. Col. 190/A3
Coast (ranges), U.S. 169, 175/C1
Coatbridge, Scot. 66/B1
Coatesville, Pa. 171/E4
Cobán, Guat. 48/B2
Cóbh, Ire. 67/B5
Coblenz, Ger., see Koblenz
Cobourg, Ont. 187/D3
Cochabamba, Bol. 56/C4
Cochinos (bay), Cuba 52/E3
Cockburn (isl.), Ont. 186/A2
Coco (riv.), Cent. Amer. 49/D2
Cocoa, Fla. 140/C4
Cocos (isls.), Austr. 93/G6
Cod (cape), Mass. 137/F2
Cody, Wyo. 177/A3
Coeur d'Alene, Idaho 143/A1
Coffeyville, Kans. 147/C4
Cohoes, N.Y. 161/F3
Coiba (isl.), Panama 49/D4
Coimbatore, India 102/C3
Coimbra, Port. 76/B2
Colchester, Eng. 67/G5
Cold Lake, Alta. 191/F2
Colebrook, N.H. 158/C1
Coleraine, N. Ire. 66/C3
College Park, Ga. 142/B1
College Park, Md. 139/E1
College Station, Texas 173/E2
Collingswood, N.J. 171/F2
Collingwood, Ont. 186/C3
Colmar, France 74/G3
Cologne, Ger. 71/B3
Colombia 56/B2
Colombo (cap.), Sri Lanka 102/C4
Colón, Pan. 49/D3
Colorado (riv.), Arg. 58/C6
Colorado (riv.), Ariz.-Calif. 44/D4
Colorado (riv.), Texas 173/E3
Colorado (state), U.S. 134
Colorado Nat'l Mon., Colo. 134/B1
Colorado Sprs., Colo. 134/B3
Columbia (cap.), S.C. 162/C4
Columbia (riv.), N. Amer. 44/B1
Columbia, Mo. 155/B2
Columbia, Pa. 171/E4
Columbia, Tenn. 148/C3
Columbus, Ga. 142/A3
Columbus, Ind. 145/B3

Columbus, Miss. 154/C2
Columbus, Nebr. 157/B4
Columbus (cap.), Ohio 166/C2
Colville (riv.), Alaska 129/A1
Communism (peak), U.S.S.R. 90/D4
Como (lake), Italy 78/B1
Comorin (cape), India 102/C4
Comoros 63/G6
Compiègne, France 74/E3
Compton, Calif. 179/C2
Conakry (cap.), Guinea 60/A4
Concepción, Chile 58/B6
Concepción, Par. 58/D5
Concord, Calif. 133/E1
Concord (cap.), N.H. 158/C3
Concord, N.C. 162/C2
Congaree Swamp Nat'l Mon., S.C. 162/C3
Congo 62/D5
Congo (riv.), Africa 62/D5
Connecticut (riv.), U.S. 136/C3, 158/B3
Connecticut (state), U.S. 136
Connellsville, Pa. 170/B4
Connersville, Ind. 145/C2
Constance (lake), Europe 81/E1
Constanța, Rom. 81/D1
Constantine, Alg. 60/C1
Conway, Ark. 131/B2
Conway, N.H. 158/C3
Conway, S.C. 163/D3
Cook (str.), N.Z. 115/F4
Cook Islands 117/K7
Cookeville, Tenn. 149/D3
Cooper (riv.), S.C. 162/C3
Cooperstown, N.Y. 161/E3
Coos Bay, Oreg. 169/C1
Copenhagen (cap.), Den. 69/C3
Copiapó, Chile 58/B5
Copper Harbor, Mich. 152/A1
Coquitlam, Br. Col. 190/B1
Coral (sea) 116/F7
Coral Gables, Fla. 141/E1
Coral Sea I. (terr.), Austr. 116/EF7
Corbin, Ky. 149/E3
Cordele, Ga. 142/B3
Córdoba, Arg. 58/C6
Córdoba, Spain 76/D4
Corfu, Greece, see Kérkira
Corinth, Greece 85/C4
Corinth, Miss. 154/C1
Cork, Ire. 67/B5
Corn (isls.), Nic. 49/D2
Corner Brook, Newf. 183/E1
Corning, N.Y. 160/D3
Cornwall, Ont. 187/F2
Coro, Ven. 56/C1
Corona, Calif. 179/C4
Coronado, Calif. 180/C4
Corpus Christi, Texas 173/E4
Corregidor (isl.), Phil. 108/C3
Corrib, Lough (lake), Ire. 67/B4
Corrientes, Arg. 58/D5
Corsica (isl.), France 75/B7
Corsicana, Texas 173/E2
Cortez, Colo. 134/C2
Cortina d'Ampezzo, Italy 78/D1
Cortland, N.Y. 161/D3
Çorum, Turkey 96/F2
Corvallis, Oreg. 169/B2
Cosenza, Italy 79/F5
Coshocton, Ohio 166/C3
Costa Brava (reg.), Spain 77/H2
Costa del Sol (reg.), Spain 76/D4
Costa Mesa, Calif. 179/C5
Costa Rica 48/C3
Côte d'Ivoire, see Ivory Coast
Côte-d'Or (mts.), France 74/F4
Cotonou, Benin 60/C4

Cottage Grove, Oreg. 169/B2
Council Bluffs, Iowa 146/C1
Council Grove, Kans. 147/B3
Courantyne (riv.), S. Amer. 57/D2
Courtenay, Br. Col. 190/B4
Courtrai, Belg. 73/B6
Coventry, Eng. 67/F4
Covington, Ky. 149/D2
Coyoacan, Mex. 47/F1
Cozumel (isl.), Mex. 47/H4
Cracow, Pol. 87/E3
Craigavon, N. Ire. 67/C3
Craiova, Rom. 84/C2
Cranbrook, Br. Col. 191/D4
Cranston, R.I. 137/D2
Crater Lake Nat'l Pk., Oreg. 169/C2
Craters of the Moon Nat'l Mon., Idaho 143/B3
Crawford, Nebr. 157/A1
Crawfordsville, Ind. 145/B2
Creston, Br. Col. 191/D4
Crete (isl.), Greece 85/D5
Crewe, Eng. 67/E4
Crimea (pen.), U.S.S.R. 89/D5
Crisfield, Md. 139/F3
Cristóbal Colón (mt.), Col. 56/B1
Crowley, La. 150/C2
Crown Point, Ind. 145/A1
Crown Point, N.Y. 161/F2
Croydon, Eng. 67/B6
Crozet (isls.), Fr. 35/L8
Ctesiphon (ruins), Iraq 100/D4
Cuba 50/B2, 52-53
Cúcuta, Col. 56/B2
Cudahy, Wis. 176/B1
Cuenca, Ecua. 56/B3
Cuernavaca, Mex. 47/F2
Cuiabá, Braz. 57/D4
Culebra (isl.), P. Rico 51/G1, 54/E1
Culiacán, Mex. 46/C2
Cullman, Ala. 128/B1
Culver City, Calif. 179/B1
Cumaná, Ven. 56/C1
Cumberland, Md. 139/D2
Cumberland (riv.), U.S. 149/D3
Cunene (riv.), Angola 62/D6
Curaçao (isl.), Neth. Ant. 50/E4, 55/N
Curitiba, Braz. 59/E5
Cusco, Peru 56/B4
Cushing, Okla. 168/B3
Custer, S. Dak. 165/E1
Custer Battlfld. Nat'l Mon., Mont. 156/C3
Cuttack, India 102/D2
Cuxhaven, Ger. 70/C2
Cuyahoga Falls, Ohio 166/B3
Cuyuni (riv.), S. Amer. 56/C2
Cyclades (isls.), Greece 85/D4
Cyprus 96/E5
Cyrenaica (reg.), Libya 61/E1
Czechoslovakia 82-83
Częstochowa, Pol. 86/D3

D

Dacca (Dhaka) (cap.), Bang. 103/D2
Dachau, Ger. 71/D4
Dahlak (arch.), Eth. 94/E6
Dahlonega, Ga. 142/A2
Daito (isls.), Japan 105/L9
Dakar (cap.), Sen. 60/A3
Dakhla (oasis), Egypt 94/B4
Dakhla, W. Sahara 60/A2
Da Lat, Viet. 111/E5
Dale Hollow (lake), U.S. 149/D3
Dalhousie, Br. 182/B1
Dalian, China 105/F2

Dallas, Texas 172/B4
Daloa, Iv. Coast 60/B4
Dalton, Ga. 142/A2
Daly City, Calif. 133/E1
Damascus (cap.), Syria 97/G6
Damavand (mt.), Iran 101/H3
Damietta, Egypt 61/F1
Da Nang, Viet. 110/E3
Danbury, Conn. 136/A3
Dandong, China 105/F1
Danli, Hond. 48/C2
Danube (riv.), Europe 64/F4
Danville, III. 144/C2
Danville, Ky. 149/D2
Danville, Va. 138/C4
Danzig (Gdańsk) (gulf), Pol. 87/D1
Danzig, Pol., see Gdańsk
Darbhanga, India 102/D2
Darby, Pa. 171/E2
Dardanelles (str.), Turkey 96/B6
Dar es Salaam (cap.), Tanz. 63/F5
Darien, Conn. 136/A4
Dariën (mts.), Pan. 49/E3
Darjeeling, India 103/E2
Darling (riv.), Austr. 115/D4
Darlington, Eng. 67/F3
Darmstadt, Ger. 71/C4
Dartmouth, N.S. 183/D4
Darwin, Austr. 114/C2
Dasht-e Kavir (des.), Iran 101/J3
Dasht-e Lut (des.), Iran 101/K5
Datong, China 105/F2
Daugavpils, U.S.S.R. 88/C3
Dauphin River, Man. 189/E3
Dauphin, Man. 189/D3
Davao, Phil. 109/E7
Davenport, Iowa 146/B4
David, Panama 49/D3
Davis (sea), Antarc. 118
Davis, Calif. 132/C1
Davis (str.), N. Amer. 40/N3
Davis (mts.), Texas 172/B2
Davos, Switz. 81/E2
Dawson, Yukon 42/C3
Dawson Creek, Br. Col. 190/C1
Dayton, Ohio 167/D3
Daytona Bch., Fla. 140/B3
De Kalb, III. 144/B1
De Land, Fla. 140/B3
De Ridder, La. 150/B1
Dead Sea, Asia 99/C4
Dearborn, Mich. 178/B4
Death Valley Nat'l Mon., U.S. 133/D3
Debra Markos, Eth. 61/F3
Debrecen, Hung. 83/F3
Decatur, Ala. 128/B1
Decatur, Ga. 142/C1
Decatur, III. 144/B3
Deccan (plat.), India 102/C3
Decorah, Iowa 146/A3
Dedham, Mass. 137/F4
Dee (riv.), Eng. 66/F2
Dee (riv.), Scot. 66/E2
Deep River, Ont. 187/D2
Deerfield, III. 178/B1
Defiance, Ohio 166/B1
Dehra Dun, India 102/C1
Deir ez Zor, Syria 97/H5
Del Mar, Calif. 180/C4
Del Rio, Texas 172/C3
Delaware, Ohio 166/C2
Delaware (bay), U.S. 159/A4
Delaware (riv.), U.S. 159/A1
Delaware (state), U.S. 139/F2
Delft, Neth. 72/D3
Delgado (cape), Moz. 63/G6
Delhi, India 102/C2
Delray Beach, Fla. 141/E4

Index

Delta, Br. Col. 190/A1
Delta, Colo. 134/B2
Deming, N. Mex. 135/F2
Den Helder, Neth. 72/E2
Denison, Texas 173/E1
Denizli, Turkey 96/C4
Denmark 69/B3
Denton, Texas (cap.) 173/E1
Denton, Texas 173/E1
Denver (cap.), Colo. 178/B4
Depew, N.Y. 160/B3
Der'a, Syria 97/G6
Derby, Eng. 67/F4
Derg, Lough (lake), Ire. 67/B4
Derna, Libya 61/E1
Derry, N.H. 158/C4
Des Moines (cap.), Iowa 146/B2
Des Moines (riv.), Iowa 146/B2
Des Plaines, Ill. 178/B4
Deschutes (riv.), Oreg. 169/A3
Deseado (riv.), Arg. 58/C7
Dessau, Ger. 70/E3
Dessye, Eth. 61/G3
Detroit, Mich. 178/C4
Deventer, Neth. 72/H3
Devil's (isl.), Fr. Guiana 57/D2
Devils Lake, N. Dak. 164/B3
Devils Tower Nat'l Mon., Wyo.
177/A1
Devon (isl.), N.W.T. 43/H1
Dewsbury, Eng. 66/H2
Dezful, Iran 100/F4
Dezhnev (cape), U.S.S.R. 91/K2
Dhahran, S. Arabia 94/F4
Dhaka (cap.), Bang. 103/D2
Dhofar (reg.), Oman 95/G6
Dhulia, India 102/C4
Diamond (head), Hawaii 129/B4
Dickinson, N. Dak. 164/C1
Diefenbaker (lake), Sask. 188/B4
Diego Garcia (isls.), Br. Ind. Oc.
Terr. 93/F6
Diego Suarez, Madag., see
Antsiranana
Dien Bien Phu, Viet. 110/C2
Dieppe, France 74/D3
Dieppe, N. Br. 182/C2
Digby, N.S. 182/C4
Dijon, France 74/F4
Dili, Indon. 113/H7
Dillon, Mont. 156/C3
Dimona, Isr. 99/C5
Dinagat (isl.), Phil. 109/E5
Dinant, Belg. 73/E7
Dinaric Alps (mts.), Yugo. 84/B3
Dingle (bay), Ire. 67/A4
Dinosaur Nat'l Mon., U.S.
134/A1, 174/C2
Dire Dawa, Eth. 61/G4
District of Columbia (U.S. 139/D1
Dixon Entrance (str.), N. Amer.
40/E4
Dixon Mounds (site), Ill. 144/B2
Dixon, Ill. 144/B1
Diyarbakır, Turkey 97/H4
Djakarta, see Jakarta
Djibouti 61/G3
Djibouti (cap.), Djibouti 61/G3
Djokjakarta, Indon., see
Yogyakarta
Dnepropetrovsk, U.S.S.R. 89/D5
Dnieper (riv.), U.S.S.R. 89/D5
Dniester (riv.), U.S.S.R. 89/C5
Dobbs Ferry, N.Y. 180/B1
Dodecanese (isls.), Greece 85/D5
Dodge City, Kans. 147/C2
Dodoma, Tanz. 63/F5
Dogo (isl.), Japan 106/D3
Doha (cap.), Qatar 95/G4
Dolomite Alps (mts.), Italy 78/C1

Dominica 51/G4, 54-55/K
Dominican Republic 50/D3,
52-53/Q-S7
Don (riv.), U.S.S.R. 89/F5
Doncaster, Eng. 67/F4
Donegal (bay), Ire. 67/B3
Donetsk, U.S.S.R. 89/E5
Dongala, Sudan 61/F3
Door (pen.), Wis. 176/C3
Dordogne (riv.), France 75/D5
Dordrecht, Neth. 72/E4
Dornbirn, Austria 82/A3
Dortmund, Ger. 70/B3
Dorval, Que. 184/A1
Dothan, Ala. 128/C3
Douai, France 74/E2
Douala, Cameroon 60/H4
Douglas, Ariz. 130/C4
Douglas (cap.), I. of Man 67/B3
Douglas, Wyo. 177/B2
Douro (riv.), Port. 76/C2
Dover (cap.), Del. 139/F2
Dover, Eng. 67/G5
Dover (str.), Europe 67/G5
Dover, N.H. 158/C3
Dover, N.J. 159/B1
Dover-Foxcroft, Maine 151/B3
Downers Grove, Ill. 178/A2
Downey, Calif. 179/B2
Doylestown, Pa. 171/F4
Drammen, Nor. 69/B3
Dráva (riv.), Europe 84/B2
Drayton Valley, Alta. 191/D2
Dresden, Ger. 71/E3
Drin (riv.), Alb. 84/C3
Drogheda, Ire. 67/C4
Drumheller, Alta. 191/E3
Drummond (isl.), Mich. 152/C2
Drummondville, Que. 185/D4
Druz, Jebel ed (mts.), Syria
97/G5
Dubai, U.A.E. 95/G4
Dubbo, Austr. 115/D4
Dublin, Ga. 142/B3
Dublin (cap.), Ire. 67/C4
Dubois, Pa. 170/B3
Dubrovnik, Yugo. 84/B3
Dubuque, Iowa 146/B4
Dudinka, U.S.S.R. 90/E2
Dudley, Eng. 67/E4
Duero (riv.), Spain 76/D2
Dufourspitze (mt.), Switz. 80/C3
Duisburg, Ger. 70/B3
Duluth, Minn. 153/C2
Dumfries, Scot. 66/E3
Duncan, Br. Col. 190/B4
Duncan, Okla. 168/C2
Duncanville, Texas 172/B4
Dundalk, Ire. 67/C3
Dundalk, Md. 139/F1
Dundas, Ont. 187/E4
Dundee, Scot. 66/E2
Dunedin, Fla. 140/C1
Dunedin, N.Z. 115/F4
Dunfermline, Scot. 66/E2
Dunkirk, N.Y. 160/A3
Dún Laoghaire, Ire. 67/D4
Dunmore, Pa. 171/E3
Durance (riv.), France 75/F6
Durango, Colo. 134/C2
Durango, Mex. 46/D3
Durant, Okla. 168/C3
Durban, S. Africa 63/F7
Durham, N.C. 163/D1
Durrës (Durazzo), Alb. 85/B3
Dushanbe, U.S.S.R. 90/D4
Düsseldorf, Ger. 71/B3
Dvina, Northern (riv.), U.S.S.R.
88/F2

Dvina, Western (riv.), U.S.S.R.
88/C3
Dzerzhinsk, U.S.S.R. 88/F3
Dzhambul, U.S.S.R. 90/D3
Dzhezkazgan, U.S.S.R. 90/D3

E

Eagan, Minn. 153/C1
Eagle Pass, Texas 172/C3
Ealing, Eng. 67/B5
E. Aurora, N.Y. 160/B3
Eastbourne, Eng. 67/G5
E. Chicago, Ind. 145/A1
East China (sea), Asia 105/F3
E. Cleveland, Ohio 167/E4
E. Detroit, Mich. 178/C4
Easter (isl.), Chile 117/Q8
E. Hampton, N.Y. 160/C4
E. Hartford, Conn. 136/B2
Eastlake, Ohio 167/F4
E. Lansing, Mich. 152/B4
E. Liverpool, Ohio 166/C4
E. London, S. Africa 63/E8
Easton, Pa. 171/F3
E. Orange, N.J. 180/A2
E. Peoria, Ill. 144/B2
East Point, Ga. 142/C1
Eastport, Maine 151/C3
E. St. Louis, Ill. 144/B3
East Siberian (sea), U.S.S.R.
91/N2
Eau Claire, Wis. 176/A3
Ebro (riv.), Spain 77/E2
Ech Cheliff, Alg. 60/C1
Ecuador 56/B3
Eddystone (rocks), Eng. 67/D5
Eden, N.C. 163/D1
Edenton, N.C. 163/F1
Edina, Minn. 153/B1
Edinburg, Texas 173/D4
Edinburgh (cap.), Scot. 66/E3
Eufrne, Turkey 96/B2
Edmonds, Wash. 175/B1
Edmonton (cap.), Alta. 191/F1
Edmundston, N. Br. 182/A1
Edson, Alta. 191/D2
Edward (lake), Africa 63/E5
Edwards (plat.), Texas 172/C2
Edwardsville, Ill. 144/B3
Eel (riv.), Calif. 132/B1
Effigy Mounds, Nat'l Mon., Iowa
146/A4
Effingham, Ill. 144/C3
Eger, Hung. 83/F3
Egypt 61/F2, 82/94
Eindhoven, Neth. 72/F5
El Asnam, Alg., see Ech Cheliff
Elat (Elath), Isr. 99/D6
Eláziğ, Turkey 97/H3
Elba (isl.), Italy 78/C3
Elbasan, Alb. 85/B3
Elbe (riv.), Ger. 70/C2
El'brus (mt.), U.S.S.R. 89/F6
Elburz (mts.), Iran 100/G2
El Cajon, Calif. 180/C4
El Centro, Calif. 133/F4
Elche, Spain 77/F3
El Dorado, Ark. 131/C2
Eldoret, Kenya 63/F4
Eleuthera (isl.), Bah. 50/C1
El Faiyûm, Egypt 61/F2
El Fasher, Sudan 61/E3
El Ferrol, Spain 76/B1
Elgin, Ill. 178/A1
Elgon (mt.), Uganda 63/F4
Elista, U.S.S.R. 89/F5
Elizabeth, N.J. 180/A2
Elizabeth City, N.C. 163/F1
Elizabethton, Tenn. 149/F3
Elizabethtown, Ky. 149/D2

El Karak, Jordan 99/E4
El Karnak, Egypt 94/C4
Elk City, Okla. 168/B2
El Kharga, Egypt 61/E2
Elkhart, Ind. 145/B1
Elkins, W. Va. 138/C2
Elk Island Nat'l Pk., Alta. 191/E2
Elko, Nev. 132/A4
Elkton, Md. 139/F2
Ellensburg, Wash. 175/B3
Ellesmere (isl.), N.W.T. 35/G1
Ellesmere Port, Eng. 66/G2
Elliot Lake, Ont. 186/B1
Ellsworth, Maine 151/B3
Elmhurst, Ill. 178/A2
El Minya, Egypt 61/F2
Elmira, N.Y. 160/C4
El Monte, Calif. 179/B3
El Morro Nat'l Mon., N. Mex. 135/D1
Elmwood Park, Ill. 178/B2
El Obeid, Sudan 61/E3
El Paso, Texas 172/A2
El Progreso, Hond. 48/C2
El Rashid, Syria 97/H4
El Reno, Okla. 168/B2
El Salvador 48/B2
Elsinore, Den., see Helsingør
Eluru, India 102/D3
Elwood, Nebr. 157/C2
Ely, Nev. 132/B4
Elyria, Ohio 166/B3
Emden, Ger. 70/B2
Emi Koussi (mt.), Chad 61/D3
Emilia-Romagna (reg.), Italy 78/C2
Emporia, Kans. 147/B4
Ems (riv.), Ger. 70/B2
Encarnación, Par. 59/D5
Enderbury (isl.), Kiribati 117/K6
Enewetak (atoll), Marshall Is. 116/G4
Enfield, Conn., see Thompsonville
Enfield, Eng. 67/B5
Engadine (valley), Switz. 81/E2
Engaño (cape), Phil. 108/D1
Engel's, U.S.S.R. 89/G4
England 66-67
Englewood, Colo. 178/A4
Englewood, N.J. 180/B1
English (chan.), Europe 64/D4
Enid, Okla. 168/A3
Ennis, Ire. 67/B5
Enniskillen, N. Ire. 67/C3
Enschede, Neth. 72/J3
Ensenada, Mex. 46/A1
Entebbe, Uganda 63/F5
Enterprise, Ala. 128/C3
Enugu, Nigeria 60/C4
Ephrata, Pa. 171/E4
Epsom and Ewell, Eng. 67/B6
Equatorial Guinea 60/C4
Erbil, Iraq 100/D3
Ereğli, Turkey 96/D2
Erfurt, Ger. 71/D3
Erie (lake), N. Amer. 45/K2, H7/43
Erie, Pa. 170/A2
Eritrea (reg.), Eth. 61/F3
Erivan, U.S.S.R., see Yerevan
Erlangen, Ger. 71/D4
Erne, Lough (lake), N. Ire. 67/C3
Erzgebirge (mts.), Europe 71/E3
Erzurum, Turkey 97/J3
Esbjerg, Den. 69/B3
Escanaba, Mich. 152/A2
Esch-sur-Alzette, Lux. 73/G8
Escondido, Calif. 180/C4
Esfahan, Iran, see Isfahan
Esher, Eng. 67/B6

Eskilstuna, Swed. 69/C3
Eskişehir, Turkey 96/D3
Española, Ont. 186/B1
Espiritu Santo (isl.), Vanuatu 116/G7
Es Salt, Jordan 99/D3
Essen, Ger. 70/B3
Essequibo (riv.), Guyana 56/D2
Essex, Md. 139/F1
Estados (isl.), Arg. 58/C5
Estevan, Sask. 188/C4
Estonian S.S.R., U.S.S.R. 88/C3
Estremadura (reg.), Spain 76/C3
Ethiopia 61/F6/4
Etna (vol.), Italy 79/E6
Etorofu (isl.), Japan 107/G1
Etosha (salt pan), Namibia 62/D6
Euboea (isl.), Greece 85/C4
Euclid, Ohio 167/E4
Eufaula, Ala. 128/C3
Eugene, Oreg. 169/B2
Eunice, La. 150/B2
Euphrates (riv.), Asia 94/D2
Eureka Springs, Ark. 131/A2
Eureka, Calif. 132/B1
Europa (isl.), Réunion 63/G7
Europe 64-65
Evanston, Ill. 178/B1
Evanston, Wyo. 177/C4
Evansville, Ind. 145/A4
Everest (mt.), Asia 103/D2
Everett, Wash. 175/B2
Everglades Nat'l Pk., Fla. 141/E4
Évora, Port. 76/C3
Évvoia (isl.), see Euboea
Ewa Beach, Hawaii 129/A4
Exeter, Eng. 67/E5
Exeter, N.H. 158/C4
Eyre (lake), Austr. 114/C3
Ez Zarqa', Jordan 99/E3

F

Faeroe (isls.), Den. 64/D2
Fairbanks, Alaska 129/B1
Fairborn, Ohio 166/C1
Fairfield, Ala. 128/B2
Fairfield, Calif. 132/C1
Fairfield, Conn. 136/A3
Fairfield, Ohio 167/E1
Fair Lawn, N.J. 180/A1
Fairmont, W. Va. 138/C2
Fairweather (mt.), N. Amer. 42/C4
Faisalabad, Pak. 102/C1
Faiyûm, Egypt, see El Faiyûm
Fajardo, P. Rico 54/D1
Falkirk, Scot. 66/B1
Falkland Islands 58-59/D8
Fallon, Nev. 132/B3
Fall River, Mass. 137/E3
Falls Church, Va. 139/D1
Falmouth, Mass. 137/E3
Famagusta, Cyprus 96/F5
Fanning (isl.), see Tabuaeran
Farewell (cape), Greenl. 40/P4
Fargo, N. Dak. 164/C4
Faribault, Minn. 153/B4
Farmers Branch, Texas 172/B4
Farmington, Maine 151/A3
Farmington, N. Mex. 134/C2
Faro, Port. 76/B4
Fayetteville, Ark. 131/A1
Fayetteville, N.C. 163/D2
Fear (cape), N.C. 163/E3
Fehmarn (isl.), Ger. 70/D1
Fergana, U.S.S.R. 90/D4
Fergus Falls, Minn. 153/A3
Ferguson, Mo. 155/A4
Fernandina Bch., Fla. 140/A3
Fernando Po, see Bioko

Fernie, Br. Col. 191/E4
Ferrara, Italy 78/C2
Ferro (Hierro) (isl.), Spain 76/A5
Fès (Fez), Mor. 60/B1
Fezzan (reg.), Libya 60/D2
Fianarantsoa, Madag. 63/G7
Fichtelgebirge (range), Ger. 71/D3
Fiji 116/H7
Findlay, Ohio 166/B2
Finger (lakes), N.Y. 160-161/C-D3
Finisterre (cape), Spain 76/B1
Finland 68-69/E2
Finland (gulf), Europe 65/G3
Firenze (Florence), Italy 78/C3
Fitchburg, Mass. 137/D1
Fiume, Yugo., see Rijeka
Flagstaff, Ariz. 130/B3
Flamborough (head), Eng. 67/G3
Flamborough, Ont. 187/E4
Flaming Gorge (res.), U.S. 174/C2, 177/C3
Flanders (provs.), Belg. 73/A-B5-6
Flathead (lake), Mont. 156/A1
Flattery (cape), Wash. 175/A1
Flemington, N.J. 159/B2
Flensburg, Ger. 70/C1
Flin Flon, Man. 189/D2
Flint, Mich. 152/C4
Floral Park, N.Y. 180/C2
Florence, Ala. 128/A1
Florence, Ky. 149/E2
Florence, Oreg. 169/B1
Florence, S.C. 163/D3
Flores (isl.), Indon. 113/G7
Flores, Guat. 48/B1
Florianópolis, Braz. 59/E5
Florida (bay), Fla. 141/F4
Florida (state), U.S. 140-141
Florida Keys (isls.), Fla. 141/F4
Florissant, Mo. 155/A4
Florissant Fossil Beds Nat'l Mon., Colo. 134/B3
Flushing, Neth. 73/C4
Fly (riv.), Papua N.G. 112/A7
Foggia, Italy 79/E4
Folkestone, Eng. 67/G5
Fond du Lac, Wis. 176/C4
Fongafale (cap.), Tuvalu 116/H6
Fonseca (gulf), Cent. Amer. 48/C2
Fontainebleau, France 74/E3
Fontana, Calif. 179/B4
Fontana (lake), N.C. 162/A2
Foochow, see Fuzhou
Fordyce, Ark. 131/C2
Forest Park, Ga. 142/C1
Forillon Nat'l Pk., Que. 185/F1
Forli, Italy 78/C2
Formentera (isl.), Spain 77/G3
Formosa, Arg. 58/D5
Formosa (Taiwan) (isl.), China 105/F3
Forrest City, Ark. 131/B3
Forsyth, Mont. 156/B4
Fortaleza, Braz. 57/F3
Ft. Assiniboine, Mont. 156/A3
Ft. Belvoir, Va. 139/E3
Ft. Benton, Mont. 156/A4
Ft. Bridger, Wyo. 177/C4
Ft. Chaffee, Ark. 131/B1
Ft. Collins, Colo. 134/A3
Ft-de-France (cap.), Martinique 51/G4, 55/J
Ft. Dodge, Iowa 146/A2
Ft. Erie, Ont. 187/F4
Ft. Eustis, Va. 138/A1
Ft. Frances, Ont. 187/D1
Forth (firth), Scot. 66/E2

Index

Ft. Kent, Maine 151/B1
Ft. Knox, Ky. 149/D2
Ft. Lauderdale, Fla. 141/D4
Ft. Leonard Wood, Mo. 155/B3
Ft. Macleod, Alta. 191/E4
Ft. Madison, Iowa 146/C4
Ft. McArthur, Calif. 179/C1
Ft. McClellan, Ala. 128/C2
Ft. McHenry Nat'l Mon., Md. 139/F1
Ft. McMurray, Alta. 42/E4
Ft. Monroe, Va. 138/A1
Ft. Myers, Fla. 141/D3
Ft. Niobrara, Nebr. 157/A2
Ft. Peck Lake (res.), Mont. 156/A3
Ft. Pierce, Fla. 141/D4
Ft. Pierre, S. Dak. 165/E2
Ft. Polk, La. 150/B1
Ft. Pulaski Nat'l Mon., Ga. 142/C3
Ft. Qu'Appelle, Sask. 188/C3
Ft. St. James, Br. Col. 190/B2
Ft. St. John, Br. Col. 190/C1
Ft. Saskatchewan, Alta. 191/F1
Ft. Smith, Ark. 131/B1
Ft. Smith, N.W.T. 42/E3
Ft. Stockton, Texas 172/B2
Ft. Story, Va. 138/B1
Ft. Sumter Nat'l Mon., S.C. 163/D4
Ft. Walton Bch., Fla. 141/F1
Ft. Wayne, Ind. 145/C2
Ft. William, Scot. 66/D2
Ft. Worth, Texas 172/A4
Fossil Butte Nat'l Mon., Wyo. 177/C4
Fostoria, Ohio 166/B2
Fountain Valley, Calif. 179/B4
Foxe (basin), N.W.T. 43/J3
Foyle, Lough (inlet), Ire. 66/C3
Framingham, Mass. 137/D2
France 74-75
Francis Case (lake), S. Dak. 165/F3
Frankfort, Ind. 145/B2
Frankfort (cap.), Ky. 149/D2
Frankfort, Mich. 152/B3
Frankfurt-am-Main, Ger. 71/C3
Frankfurt-an-der-Oder, Ger. 70/F2
Franklin, Pa. 170/A3
Franklin, Tenn. 148/C4
Franklin, Va. 139/E4
Franklin, Wis. 176/B1
Franklin D. Roosevelt (lake), Wash. 175/A4
Franz Josef Land (isls.), U.S.S.R. 90/C1
Fraser (riv.), Br. Col. 190/C3
Fraserburgh, Scot. 66/E2
Fredericia, Den. 69/B3
Frederick, Md. 139/E2
Fredericksburg, Texas 173/F3
Fredericksburg, Va. 139/E3
Fredericton (cap.), N. Br. 182/B2
Frederik VI Coast, Greenl. 40/P3
Frederikshavn, Den. 69/B3
Freehold, N.J. 159/C2
Freeport, Ill. 144/B1
Freeport, N.Y. 160/B4
Freeport, Texas 173/F3
Freetown (cap.), S. Leone 60/A4
Freiburg im Breisgau, Ger. 71/B5
Fremantle, Austr. 114/A4
Fremont, Calif. 133/F2
Fremont, Nebr. 157/B4
Fremont, Ohio 166/B2
French Guiana 57/D2
French Polynesia 117/M8
Fresno, Calif. 133/D2

Fria (cape), Namibia 62/D6
Fribourg, Switz. 80/C2
Fridley, Minn. 153/C1
Friedrichshafen, Ger. 71/C5
Friesland (prov.), Neth. 72/G1
Frio (cape), Braz. 59/E5
Frisian (isls.), Ger. 70/C1
Friuli-Venezia Giulia (reg.), Italy 78/D1
Frobisher Bay, N.W.T. 43/L3
Frome (lake), Austr. 115/D4
Front Royal, Va. 139/D2
Frontenac Prov. Pk., Que. 185/E4
Frunze, U.S.S.R. 90/D3
Fuerteventura (isl.), Spain 76/C4
Fuji (mt.), Japan 107/F2
Fujian (Fukien) (prov.), China 105/E3
Fukui, Japan 106/D3
Fukuoka, Japan 106/C4
Fukushima, Japan 107/F3
Fukuyama, Japan 106/D3
Fulda, Ger. 71/C3
Fullerton, Calif. 179/C3
Fulton, Mo. 155/B3
Fulton, N.Y. 161/D2
Funabashi, Japan 107/H2
Funafuti (isls.), Tuvalu 116/J6
Funchal, Port. 76/A2
Fundy (bay), N. Amer. 182/B3
Fundy Nat'l Pk., N. Br. 182/C3
Furneaux Group (isls.), Austr. 115/D4
Fürth, Ger. 71/D4
Fushun, China 105/F1
Füssen, Ger. 71/D5
Fuxin, China 105/F1
Fuzhou, China 105/E3

G

Gabès, Tun. 60/D1
Gabon 62/D5
Gaborone (cap.), Bots. 63/E7
Gabrovo, Bulg. 84/D3
Gadsden, Ala. 128/C1
Gaffney, S.C. 162/B2
Gainesville, Fla. 140/B2
Gainesville, Ga. 142/B2
Gairdner (lake), Austr. 114/C4
Gaithersburg, Md. 139/E2
Galápagos (isls.), Ecua. 34/F6
Galați, Rom. 84/D2
Galena, Ill. 144/A1
Galesburg, Ill. 144/A2
Galicia (reg.), Spain 76/B1
Galilee, Sea of (lake), Isr. 98/D2
Galle, Sri Lanka 102/C4
Gallipoli, see Gelibolu
Gallipolis, Ohio 167/E3
Gallup, N. Mex. 135/D2
Galveston, Texas 173/F3
Galway, Ire. 67/B4
Galway (bay), Ire. 67/B4
Gambia 60/A3
Gambier (isls.), Fr. Poly. 117/N8
Gananoque, Ont. 187/E3
Gander, Newf. 183/F1
Ganges (riv.), Asia 102/D2
Gangtok, India 103/D2
Gansu (prov.), China 104/D2
Gao, Mali 60/C3
Garda (lake), Italy 78/C2
Garden City, Kans. 147/B1
Garden City, Mich. 178/B4
Garden City, N.Y. 180/C2
Garden Grove, Calif. 179/C3
Gardena, Calif. 179/B1
Garfield, N.J. 180/A2
Garfield Hts., Ohio 167/F4

Garland, Texas 172/C4
Garmisch-Partenkirchen, Ger. 71/D5
Garonne (riv.), France 75/C5
Gary, Ind. 145/A1
Gaspé, Que. 185/F1
Gaspé (pen.), Que. 185/E1
Gastonia, N.C. 162/C2
Gates of the Arctic Nat'l Pk., Alaska 129/B1
Gateshead, Eng. 66/F3
Gatineau, Que. 184/C4
Gatineau Pk., Que. 184/B4
Gatlinburg, Tenn. 149/E4
Gauhati, India 103/E2
Gävle, Swed. 69/C2
Gaya, India 102/D2
Gaza, Gaza Strip 94/G3, 99/A4
Gaza Strip 99/A4
Gaziantep, Turkey 97/G4
Gdańsk, Pol. 86/D1
Gdańsk (gulf), Pol. 86/D1
Gdynia, Pol. 86/D1
Gedaref, Sudan 61/F3
Geelong, Austr. 115/D4
Gejiu, China 104/D3
Gelibolu, Turkey 96/C6
Gelsenkirchen, Ger. 70/B3
Genesee (riv.), N.Y. 160/B3
Geneva (lake), Europe 80/B2
Geneva, N.Y. 160/C3
Geneva, Switz. 80/B2
Genk, Belg. 73/G6
Genoa (Genova), Italy 78/B2
Georgetown (cap.), Cayman Is. 50/A3
Georgetown, Del. 139/F2
Georgetown (cap.), Guyana 57/D2
George Town, Malaysia 112/B4
Georgetown, S.C. 163/D3
George Washington Birthplace Nat'l Mon., Va. 139/E3
G.W. Carver Nat'l Mon., Mo. 155/C2
Georgia (str.), Br. Col. 190/B3
Georgia (state), U.S. 142
Georgian (bay), Ont. 186/B2
Georgian Bay Is. Nat'l Pk., Ont. 186/B2
Georgian S.S.R., U.S.S.R. 89/F6
Gera, Ger. 71/D3
Geraldton, Austr. 114/A3
Gerlachovka (mt.), Czech. 83/F2
Germany 70-71
Germiston, S. Africa 63/E7
Gettysburg, Pa. 171/D4
Ghana 60/C4
Ghazni, Afghan. 102/B3
Ghent, Belg. 73/C5
Gibraltar 76/D4
Gibraltar (str.) 76/D5
Gibson (des.), Austr. 114/B3
Gifu, Japan 106/E4
Gijón, Spain 76/D1
Gila (riv.), U.S. 135/F1
Gila Cliff Dwellings Nat'l Mon., N. Mex. 135/E1
Gilbert Is., see Kiribati
Gillette, Wyo. 177/A2
Girona (Gerona), Spain 77/H1
Gironde (riv.), France 75/C5
Giza, Egypt 94/C4
Glace Bay, N.S. 183/F2
Glacier Bay Nat'l Pk., Alaska 129/C2
Glacier Nat'l Pk., Br. Col. 191/D3
Glacier Nat'l Pk., Mont. 156/A1
Gladstone, Mich. 152/A2
Gladstone, Mo. 155/C1
Glarus, Switz. 81/D1

Glasgow, Ky. 149/D3
Glasgow, Mont. 156/A4
Glasgow, Scot. 66/E3
Glassboro, N.J. 159/A3
Glazov, U.S.S.R. 88/H3
Glencoe, Ill. 178/B1
Glen Cove, N.Y. 180/C1
Glendale, Ariz. 130/A1
Glendale, Calif. 179/A2
Glens Falls, N.Y. 161/F2
Glenwood Springs, Colo. 134/A2
Gliwice, Pol. 86/A4
Globe, Ariz. 130/C3
Gloucester, Eng. 67/F5
Gloucester, Mass. 137/E1
Gloversville, N.Y. 161/E3
Gniezno, Pol. 86/C2
Gobi (des.), Asia 104/D1
Godavari (riv.), India 102/D3
Goderich, Ont. 186/B3
Godthab (Nuuk) (cap.), Greenl. 40/N3
Godwin Austen (K2) (mt.), India 102/C1
Goiânia, Braz. 57/E4
Golan Heights 98/D1
Golden, Br. Col. 191/D3
Golden, Colo. 178/A4
Goldsboro, N.C. 163/E2
Golmud, China 104/C2
Gomel', U.S.S.R. 89/D4
Gomera (isl.), Spain 76/A5
Gonaïves, Haiti 52/P6
Gonâve (isl.), Haiti 50/D3, 52/N7
Gondar, Eth. 61/F3
Good Hope (cape), S. Africa 63/D8
Goodland, Kans. 147/A1
Goose (lake), U.S. 132/A2
Goose Bay, Newf. 43/L5
Gorakhpur, India 102/D2
Gorgan, Iran 101/J2
Gorham, N.H. 158/C2
Gor'kiy, U.S.S.R. 88/F3
Gorlovka, U.S.S.R. 89/E5
Goshen, Ind. 145/B1
Goslar, Ger. 70/D3
Gosport, Eng. 67/F5
Göta (canal), Swed. 69/C3
Göteborg, Swed. 69/B3
Gotland (isl.), Swed. 69/D3
Göttingen, Ger. 70/C3
Gouda, Neth. 72/E3
Gough (isl.), U.K. 35/J8
Gouin (res.), Que. 184/C2
Gracias a Dios (cape), Cent. Amer. 49/D2
Grafton, N. Dak. 164/A4
Graham Land, Antarc. 118
Grahamstown, S. Africa 63/E8
Granada, Nic. 48/C3
Granada, Spain 76/E4
Granby, Que. 185/D4
Gran Canaria (isl.), Spain 76/B5
Gran Chaco (reg.), S. Amer. 58/C5
Grand (canal), China 105/E2
Grand (lake), N.Y. 160/A1
Grand Bahama (isl.), Bah. 50/B1
Grand Canyon Nat'l Pk., Ariz. 130/B2
Grand Cayman (isl.), Cayman Is. 50/B3
Grand Coulee (dam), Wash. 175/B4
Grande (riv.), Braz. 59/E5
Grande (riv.), Nic. 48/C2
Grande, Rio (riv.), N. Amer. 41/J7
Grande Cache, Alta. 190/C2
Grande Prairie, Alta. 191/D2

Grand Erg Occidental (des.), Africa 60/C1
Grand Erg Oriental (des.), Africa 60/C1
Grande-Rivière, Que. 185/F1
Grand Falls, N. Br. 182/A2
Grand Forks, N. Dak. 164/B4
Grand Island, Nebr. 157/B3
Grand Isle, La. 150/C3
Grand Junction, Colo. 134/B2
Grand Manan (isl.), N. Br. 182/B4
Grand Marais, Minn. 153/A1
Grand Portage Nat'l Mon., Minn. 153/B1
Grand Prairie, Texas 172/B4
Grand Rapids, Mich. 152/B4
Grand Teton Nat'l Pk., Wyo. 177/A4
Grandview, Mo. 155/C1
Granite City, Ill. 144/A3
Grants, N. Mex. 135/D2
Grants Pass, Oreg. 169/C1
Grasslands Nat'l Pk., Sask. 188/B4
'sGravenhage (The Hague) (cap.), Neth. 72/D3
Gravenhurst, Ont. 186/C2
Gravesend, Eng. 67/C6
Graz, Austria 82/C3
Great Abaco (isl.), Bah. 50/C1
Great Australian (bight), Austr. 114/B4
Great Barrier (reef), Austr. 115/D-E3-F3
Great Basin Nat'l Pk., Nev. 132/C4
Great Bear (lake), N.W.T. 42/D2
Great Bend, Kans. 147/B2
Great Britain & Northern Ireland (United Kingdom) 66-67
Great Dividing (range), Austr. 115/D3
Great Exuma (isl.), Bah. 50/C2
Great Falls, Mont. 156/B2
Great Inagua (isl.), Bah. 50/D2
Great Miami (riv.), Ohio 166/C1
Great Neck, N.Y. 180/C2
Great Salt (lake), Utah 174/A2
Great Salt Lake (des.), Utah 174/A2
Great Sand Dunes Nat'l Mon., Colo. 134/C3
Great Sandy (des.), Austr. 114/B3
Great Slave (lake), N.W.T. 42/E3
Great Smoky Mts. Nat'l Pk., U.S. 149/E4, 162/A2
Great Victoria (des.), Austr. 114/B3
Great Wall, China 104-105/D-E1-2
Great Yarmouth, Eng. 67/G4
Greece 85/C3
Greece, N.Y. 160/B1
Greeley, Colo. 134/A3
Green (riv.), U.S. 177/C4
Green (mts.), Vt. 158/A4
Green Bay, Wis. 176/C3
Greenbelt, Md. 139/E3
Greeneville, Tenn. 149/F3
Greenfield, Mass. 136/B1
Greenfield, Wis. 176/A1
Greenland 40/P2
Greenland (sea) 35/J2
Greenock, Scot. 66/A1
Green River, Utah 174/C3
Green River, Wyo. 177/C3
Greensboro, N.C. 163/F4
Greensburg, Pa. 170/B4
Greenville, Miss. 154/A2
Greenville, N.C. 163/E2

Greenville, S.C. 162/B2
Greenville, Texas 173/E1
Greenwich, Conn. 136/A4
Greenwich, Eng. 67/B5
Greenwood, Ind. 145/B3
Greenwood, Miss. 154/B2
Greenwood, S.C. 162/B3
Greer, S.C. 162/B2
Grenada 51/F4, 55/R
Grenada, Miss. 154/B2
Grenadines (isls.), see St. Vincent & the Grenadines
Grenoble, France 75/F5
Gresham, Oreg. 180/B4
Gretna, La. 150/B4
Greybull, Wyo. 177/A3
Griffin, Ga. 142/A3
Grimsby (Great Grimsby), Eng. 67/G4
Grimsby, Ont. 187/E4
Grindelwald, Switz. 80/C2
Grodno, U.S.S.R. 89/B4
Groningen, Neth. 72/H1
Groote Eylandt (isl.), Austr. 114/C2
Gros Morne Nat'l Pk., Newf. 183/E1
Grossglockner (mt.), Austria 82/B3
Groton, Conn. 136/C3
Groznyy, U.S.S.R. 89/G6
Grudziądz, Pol. 86/D2
Gruyères, Switz. 80/B2
Gstaad, Switz. 80/B2
Guadalajara, Mex. 46/D4
Guadalajara, Spain 77/E2
Guadalcanal (isl.), Sol. Is. 116/F7
Guadalquivir (riv.), Spain 76/C4
Guadalupe Mts. Nat'l Pk., Texas 172/B2
Guadeloupe 51/F3, 54-55/H
Guadiana (riv.), Europe 76/C3
Guainía (riv.), S. Amer. 56/C2
Guajira (pen.), S. Amer. 56/B1
Guam, U.S. 116/E4
Guanabacoa, Cuba 50/A2, C1/S2
Guangdong (prov.), China 105/E3
Guangxi Zhuangzu (reg.), China 104/D3
Guangzhou (Canton), China 105/E3
Guantánamo, Cuba 53/K5
Guantánamo (bay), Cuba 53/K5
Guaporé (riv.), S. Amer. 56/C4
Guardafui, Somalia, see Ras Asēr
Guatemala 48/B2
Guatemala (cap.), Guat. 48/B2
Guaviare (riv.), Col. 56/B2
Guayaquil, Ecua. 56/A3
Guaynabo, P. Rico 54/C1
Guelph, Ont. 187/E4
Guernsey (isl.), Chan. Is. 67/E6
Guiana (highlands), S. Amer. 56-57/C-D2
Guilford, Conn. 136/B3
Guinea 60/A3
Guinea (gulf), Africa 60/C4
Guinea-Bissau 60/A3
Guiyang, China 104/D3
Guizhou (prov.), China 104/D3
Gulbarga, India 102/C3
Gulfport, Miss. 154/C4
Guntur, India 102/C3
Guri (res.), Ven. 56/C2
Gur'yev, U.S.S.R. 90/C3
Guthrie, Okla. 168/B3
Guyana, P. Rico 54/C1
Guyana 56/D2
Guymon, Okla. 168/A2
Gwalior, India 102/C2

Index

Gweru, Zimb. 63/F6
Gyangzê, China 104/C3
Gyor, Hung. 83/D3

H

Haarlem, Neth. 72/E3
Hachinohe, Japan 107/F2
Hachioji, Japan 107/H2
Haddonfield, N.J. 171/F2
Hadhramaut (reg.), Yemen 94-95/F-G6-7
Haeju, N. Korea 106/B3
Hagen, Ger. 70/B3
Hagerstown, Md. 139/E2
Hague, The (cap.), Neth. 72/D3
Haifa, Isr. 98/C1
Haikou, China 105/E4
Hail, S. Arabia 94/E4
Hainan (isl.), China 104-105/D4
Haiphong, Viet. 110/D2
Haiti 50/D3, 52/H6
Hakodate, Japan 107/F2
Haleakala Nat'l Pk., Hawaii 129/C3
Haleb (Aleppo), Syria 97/G4
Halifax, Eng. 66/G3
Halifax (cap.), N.S. 183/D4
Hallandale, Fla. 141/D1
Halle, Ger. 70/D3
Halmahera (isl.), Indon. 113/H5
Hälsingborg, Swed. 69/C3
Haltom City, Texas 172/A4
Hama, Syria 97/G5
Hamadan, Iran 100/F3
Hamamatsu, Japan 107/E4
Hamburg, Ger. 70/D2
Hamden, Conn. 136/B3
Hamhung, N. Korea 106/B3
Hamilton (cap.), Bermuda 51/B3
Hamilton, N.Z. 115/F3
Hamilton, Ohio 167/A4
Hamilton, Ont. 187/E4
Hamilton, Scot. 66/B1
Hamm, Ger. 70/B3
Hammerfest, Nor. 68/D1
Hammond, Ind. 145/A1
Hammond, La. 150/B3
Hammondsport, N.Y. 160/C3
Hampton, Va. 138/A1
Han (riv.), S. Korea 106/B3
Hana, Hawaii 129/C3
Handan, China 105/E2
Hanford, Calif. 133/D2
Hangzhou (Hangchow), China 105/F2
Hannibal, Mo. 155/A3
Hannover, Ger. 70/C2
Hanoi (cap.), Viet. 110/D2
Hanover, N.H. 158/B3
Hanover, Pa. 171/D4
Harar, Eth. 61/G4
Harare (cap.), Zim. 63/F6
Harbin, China 105/F1
Hardanger (fjord), Nor. 69/B2
Hargeysa, Somalia 61/G4
Harlan, Ky. 149/E3
Harlingen, Texas 173/E4
Harriman, Tenn. 149/E4
Harris (dist.), Scot. 66/C2
Harrisburg (cap.), Pa. 171/D4
Harrison, N.Y. 180/C2
Harrisonburg, Va. 139/D3
Harrodsburg, Ky. 149/D2
Harrogate, Eng. 67/F3
Harrow, Eng. 67/B5
Hartford (cap.), Conn. 136/B2
Harz (mts.), Ger. 70/D3
Hasa (reg.), S. Arabia 94/F4

Hasselt, Belg. 73/F6
Hastings, Eng. 67/G5
Hastings, Minn. 153/C4
Hastings, Nebr. 157/C3
Hastings, N.Z. 115/F4
Hatteras (cape), N.C. 163/F2
Hattiesburg, Miss. 154/C4
Havana (cap.), Cuba 50/A2; 52/C1
Havel (riv.), Ger. 70/E2
Haverford, Pa. 171/E1
Haverhill, Mass. 137/D1
Havre, Mont. 156/A3
Havre de Grace, Md. 139/F2
Hawaii (isl.), Hawaii 129/C4
Hawaii (state), U.S. 129
Hawaii Volcanoes Nat'l Pk., Hawaii 129/C4
Hawaiian (isls.), U.S. 117/K3
Hawkesbury, Ont. 187/F2
Hawthorne, Calif. 179/B1
Hawthorne, Nev. 132/C3
Hawthorne, N.J. 180/A1
Hay River, N.W.T. 42/E3
Hays, Kans. 147/B2
Hayward, Calif. 133/E1
Hayward, Wis. 176/A2
Hazleton, Pa. 171/E3
Heard (isls.), Austr. 35/M8
Hearst, Ont. 187/F1
Hebei (prov.), China 105/E2
Hebrides, Outer (isls.), Scot. 66/C1-2
Hebron, West Bank 99/C4
Heerlen, Neth. 73/G6
Hefei, China 105/E2
Hegang, China 105/G1
Heidelberg, Ger. 71/C4
Heilbronn, Ger. 71/C4
Heilongjiang (prov.), China 105/F1
Hejaz (reg.), Saudi Arabia 94/D4-5
Helena (cap.), Mont. 156/B2
Helgoland (isl.), Ger. 70/C1
Helmand (riv.), Afghan. 102/B1
Helsingör, Den. 69/C3
Helsinki (cap.), Fin. 69/D2
Henan (prov.), China 105/E2
Henderson, Ky. 148/C2
Henderson, Nev. 133/D4
Henderson, N.C. 163/D1
Hengelo, Neth. 72/J3
Hengyang, China 105/E3
Henzada, Burma 110/A3
Herat, Afghan. 102/B1
Herbert Hoover Nat'l Hist. Site, Iowa 146/B3
Hereford, Eng. 67/E4
Hereford, Texas 172/A1
Hermon (mt.), Asia 98/D1
Hermosillo, Mex. 46/B2
Hershey, Pa. 171/D4
Hertford, Eng. 67/G5
's Hertogenbosch, Neth. 72/G4
Herzeliyya, Isr. 98/B3
Hesse (state), Ger. 71/C3
Hever City, Utah 174/B2
Hialeah, Fla. 141/D1
Hibbing, Minn. 153/B2
Hickory, N.C. 162/C2
Hierro (isl.), Spain 76/A5
Higashiosaka, Japan 107/E4
Highland Park, Ill. 178/B1
High Point, N.C. 163/E4
High River, Alta. 191/E3
Hildesheim, Ger. 70/D2
Hilla, Iraq 100/D4
Hillcrest Hts., Md. 139/E1
Hillsboro, N.H. 158/B4
Hillsboro, Oreg. 180/A4

Hilo, Hawaii 129/C4
Hilton Head Island, S.C. 162/C4
Hilversum, Neth. 72/F3
Himalaya (mts.), Asia 102-103/C-E1-2
Himeji, Japan 106/D4
Hinckley, Minn. 153/C3
Hindu Kush (mts.), Asia 102/C1
Hingham, Mass. 137/E2
Hinton, Alta. 191/D2
Hirakata, Japan 107/E4
Hiroshima, Japan 106/C4
Hispaniola (isl.), W. Indies 52-53
Hitachi, Japan 107/F3
Hivaoa (isl.), Fr. Poly. 117/N6
Hobart, Austr. 115/D5
Hobart, Ind. 145/A1
Hobbs, N. Mex. 135/F4
Hoboken, N.J. 180/B2
Ho Chi Minh City, Viet. 111/D5
Hocking (riv.), Ohio 167/D3
Hodeida, Yemen 94/E7
Hofuf, Saudi Arabia 94/F4
Hohhot, China 105/E1
Hokkaido (isl.), Japan 107/G2
Holbrook, Ariz. 130/C3
Holguin, Cuba 50/C2, J4/53
Holladay, Utah 174/C1
Holland, Mich. 152/A4
Holland, see Netherlands
Hollidaysburg, Pa. 170/C4
Hollywood, Calif. 179/C1
Hollywood, Fla. 141/D1
Holon, Isr. 98/B3
Holyoke, Mass. 136/B2
Homer, Alaska 129/A2
Homestead, Fla. 141/E4
Homestead, Pa. 170/B1
Homestead Nat'l Mon., Nebr. 157/C4
Homewood, Ala. 128/B2
Homs, Libya 60/D1
Homs, Syria 97/G5
Honan, China, see Henan
Honduras 48/C2
Honduras (gulf), Cent. Amer. 48/B1
Honesdale, Pa. 171/F2
Hong Kong 105/E3
Honiara (cap.), Sol. Is. 116/G6
Honolulu (cap.), Hawaii 129/B4
Honshu (isl.), Japan 107/F3
Hood (mt.), Oreg. 169/A2
Hood River, Oreg. 169/A2
Hoover (dam), U.S. 133/D4
Hopatcong (lake), N.J. 159/B1
Hope, Ark. 131/B2
Hope, Br. Col. 190/C4
Hopei, China, see Hebei
Hopewell, Va. 139/E4
Hopkinsville, Ky. 148/C2
Hoquiam, Wash. 175/B22
Hormuz (str.), Asia 101/K7
Horn (cape), Chile 58/C8
Horsens, Den. 69/B3
Horseshoe Bend Nat'l Mil. Pk., Ala. 128/C2
Hospitalet, Spain 77/H2
Hoste (isl.), Chile 58/B8
Hot Springs, Ark. 131/B2
Hot Springs, S. Dak. 165/E1
Hot Springs Nat'l Pk., Ark. 131/B2
Houghton, Mich. 152/C1
Houlton, Maine 151/C2
Houma, La. 150/C3
Houston, Texas 173/F4
Hove, Eng. 67/F5
Hoverweep Nat'l Mon., U.S. 174/C4
Howland (isl.), U.S. 117/J5
Howrah, India 103/D2

Hradec Králové, Czech. 82/D1
Huainan, China 105/E2
Huallaga (riv.), Peru 56/B3
Huambo, Angola 62/D6
Huancayo, Peru 56/B4
Huang (Hwang) He (Yellow) (riv.), China 105/E2
Huanuco, Peru 56/B3
Huaráz, Peru 56/B3
Huascarán (mt.), Peru 56/B3
Hubei (prov.), China 105/E2
Hubli, India 102/C3
Huddersfield, Eng. 66/G1
Hudson (bay), Can. 43/H3
Hudson (str.), Can. 43/J3
Hudson, N.Y. 161/F3
Hudson (riv.), U.S. 161/F4
Hue, Viet. 110/D3
Huelva, Spain 76/C4
Huesca, Spain 77/F1
Huila (mt.), Col. 56/B2
Hull, Eng. 67/F4
Hull, Que. 184/C4
Humacao, P. Rico 54/D1
Humboldt, Tenn. 148/B4
Hunan (prov.), China 105/E3
Hüngnam, N. Korea 106/B3
Hunsrück (mts.), Ger. 71/B4
Huntingdon, Pa. 170/C4
Huntington, Ind. 145/C2
Huntington, N.Y. 160/B4
Huntington, W. Va. 138/B3
Huntington Bch., Calif. 179/C2
Huntsville, Ala. 128/B1
Huntsville, Ark. 131/B2
Huntsville, Ont. 186/C2
Huntsville, Texas 173/E2
Huon (gulf), Papua N.G. 112/C7
Hupei, China, see Hubei
Huron (lake), N. Amer. 43/H7, 45/K2
Huron, S. Dak. 165/E3
Hurst, Texas 172/E4
Hutchinson, Kans. 147/B3
Hwange, Zimb. 63/E6
Hyannis, Mass. 137/F3
Hyannis, Nebr. 157/B2
Hyattsville, Md. 139/E1
Hyde, Eng. 66/G2
Hyderabad, India 102/C2
Hyderabad, Pak. 102/B2

Iaşi, Rom. 84/D2
Ibadan, Nigeria 60/C4
Ibague, Col. 56/B2
Ibiza (isl.), Spain 77/G3
Ica, Peru 56/B4
Iceland 64/C2
Ichang, China, see Yichang
Ichikawa, Japan 107/H2
Idabell, Okla. 168/C4
Idaho (state), U.S. 143
Idaho City, Idaho 143/A3
Idaho Falls, Idaho 143/D2
Iguaçu (riv.), S. Amer. 59/D5
Iguazú (falls), S. Amer. 59/D5
IJsselmeer (lake), Neth. 72/F2
Ile Bizard, Que. 184/A1
Iliamna (lake), Alaska 129/A2
Iligan, Phil. 109/E6
Illinois (riv.), Ill. 144/A3
Illinois (state), U.S. 144
Iloilo, Phil. 109/D5
Ilorin, Nigeria 60/C4
Imphal, India 103/E2
Inarijärvi (lake), Fin. 68/E1
Inch'ŏn, S. Korea 106/B3
Independence, Kans. 147/C4

Independence, Mo. 155/C1
India 102-103
Indian (lake), Mich. 152/A2
Indiana, Pa. 170/B3
Indiana (state), U.S. 145
Indiana Dunes Nat'l Lakeshore, Ind. 145/A1
Indianapolis (cap.), Ind. 145/B3
Indian Ocean 93/F-G6
Indigirka (riv.), U.S.S.R. 91/H2
Indio, Calif. 133/F4
Indochina (reg.), Asia 110-111/D2-5
Indonesia 112-113/C-H6-7
Indore, India 102/C2
Indus (riv.), Asia 102/B2
Inglewood, Calif. 179/B1
Inhambane, Moz. 63/F7
Inn (riv.), Europe 82/B2
Inner Mongolia (reg.), China 104-105/D-E1
Innisfail, Alta. 191/E3
Innsbruck, Austria 82/A3
In Salah, Alg. 60/C2
Insein, Burma 110/A3
Interlaken, Switz. 80/C2
International Falls, Minn. 153/B2
International Peace Garden, N. Amer. 164/A3, 189/D4
Inuvik, N.W.T. 42/C2
Invercargill, N.Z. 115/E4
Inverness, Scot. 66/D2
Ionian (isls.), Greece 85/C4
Iowa (state), U.S. 146
Iowa City, Iowa 146/E3
Ipoh, Malaysia 112/C5
Ipswich, Eng. 67/G4
Iquique, Chile 56/B5
Iquitos, Peru 56/B3
Iráklion, Greece 85/D5
Iran 100-101
Irapuato, Mex. 46/E4
Iraq 100
Irbid, Jordan 98/D2
Ireland 67/BC4
Ireland, Northern, U.K. 67/C3
Iringa, Tanz. 63/F5
Irish (sea), Europe 67/D4
Irkutsk, U.S.S.R. 91/F3
Irondequoit (bay), N.Y. 160/C1
Iron Mountain, Mich. 152/C1
Ironton, Ohio 167/E3
Iroquois Falls, Ont. 187/F1
Irrawaddy (riv.), Burma 110/A2
Irtysh (riv.), U.S.S.R. 90/D3
Irvine, Calif. 179/C2
Irving, Texas 172/E4
Irvington, N.J. 180/A2
Isar (riv.), Ger. 71/E4
Ischia (isl.), Italy 79/D4
Ise, Japan 106/E4
Ise (bay), Japan 106/E4
Isère (riv.), France 75/F5
Isfahan, Iran 101/G4
Ishim (riv.), U.S.S.R. 90/D3
Ishpeming, Mich. 152/C1
Iskenderun, Turkey 97/G4
Islamabad (cap.), Pak. 102/C1
Islamorada, Fla. 141/E5
Isle of Man 67/D3
Isle Royale Nat'l Pk., Mich. 152/A1
Isparta, Turkey 96/D4
Israel 98-99
Issyk-Kul' (lake), U.S.S.R. 90/D3
Istanbul, Turkey 96/C2
Itaipu (res.), S. Amer. 59/D5
Italy 78-79
Ithaca, N.Y. 161/D3
Itháki (Ithaca) (isl.), Greece 85/C4
Ivano-Frankovsk, U.S.S.R. 89/B5

Ivanovo, U.S.S.R. 88/F3
Ivory Coast 60/B4
Iwaki, Japan 107/F3
Iwo (isl.), Japan 107/G3
Izabal (lake), Guat. 48/B2
Izhevsk, U.S.S.R. 88/H3
Izmail, U.S.S.R. 89/C5
Izmir, Turkey 96/B3
Izmit, Turkey 96/C2
Izu (isls.), Japan 107/E4

J

Jabalpur, India 102/D2
Jackman, Maine 151/A2
Jackson, Mich. 152/B4
Jackson (cap.), Miss. 154/A4
Jackson, Tenn. 148/B4
Jackson, Wyo. 177/B4
Jackson (lake), Wyo. 177/A4
Jacksonville, Ark. 131/B2
Jacksonville, Fla. 140/A3
Jacksonville, Ill. 144/A3
Jacksonville, N.C. 163/E2
Jacksonville Bch., Fla. 140/A3
Jaén, Spain 76/D4
Jaffa, Isr., see Tel Aviv-Jaffa
Jaffna, Sri Lanka 102/D4
Jaipur, India 102/C2
Jakarta (cap.), Indon. 113/H1
Jalalabad, Afgh. 102/B1
Jalapa, Mex. 47/H1
Jamaica 50,53
Jambi, Indon. 112/C6
James (bay), Can. 43/H5
James (riv.), N. Dak., S. Dak. 164/C3, 165/E4
James (riv.), Va. 139/D3
Jamestown, N.Y. 160/A4
Jamestown, N. Dak. 164/C3
Jammu, India 102/C1
Jamnagar, India 102/B2
Jamshedpur, India 102/D2
Janesville, Wis. 176/B4
Jan Mayen (isl.), Nor. 35/J2
Japan 106-107
Japan (sea), Asia 92/J4
Japurá (riv.), Braz. 56/C3
Jarash, Jordan 98/D3
Jars (plain), Laos 110/C3
Jarvis (isl.), Pacific 117/L6
Jasper Nat'l Park, Alta. 191/D2
Java (isl.), Indon. 112/DE7
Java (sea), Indon. 112/DE6
Jaworzno, Pol. 87/D3
Jayapura, Indon. 113/K6
Jefferson City (cap.), Mo. 155/B3
Jeffersontown, Ky. 149/F1
Jeffersonville, Ind. 145/C4
Jena, Ger. 71/D3
Jerez de la Frontera, Spain 76/C4
Jericho, West Bank 99/C4
Jersey (isl.), Chan. Is. 67/E6
Jersey City, N.J. 180/B2
Jerusalem (cap.), Isr. 99/C4
Jewel Cave Nat'l Mon., S. Dak. 165/E1
Jhansi, India 102/C2
Jiamusi, China 105/F1
Jiangsu (prov.), China 105/F2
Jiangxi (prov.), China 105/E3
Jidda, Saudi Arabia 94/D5
Jilin, China 105/F1
Jilin (prov.), China 105/F1
Jimma, Eth. 61/F4
Jinan, China 105/E2
Jingdezhen, China 105/E3
Jinja, Uganda 63/F4
Jinmen (isl.), China 105/E3
Jinzhou, China 105/F1
Jixi, China 105/G1

Index

João Pessoa, Braz. 57/F3
Jodhpur, India 102/C2
Johannesburg, S. Africa 63/E7
John Day (riv.), Oreg. 169/B3
John Day Fossil Beds Nat'l Mon., Oreg. 169/B3
John Muir Nat'l Hist. Site, Calif. 133/E1
Johnson City, N.Y. 161/D3
Johnson City, Tenn. 149/D3
Johnson Space Center, Texas 173/F4
Johnston (atoll), U.S. 117/K4
Johnstown, N.Y. 161/E3
Johnstown, Pa. 170/B4
Johore Baharu, Malaysia 111/C7
Joinvile, Braz. 59/E5
Joliet, Ill. 178/A4
Joliette, Que. 185/D4
Jolo (isl.), Phil. 109/C8
Jonesboro, Ark. 131/A3
Jönköping, Sweden 69/C3
Jonquière, Que. 185/E2
Joplin, Mo. 155/C2
Jordan 98-99
Jordan (riv.), Asia 98/D3
Jos, Nigeria 60/C4
Joshua Tree Nat'l Mon., Calif. 133/E4
Juan de Fuca (str.), N. Amer. 175/A2, 190/B4
Juan de Nova, Réunion 63/G6
Juan Fernández (isls.), Chile 58/B6
Juba, Sudan 61/F4
Jubbulpore, India, see Jabalpur
Judaea (reg.), Asia 99/B-C4-5
Juiz de Fora, Braz. 59/E5
Jujuy, Arg. 58/C5
Julesburg, Nebr. 157/B1
Julianehåb, Greenl., see Qaqortoq
Jullundur, India 102/C1
Jumna (riv.), India 102/C2
Junagadh, India 102/B2
Junction City, Kans. 147/B3
Juneau (cap.), Alaska 129/C2
Jungfrau (mt.), Switz. 80/D2
Jupiter, Fla. 141/F4
Jura (mts.), Europe 74-75/F-G4
Juruá (riv.), Braz. 56/C3
Juventud (isl.), Cuba 50/A2, C2/52
Jyväskylä, Fin. 69/E2

K

K2 (mt.), Asia 102/C1
Kabul (cap.), Afghan. 102/B1
Kabwe, Zambia 63/E6
Kadıköy, Turkey 96/D6
Kadoma, Zimb. 63/E6
Kaduna, Nigeria 60/C4
Kaédi, Maur. 60/A3
Kaesŏng, N. Korea 106/B3
Kagoshima, Japan 106/C5
Kahoolawe (isl.), Hawaii 129/B4
Kahului, Hawaii 129/B4
Kaifeng, China 105/E2
Kailua, Hawaii 129/B4
Kaiserslautern, Ger. 71/B4
Kakinada, India 102/D5
Kalaallit Nunaat (Greenland) 40/P7
Ka Lae (cape), Hawaii 129/C4
Kalahari (des.), Africa 63/E7
Kalamai, Greece 85/C4
Kalamazoo, Mich. 152/B4
Kalaupapa Nat'l Hist. Pk., Hawaii 129/B3
Kalemie, Zaire 63/E5

Kalgan, China, see Zhangjiakou
Kalimantan (reg.), Indon. 112/E5
Kalinin, U.S.S.R. 88/D3
Kaliningrad, U.S.S.R. 88/B4
Kalispell, Mont. 156/A1
Kalisz, Pol. 86/D3
Kaloko-Honokohau Nat'l Hist. Pk., Hawaii 129/B4
Kaluga, U.S.S.R. 89/E4
Kama (riv.), U.S.S.R. 88/H2
Kamakura, Japan 107/H2
Kamaran (isl.), Yemen 94/E6
Kamchatka (pen.), U.S.S.R. 91/H3
Kamenets-Podol'skiy, U.S.S.R. 89/C5
Kamina, Zaire 63/E5
Kamloops, Br. Col. 190/C3
Kampala (cap.), Uganda 63/F4
Kampuchea, see Cambodia
Kamyshin, U.S.S.R. 89/F4
Kananga, Zaire 63/E5
Kanata, Ont. 186/A1
Kanawha (riv.), W. Va. 138/B3
Kanazawa, Japan 106/E3
Kanchipuram, India 102/D3
Kandahar, Afghan., see Qandahar
Kandy, Sri Lanka 102/D3
Kaneohe, Hawaii 129/B3
Kangaroo (isl.), Austr. 114/C4
Kanin (pen.), U.S.S.R. 90/C2
Kankakee, Ill. 144/C2
Kankan, Guinea 60/B3
Kannapolis, N.C. 162/C2
Kano, Nigeria 60/C3
Kanpur, India 102/C2
Kansas (state), U.S. 147
Kansas City, Kans. 147/A4
Kansas City, Mo. 155/C2
Kansk, U.S.S.R. 91/E3
Kansu, China, see Gansu
Kanton (isl.), Kiribati 117/J6
Kaohsiung, China 105/F3
Kaolack, Sen. 60/A3
Kapingamarangi, Micronesia 116/E5
Kaposvár, Hung. 83/D3
Kapuas (riv.), Indon. 112/E6
Kapuskasing, Ont. 187/F1
Kara (sea), U.S.S.R. 90/D2
Kara-Kum (des.), U.S.S.R. 90/C3
Karachi, Pak. 102/B2
Karaganda, U.S.S.R. 90/D3
Karaj, Iran 100/G3
Karak, Jordan, see El Karak
Karakoram (mts.), Asia 102/C1
Karakorum (ruins), Mong. 104/D1
Karbala, Iraq 100/C4
Kariba (lake), Africa 63/E6
Karimata (isl.), Indon. 112/D6
Karlsruhe, Ger. 71/C4
Karnak, Egypt, see El Karnak
Kárpathos (isl.), Greece 85/D5
Karshi, U.S.S.R. 90/D4
Karun (riv.), Iran 100/F5
Karviná, Czech. 83/E2
Kasai (riv.), Africa 63/E5
Kasama, Zambia 63/F6
Kashan, Iran 101/G3
Kashi (Kashgar), China 104/A2
Kassala, Sudan 61/F3
Kassel, Ger. 70/C2
Katahdin (mt.), Maine 151/B2
Katanga (reg.), Zaire 63/E5
Kathmandu (cap.), Nepal 102/D2
Katmai Nat'l Pk., Alaska 129/A2
Katowice, Pol. 86/B4
Katsina, Nigeria 60/C4
Kattegat (str.), Europe 69/B3
Kauai (isl.), Hawaii 129/A3

Kaunas, U.S.S.R. 88/C3
Kavália, Greece 85/D3
Kawaguchi, Japan 107/H2
Kawartha (lake), Ont. 187/D3
Kawasaki, Japan 107/H2
Kayenta, Ariz. 130/C2
Kayes, Mali 60/A3
Kayseri, Turkey 97/F3
Kazakh S.S.R., U.S.S.R. 90/EF3
Kazan', U.S.S.R. 88/G3
Kearney, Nebr. 157/C3
Kearny, N.J. 180/A2
Kecskemét, Hung. 83/E3
Kediri, Indon. 113/K2
Keelung, China 105/F3
Keene, N.H. 158/B4
Keetmanshoop, Namibia 63/D7
Kefallinia (isl.), Greece 85/B4
Kefar Sava, Isr. 98/B3
Kejimkujik Nat'l Pk., N.S. 182/B3
Kelang, Malaysia 111/C7
Kelantan (state), Malaysia 111/C6
Kellys (isl.), Ohio 166/A3
Kelowna, Br. Col. 190/C4
Kelso, Wash. 175/C2
Kemerovo, U.S.S.R. 90/E3
Kemmerer, Wyo. 177/C1
Kenai, Alaska 129/B2
Kenai Fjords Nat'l Pk., Alaska 129/B2
Kenitra, Mor. 60/B1
Kenmore, N.Y. 160/A1
Kennebec (riv.), Maine 151/A3
Kennebunk, Maine 151/A4
Kenner, La. 150/A3
Kennewick, Wash. 175/C3
Kenora, Ont. 187/D3
Kenosha, Wis. 176/C4
Kent, Ohio 166/B4
Kent, Wash. 175/C1
Kentucky (lake), U.S. 148/B3
Kentucky (state), U.S. 148-149
Kentville, N.S. 182/C3
Kentwood, Mich. 152/B4
Kenya 63/F4
Kenya (mt.), Kenya 63/F4
Keokuk, Iowa 146/C4
Kerch, U.S.S.R. 89/E5
Kérkira (isl.), Greece 85/B4
Kerkrade, Neth. 73/H6
Kermadec (isls.), N.Z. 117/J9
Kerman, Iran 101/K5
Kerrville, Texas 173/D3
Ketchikan, Alaska 129/C2
Kettering, Eng. 67/F4
Kettering, Ohio 267/D1
Keuka (lake), N.Y. 160/C3
Kewaunee, Wis. 176/C2
Keweenaw (pen.), Mich. 152/C1
Key Biscayne, Fla. 141/E1
Key Largo, Fla. 141/F4
Key West, Fla. 141/F3
Khabarovsk, U.S.S.R. 91/G3
Khalkís, Greece 85/C4
Khanty-Mansiysk, U.S.S.R. 90/D2
Khan Yunis, Gaza Strip 99/A5
Kharagpur, India 102/D2
Khârga (oasis), Egypt 94/C4
Khartoum (cap.), Sudan 61/F3
Khartoum North, Sudan 61/F3
Khar'kov, U.S.S.R. 89/E5
Khaskovo, Bulg. 84/D3
Kherson, U.S.S.R. 89/D5
Khíos (isl.), Greece 85/D4
Khirbet Qumran, West Bank 99/C4
Khmel'nitskiy, U.S.S.R. 89/C5
Khon Kaen, Thai. 110/C3
Khorramabad, Iran 100/F4
Khorramshahr, Iran 100/F5
Khvoy, Iran 100/D1

Khyber (pass), Pak. 102/C1
Kiangsi, China, see Jiangxi
Kiangsu, China, see Jiangsu
Kiel (Nord Ostsee) (canal), Ger.
70/C1
Kiel, Ger. 70/C1
Kielce, Pol. 87/E3
Kiev, U.S.S.R. 89/D4
Kigali (cap.), Rwanda 63/F5
Kigoma, Tanz. 63/F5
Kikwit, Zaire 63/D5
Kilgore, Texas 173/F2
Kilimanjaro (mt.), Tanz. 63/F5
Kilkenny, Ire. 67/C4
Killarney, Ire. 67/B4
Kilmarnock, Scot. 66/D3
Kimball, Nebr. 157/B1
Kimberley, S. Africa 63/E7
Kinabalu (mt.), Malaysia 113/F4
Kinbasket (lake), Br. Col. 191/D3
Kincardine, Ont. 186/B3
Kindersley, Sask. 188/A3
Kindia, Guinea 60/A3
Kineshma, U.S.S.R. 88/F3
King (isl.), Austr. 114/D5
King Christian IX Land, Greenl.
40/Q3
King Christian X Land, Greenl.
40/Q3
Kingman, Ariz. 130/A3
Kings Canyon Nat'l Pk., Calif.
133/D3
King's Lynn, Eng. 67/G4
Kings Mountain, N.C. 162/C2
Kings Mountain Nat'l Mil. Pk.,
S.C. 162/C2
Kings Point, N.Y. 180/C2
Kingsport, Tenn. 149/F3
Kingston (cap.), Jam. 50/C3,
53/W10
Kingston, N.Y. 161/F4
Kingston, Ont. 187/E3
Kingston, Pa. 171/E3
Kingston upon Thames, Eng.
67/B6
Kingstown (cap.), St. Vinc. &
Grens. 50/G4, 55/P
Kingsville, Texas 173/F8
Kinshasa (cap.), Zaire 62/B5
Kinston, N.C. 163/E2
Kirgiz S.S.R., U.S.S.R. 90/D3
Kiribati 117/J6
Kirikkale, Turkey 96/E3
Kirin, China, see Jilin
Kiritimati (isl.), Kiribati 117/L5
Kirkcaldy, Scot. 66/E2
Kirkland, Wash. 175/B1
Kirkland Lake, Ont. 187/F1
Kirksville, Mo. 155/A2
Kirkuk, Iraq 100/D3
Kirkwall, Scot. 66/E1
Kirkwood, Mo. 155/B4
Kirov, U.S.S.R. 88/G3
Kirovabad, U.S.S.R. 89/G6
Kirovograd, U.S.S.R. 89/D5
Kiryu, Japan 107/F3
Kisangani, Zaire 63/E4
Kishinev, U.S.S.R. 89/C5
Kishiwada, Japan 107/E5
Kisimayu, Somalia, see
Chisimayu
Kissimmee, Fla. 140/D3
Kistna (riv.), India 102/C3
Kisumu, Kenya 63/F5
Kitakyushu, Japan 106/C4
Kitchener, Ont. 187/D4
Kitimat, Br. Col. 190/A2
Kittery, Maine 151/A4
Kitty Hawk, N.C. 163/F1
Kitwe, Zambia 63/E6
Kitzbühel, Austria 82/B3

Kivu (lake), Africa 63/E5
Kızılırmak (riv.), Turkey 96/E2
Kjölen (mts.), Europe 68/C-D1-2
Klagenfurt, Austria 82/C3
Klaipėda, U.S.S.R. 88/B3
Klamath (riv.), U.S. 132/A1,
169/C2
Klamath Falls, Oreg. 169/C2
Klosters, Swit. 81/E2
Kluane Nat'l Pk., Yukon 129/B2
Knife River Indian Villages Nat'l
Hist. Site, N. Dak. 164/B2
Knoxville, Tenn. 149/E4
Kobe, Japan 106/D4
Koblenz, Ger. 71/B3
Kobuk Valley Nat'l Pk., Alaska
129/A1
Kochi, Japan 106/D4
Kodiak, Alaska 129/B2
Kodiak (isl.), Alaska 129/A2
Kofu, Japan 107/E4
Kōje (isl.), S. Korea 106/C4
Kokchetav, U.S.S.R. 90/D3
Kokomo, Ind. 145/B2
Kola (pen.), U.S.S.R. 88/E1
Kolar Gold Fields, India 102/C3
Kolding, Den. 69/C4
Kolhapur, India 102/C3
Köln (Cologne), Ger. 71/B3
Kolomna, U.S.S.R. 89/E4
Kolonia (cap.), Micronesia 116/F5
Kolwezi, Zaire 63/E6
Kolyma (range), U.S.S.R. 91/H2
Kolyma (riv.), U.S.S.R. 91/H2
Kompong Cham, Camb. 111/D5
Komsomol'sk, U.S.S.R. 91/G3
Königsberg (Kaliningrad),
U.S.S.R. 88/B4
Königssee (lake), Ger. 71/E5
Konotop, U.S.S.R. 89/D4
Kontum, Viet. 110/E4
Konya, Turkey 96/E4
Kootenay (lake), Br. Col. 191/D4
Kootenay Nat'l Pk., Br. Col.
191/D3
Korçë, Alb. 85/C3
Korea, North 106/C2
Korea, South 106/C3
Korea (str.), Asia 106/C4
Koriyama, Japan 107/F3
Kortrijk, Belg., see Courtrai
Koryak (range), U.S.S.R. 91/J2
Kos (isl.), Greece 85/D4
Košice, Czech. 83/F2
Kosti, Sudan 61/F3
Kostroma, U.S.S.R. 88/F3
Koszalin, Pol. 86/C1
Kota, India 102/C2
Kota Baharu, Malaysia 111/C6
Kota Kinabalu, Malaysia 112/F4
Kotka, Fin. 69/E2
Kottbus, Ger. 70/F3
Kouchibouguac Nat'l Pk., N. Br.
182/C2
Kozhikode, India 102/C3
Kra (isth.), Thai. 111/B5
Kragujevac, Yugo. 84/C2
Krakatau (isl.), see Rakata
Kraków, Pol., see Cracow
Kralendijk, Neth. Ant. 55/M
Krasnodar, U.S.S.R. 89/E6
Krasnoyarsk, U.S.S.R. 91/E3
Krefeld, Ger. 70/B3
Kremenchug, U.S.S.R. 89/D5
Kristiansand, Nor. 69/B3
Krivoy Rog, U.S.S.R. 89/D5
Krung Thep, Thai., see Bangkok
Kuala Lumpur (cap.), Malaysia
111/C7
Kuala Terengganu, Malaysia
111/C6

Kuantan, Malaysia 111/C7
Kuching, Malaysia 112/D5
Kudymkar, U.S.S.R. 88/H3
Kufra (oasis), Libya 61/E2
Kumamoto, Japan 106/C4
Kumasi, Ghana 60/B4
Kunashiri (isl.), Japan 107/G1
Kunlun Shan (mts.), Asia
104/AC2
Kunming, China 104/D3
Kunsan, S. Korea 106/B4
Kuopio, Fin. 68/E2
Kurdistan (reg.), Asia 94/EF2
Kure, Japan 106/D4
Kurgan, U.S.S.R. 90/D3
Kuria Muria (isls.), Oman 95/H6
Kuril (isls.), Asia 91/H3
Kurnool, India 102/C3
Kursk, U.S.S.R. 89/E4
Kushiro, Japan 107/G2
Kuskokwim (mts.), Alaska 129/A2
Kustanay, U.S.S.R. 9D/B3
Kut, Iraq 100/D4
Kütahya, Turkey 96/C3
Kutaisi, U.S.S.R. 89/F6
Kutch, Rann of (salt marsh), India
102/C2
Kutztown, Pa. 171/E4
Kuwait 94/F4
Kuybyshev, U.S.S.R. 89/H4
Kuznetsk, U.S.S.R. 89/G4
Kwajalein (atoll), Marshall Is.
116/G5
Kwangju, S. Korea 106/B4
Kwangsi Chuang, China, see
Guangxi Zhuangzu
Kwangtung, China, see
Guangdong
Kweichow, China, see Guizhou
Kwekwe, Zimb. 63/E6
Kyoto, Japan 107/E4
Kyushu (isl.), Japan 106/D4
Kyzyl, U.S.S.R. 91/E3
Kyzyl-Kum (des.), U.S.S.R. 90/D3
Kzyl-Orda, U.S.S.R. 90/D3

L

Laayoune, W. Sahara 60/A2
La Baie, Que. 185/E2
Labrador (dist.), Newf. 40/M4
Labuan (isl.), Malaysia 112/E4
Lac-Mégantic, Que. 185/E4
Laccadive, India, see Cannanore
La Ceiba, Hond. 48/C2
La Chaux-de-Fonds, Switz. 80/B1
Lachine, Que. 184/A1
La Chorrera, Panama 49/D3
Lackawanna, N.Y. 160/B3
Lacombe, Alta. 191/E3
Laconia, N.H. 158/C3
La Coruña, Spain 76/B1
La Crosse, Wis. 176/A4
Ladoga (lake), U.S.S.R. 88/D2
Lae, Papua N.G. 116/E6
Lafayette, Ind. 145/B2
Lafayette, La. 150/C2
La Follette, Tenn. 149/E3
Laghouat, Alg. 60/C1
Lagos (cap.), Nigeria 60/C4
La Grande, Oreg. 169/A4
La Grange, Ga. 142/A3
La Guaira, Ven. 56/C1
La Habra, Calif. 179/D3
Lahaina, Hawaii 129/B3
Lahn (riv.), Ger. 71/C3
Lahore, Pak. 102/C1
Lahti, Fin. 69/E2
Laie, Hawaii 129/A4
La Jolla, Calif. 180/C4
La Junta, Colo. 134/C4

Index

Lake Bluff, Ill. 178/B1
Lake Buena Vista, Fla. 140/B4
Lake Charles, La. 150/C1
Lake Chelan Nat'l Rec. Area, Wash. 175/A3
Lake Clark Nat'l Pk., Alaska 129/A2
Lake Forest, Ill. 178/B1
Lake George, N.Y. 161/F2
Lake Havasu City, Ariz. 130/A3
Lakeland, Fla. 141/D4
Lake Louise, Alta. 191/D3
Lake Mead Nat'l Rec. Area, U.S. 130/A2, 133/D4
Lake Placid, N.Y. 161/F2
Lakeview, Oreg. 169/C3
Lake Wales, Fla. 140/C3
Lakewood, Calif. 179/C2
Lakewood, Colo. 178/A4
Lakewood, Ohio 178/F3
Lakewood, N.J. 159/D3
Lake Worth, Fla. 141/D4
Lakshadweep, India, see Cannanore
Lalitpur, Nepal 102/D2
La Louvière, Belg. 73/D7
La Manche (English) (chan.), Europe 74/C2
La Mauricie Nat'l Pk., Que. 185/J3
Lambaréné, Gabon 62/D5
La Mesa, Calif. 180/C4
La Mesa, Texas 172/C2
Lamon (bay), Phil. 108/D3
Lanai (isl.), Hawaii 129/B3
Lancaster, Calif. 133/E3
Lancaster, Eng. 67/E3
Lancaster, N.H. 158/C2
Lancaster, Ohio 167/D3
Lancaster, Pa. 171/E4
Lancaster, S.C. 162/C2
Land's End (prom.), Eng. 67/D5
Legnica (Liegnitz), Pol. 86/B3
Le Havre, France 74/C3
Lander, Wyo. 177/E3
Langley, Br. Col. 190/B1
Lansing, Ill. 178/B3
Lansing (cap.), Mich. 152/B4
Lanzarote (isl.), Spain 76/C4
Lanzhou (Lanchow), China 104/D2
Laos 110/D3
La Palma (isl.), Spain 76/A4
La Paz (cap.), Bol. 56/C4
Lapland (reg.), Europe 68/CF1
La Plata, Arg. 58/D5
LaPorte, Ind. 145/B1
Lappeenranta, Fin. 69/E2
Laptev (sea), U.S.S.R. 91/G2
La Puente, Calif. 179/D3
Laramie (mts.), U.S. 177/C2
Laramie, Wyo. 177/C2
Laredo, Texas 173/D4
Largo, Fla. 140/C1
La Rioja, Arg. 58/C5
Lárisa, Greece 85/C4
Lárnaca, Cyprus 96/E5
Larne, N. Ire. 67/D3
La Rochelle, France 75/C4
La Romana, Dom. Rep. 53/T7
La Ronge, Sask. 188/C1
Las Cruces, N. Mex. 135/F2
La Serena, Chile 58/B5
Las Palmas, Spain 76/B4
La Spezia, Italy 78/B2
Lassen Volcanic Nat'l Pk., Calif. 132/B2
Las Vegas, N. Mex. 135/D3
Las Vegas, Nev. 133/D4
Latakia, Syria 97/G5

Latium (reg.), Italy 78/D3
La Tuque, Que. 185/D3
Latvian S.S.R., U.S.S.R. 88/C3
Launceston, Austr. 115/D5
Laurel, Del. 139/E3
Laurel, Md. 139/E2
Laurel, Miss. 154/C3
Lausanne, Switz. 80/B2
Lava Beds Nat'l Mon., Calif. 132/A2
Laval, Que. 184/A1
La Vega, Dom. Rep. 52/R6
Lawrence, Kans. 147/B4
Lawrence, Mass. 137/D1
Lawrenceburg, Tenn. 148/C3
Lawton, Okla. 168/C2
Lead, S. Dak. 165/E1
Leadville, Colo. 134/B2
Leamington, Ont. 186/A4
Leavenworth, Kans. 147/A4
Lebanon 96/F6
Lebanon, N.H. 158/B3
Lebanon, Pa. 171/E4
Lebanon, Tenn. 148/C3
Leduc, Alta. 191/F1
Leech (lake), Minn. 153/B3
Leeds, Eng. 67/F4
Leesburg, Fla. 140/B3
Leeuwarden, Neth. 72/G1
Leeward (isls.), W. Indies 51/F3
Leghorn, Italy 78/C3
Leicester, Eng. 67/F4
Leiden, Neth. 72/E3
Leipzig, Ger. 71/E3
Leizhou Bandao (pen.), China 105/E3
Lelystad, Neth. 72/F3
Le Mans, France 74/D3
Lena (riv.), U.S.S.R. 91/G2
Leninakan, U.S.S.R. 89/F6
Leningrad, U.S.S.R. 88/D3
Leninsk, U.S.S.R. 90/E3
Leninsk-Kuznetskiy, U.S.S.R. 90/E3
Lenox, Mass. 136/A1
Lens, France 74/E2
Leominster, Mass. 137/D1
León, Mex. 46/E4
León, Nic. 48/C3
León, Spain 76/D1
Lérida (Lleida), Spain 77/G2
Lerwick, Scot. 66/G1
Les Cayes, Haiti 52/N7
Leskovac, Yugo. 84/C3
Lesotho 63/E7
Lesser Antilles (isls.), W. Indies 51/F4
Lesser Slave (lake), Alta. 191/D1
Lésvos (isl.), Greece 85/D4
Lethbridge, Alta. 191/F4
Letterkenny, Ire. 66/B3
Leverkusen, Ger. 71/B4
Lewes, Del. 139/F3
Lewis (dist.), Scot. 66/C1
Lewis and Clark (lake), Nebr. 157/A8
Lewis and Clark Mem., Mont. 156/C2
Lewisburg, Pa. 171/D3
Lewisburg, Tenn. 148/C4
Lewisburg, W. Va. 138/C3
Lewiston, Idaho 143/A2
Lewiston, Maine 151/A3
Lewistown, Mont. 156/D3
Lewistown, Pa. 170/C3
Lexington, Ky. 149/E2
Lexington, N.C. 162/C2
Leyte (gulf), Phil. 109/E5
Leyte (isl.), Phil. 109/E5
Lhasa, China 104/C3

Lianyungang, China 105/E2
Liaodong Bandao (pen.), China 105/F2
Liaoning (prov.), China 105/F1
Liaoyuan, China 105/F1
Libby, Mont. 156/A1
Liberal, Kans. 147/C1
Liberec, Czech. 82/C1
Liberia 60/B4
Liberty, Mo. 155/B1
Libreville (cap.), Gabon 62/C4
Libya 60-61/D2
Libyan (des.), Africa 61/E2
Liechtenstein 81/E1
Liège, Belg. 73/G6
Liepāja, U.S.S.R. 88/B3
Liguria (reg.), Italy 78/B2
Ligurian (sea), Italy 78/B2
Lihue, Hawaii 129/A3
Likasi, Zaire 63/E6
Lille, France 74/E2
Lilongwe (cap.), Malawi 63/F6
Lima, Ohio 166/B3
Lima (cap.), Peru 56/B4
Limassol, Cyprus 97/E5
Limerick, Ire. 67/B4
Limnos (isl.), Greece 85/D4
Limoges, France 75/D5
Limón, C. Rica 49/D3
Limpopo (riv.), Africa 63/E7
Lincoln (sea), Arctic 40/M1
Lincoln, Eng. 67/F4
Lincoln, Ill. 144/B2
Lincoln (cap.), Nebr. 157/B4
Lincoln Boyhood Nat'l Mem., Ind. 145/B4
Lincoln Park, Mich. 178/C4
Lindau, Ger. 71/C5
Linden, N.J. 180/A3
Lindesnes (cape), Nor. 69/B3
Lindi, Tanz. 63/F5
Lindsay, Ont. 186/C3
Lindsborg, Kans. 147/B3
Lingayen (gulf), Phil. 108/C2
Linköping, Swed. 69/C3
Linz, Austria 82/C2
Lions (gulf), France 75/E6
Lipari (isls.), Italy 79/E5
Lipetsk, U.S.S.R. 89/E4
Lippe (riv.), Ger. 70/C3
Lisbon (cap.), Port. 76/B3
Lisburn, N. Ire. 67/D3
Lisle, Ill. 178/A2
Lismore, Austr. 115/E3
Listowel, Ont. 186/B3
Litchfield, Conn. 136/A3
Litchfield, Minn. 153/B4
Lithuanian S.S.R., U.S.S.R. 88/B3
Little America, Antarc. 118
Little Cayman (isl.), Cayman Is. 50/B3
Little Current, Ont. 186/A2
Little Missouri (riv.), U.S. 164/C1
Little Rock (cap.), Ark. 131/B2
Littleton, N.H. 158/B2
Liuzhou, China 104/D3
Livermore, Calif. 132/C1
Liverpool, Eng. 67/E4
Liverpool, N.S. 182/C4
Livingston, Mont. 156/C2
Livingston, N.J. 180/A2
Livingston, Scot. 66/C1
Livingstone, Zambia 63/E6
Livonia, Mich. 178/B4
Livorno (Leghorn), Italy 78/C3
Ljubljana, Yugo. 84/A2
Llanos (plains), S. Amer. 56/B2
Lleida, Spain 77/G2
Lloydminster, Alta. 191/F2

Lloydminster, Sask. 188/A2
Llullaillaco (vol.), Chile 58/C5
Lobito, Angola 62/D6
Locarno, Switz. 81/D2
Lock Haven, Pa. 171/C3
Lockport, N.Y. 160/B1
Lod (Lydda), Isr. 99/B4
Lodi, Calif. 132/C2
Lodi, N.J. 180/B2
Łódź, Pol. 87/D3
Lofoten (isls.), Nor. 68/C1
Logan, Utah 174/B2
Logan (mt.), Yukon 129/B2
Logansport, Ind. 145/B2
Logroño, Spain 77/E1
Loire (riv.), France 74/C4
Lombard, Ill. 178/A2
Lombardy (reg.), Italy 78/B2
Lombok (isl.), Indon. 112/F7
Lomé (cap.), Togo 60/C4
Lomond, Loch (lake), Scot. 66/A1
Lompoc, Calif. 133/C4
London, Eng. (cap.), U.K. 67/F5
London, Ont. 186/B4
Londonderry, N. Ire. 66/C3
Londrina, Braz. 59/D5
Long (isl.), Bah. 50/C2
Long (isl.), N.Y. 160/B4
Long Beach, Calif. 179/C2
Long Beach, N.J. 159/C3
Long Beach, N.Y. 180/C2
Long Branch, N.J. 159/C2
Long Island (sound), U.S. 160/B4
Longmont, Colo. 134/A3
Long Point (bay), Ont. 186/C4
Longueuil, Que. 184/B1
Longview, Texas 173/F2
Longview, Wash. 175/C2
Lookout (cape), N.C. 163/F2
Lop Nur (Lop Nor) (dry lake), China 104/C1
Lopatka (cape), U.S.S.R. 91/N3
Lorain, Ohio 166/A3
Lord Howe (isl.), Austr. 116/G9
Lorient, France 74/B4
Lorraine (prov.), France 74/G3
Lorraineville, Que. 184/A3
Los Alamos, N. Mex. 135/D3
Los Altos, Calif. 133/F1
Los Angeles, Calif. 133/E3
Los Gatos, Calif. 133/D1
Los Teques, Ven. 56/C1
Loughborough, Eng. 67/F4
Louisbourg, N.S. 183/F3
Louisiana (state), U.S. 150
Louisville, Ky. 149/E1
Lourdes, France 75/D6
Louvain (Leuven), Belg. 73/E6
Lovington, N. Mex. 135/E4
Lowell, Mass. 137/D1
Lower Red (lake), Minn. 153/B2
Lower Saxony (state), Ger. 70/C2
Lower Tunguska (riv.), U.S.S.R. 91/E2
Lowestoft, Eng. 67/G4
Loyalty (isls.), New Caledonia 116/G8
Lualaba (riv.), Zaire 63/E5
Luanda (cap.), Angola 62/D5
Luang Prabang, Laos 110/D3
Lubango, Angola 62/D6
Lubbock, Texas 172/C1
Lubec, Maine 151/H3
Lübeck, Ger. 70/D2
Lublin, Pol. 87/F3
Lubumbashi, Zaire 63/E6
Lucca, Italy 78/C3
Lucerne (lake), Switz. 81/D2
Lucerne (Luzern), Switz. 81/D1
Lucknow, India 102/C2
Lüda (Dalian), China 105/F2

Lüderitz, Namibia 62/D7
Ludhiana, India 102/C1
Ludington, Mich. 152/A3
Ludwigshafen, Ger. 71/C4
Lufkin, Texas 173/F2
Lugano, Switz. 81/D2
Lugo, Spain 76/C1
Lumberton, N.C. 163/D2
Lund, Swed. 69/C3
Lundy (isl.), Eng. 67/D5
Lüneburger Heide (dist.), Ger. 70/C2
Luoyang, China 105/E2
Luray, Va. 139/D3
Lusaka (cap.), Zambia 63/E6
Lusk, Wyo. 177/B1
Luton, Eng. 67/F5
Lutsk, U.S.S.R. 89/B4
Luverne, Minn. 153/A4
Luxembourg 73/H8
Luxembourg (cap.), Lux. 73/H8
Luxor, Egypt 61/F2
Luzon (isl.), Phil. 108/C2
L'vov, U.S.S.R. 89/B5
Lyallpur, Pak., see Faisalabad
Lydda, Isr. 99/B4
Lynchburg, Va. 139/D3
Lyndon B. Johnson Nat'l Hist. Site, Texas 173/D3
Lynn, Mass. 137/F4
Lynnwood, Wash. 175/B1
Lynwood, Calif. 179/B2
Lyons, France 75/F5

M

Ma'an, Jordan 99/E5
Maas (riv.), Neth. 72/F4
Maastricht, Neth. 73/G6
Macapá, Braz. 57/D2
Macau 105/E3
Macclesfield, Eng. 66/G2
Maceió, Braz. 57/F3
Machala, Ecuador 56/B3
Machias, Maine 151/H3
Machida, Japan 107/H2
Machilipatnam, India 102/D3
Mackay, Austr. 115/D3
Mackenzie (riv.), N.W.T. 42/C2
Mackenzie, Br. Col. 190/C2
Mackinac (isl.), Mich. 152/B2
Mackinaw City, Mich. 152/B2
Macomb, Ill. 144/A2
Macon, Ga. 142/B3
Ma'daba, Jordan 99/D4
Madagascar 6-7 63/G4
Madang, Papua N.G. 112/B7
Madawaska (riv.), Ont. 187/D2
Madawaska, Maine 151/B1
Madeira (isl.), Port. 76/A2
Madeira (riv.), Braz. 56/C3
Madera, Calif. 133/D2
Madison, Ind. 145/C4
Madison, S. Dak. 165/E4
Madison (cap.), Wis. 176/B4
Madisonville, Ky. 148/C3
Madiun, Indon. 113/J2
Madras, India 102/D3
Madre de Dios (riv.), S. Amer. 56/C4
Madrid (cap.), Spain 76/E2
Madura (isl.), Indon. 113/K2
Madurai, India 102/C4
Maebashi, Japan 106/E2
Maestra, Sierra (mts.), Cuba 53/J4

Magadan, U.S.S.R. 91/H3
Magdalena (riv.), Col. 56/B2
Magdeburg, Ger. 70/D2
Magelang, Indon. 113/J2

Magellan (str.), S. Amer. 58/C8
Maggiore (lake), Europe 81/D3
Magnitogorsk, U.S.S.R. 90/D3
Magnolia, Ark. 131/C2
Magog, Que. 185/D4
Mahajanga, Madag. 63/G6
Maidstone, Eng. 67/G5
Maiduguri, Nigeria 60/D3
Main (riv.), Ger. 71/C4
Maine (state), U.S. 151
Mainz, Ger. 71/C4
Maiquetia, Ven. 56/C1
Majorca (Mallorca) (isl.), Spain 77/H3
Majuro (atoll), Marshall Is. 116/H5
Makale, Eth. 61/F3
Makassar, Indon., see Ujung Pandang
Makassar (str.), Indon. 112-113/F6
Makeyevka, U.S.S.R. 89/E5
Makhachkala, U.S.S.R. 89/G6
Malabo (cap.), Equat. Guin. 60/C4
Malacca (str.), Asia 111/B7
Málaga, Spain 76/D4
Malakal, Sudan 61/F4
Malang, Indon. 113/K2
Malange, Angola 62/B5
Malatya, Turkey 97/H3
Malawi 63/F6
Malay (pen.), Asia 111/C6
Malaya (state), Malaysia 111/C7
Malaysia 111/C6, 112/D5
Malden, Mass. 137/F4
Maldives 93/F5
Male (cap.), Maldives 93/F5
Malheur (lake), Oreg. 169/C3
Mali 60/B2
Malibu, Calif. 179/B1
Malines (Mechelen), Belg. 73/E6
Malmédy, Belg. 73/H7
Malmö, Sweden 69/C3
Malone, N.Y. 161/E1
Malta 79/E7
Malvern, Ark. 131/B2
Malvinas (isls.), see Falkland (isls.)
Mamaroneck, N.Y. 180/C1
Mammoth Cave Nat'l Pk., Ky. 148/C3
Mamoré (riv.), S. Amer. 56/C4
Man, Isle of 67/D3
Man, Iv. Coast 60/B4
Manado, Indon. 113/G5
Managua (cap.), Nic. 48/C2
Managua (lake), Nic. 48/C2
Manama (cap.), Bahrain 95/G4
Manassas, Va. 139/E2
Manaus, Braz. 56/D3
Mancha, La (reg.), Spain 77/E3
Manchester, Conn. 136/C2
Manchester, Eng. 67/E4
Manchester, N.H. 158/C4
Manchester Center, Vt. 158/A3
Mandalay, Burma 110/B2
Mandan, N. Dak. 164/C2
Mandeb, Bab el (str.) 94/E7
Mangalore, India 102/C3
Manhattan, Kans. 147/A3
Manhattan (borough), N.Y. 180/B2
Manhattan Beach, Calif. 179/C1
Manila (cap.), Phil. 108/C3
Manisa, Turkey 96/B3
Manistee, Mich. 152/A3
Manistique, Mich. 152/A2
Manitoba (prov.), Can. 189
Manitoba (lake), Man. 189/E4
Manitou Spring, Colo. 134/B3

Index

Manitoulin (isl.), Ont. 186/A2
Manitowoc, Wis. 176/C3
Maniwaki, Que. 184/B4
Manizales, Col. 56/B2
Mankato, Minn. 153/B4
Mannar (gulf), Asia 102/C4
Mannheim, Ger. 71/C4
Mansfield, Eng. 67/F4
Mansfield, Ohio 166/B3
Mansfield, Pa. 171/D2
Mansfield (mt.), Vt. 158/A2
Manteo, N.C. 163/F1
Mantua, Italy 78/C2
Maple Creek, Sask. 188/A4
Maple Heights, Ohio 167/F4
Maple Ridge, Br. Col. 190/B1
Maplewood, Minn. 153/C1
Maplewood, N.J. 180/A2
Maputo (cap.), Moz. 63/F7
Mar del Plata, Arg. 59/D6
Maracaibo, Ven. 56/B1
Maracaibo (lake), Ven. 56/B2
Maracay, Ven. 56/D1
Maradi, Niger 60/C3
Marajó (isl.), Braz. 57/E3
Marañón (riv.), Peru 56/B3
Maras, Turkey 97/G4
Marathon, Fla. 141/F3
Marburg, Ger. 71/C3
Marche (reg.), Italy 78/D3
Marco Island, Fla. 141/E3
Marcus (isls.), Japan 116/F3
Mardan, Pak. 102/C1
Margarita (isl.), Ven. 56/C1
Margate, Eng. 67/G5
Marianao, Cuba 50/A2, C1/52
Marianas, Northern 116/E4
Maribor, Yugo. 84/B2
Marie-Galante (isl.), Guad. 55/H
Mariel, Cuba 52/C1
Marietta, Ga. 142/B1
Marietta, Ohio 167/D4
Marinduque (isl.), Phil. 108/C4
Marinette, Wis. 176/C3
Marion, Ind. 145/C2
Marion, Iowa 146/B3
Marion, Ohio 166/C2
Marion (lake), S.C. 162/C3
Maritime Alps (mts.), Europe 75/G3
Mariupol, U.S.S.R. 89/E5
Marka, Somalia 61/G4
Marken (isl.), Neth. 72/F3
Markham, Ont. 187/F3
Marlborough, Mass. 137/D2
Marne (riv.), France 74/E3
Maroni (riv.), S. Amer. 57/D2
Maroua, Cam. 60/D3
Marquesas (isls.), Fr. Poly. 117/N6
Marquette, Mich. 152/C1
Marrakech, Mor. 60/B1
Marseille, France 75/F6
Marshall, Texas 173/F1
Marshall Islands 116/G4
Marshalltown, Iowa 146/B3
Marshfield, Wis. 176/B3
Martha's Vineyard (isl.), Mass. 137/E3
Martin, Tenn. 148/B3
Martinique 50/G4, 54-55/J
Martinsburg, W. Va. 139/D2
Martinsville, Va. 138/C4
Mary (Merv), U.S.S.R. 90/D4
Maryland (state), U.S. 139
Marysville, Ohio 166/C2
Masan, S. Korea 106/C4
Masaya, Nic. 48/C3
Masbate (isl.), Phil. 108/D4
Mascouche, Que. 184/B1

Maseru (cap.), Lesotho 63/E8
Mashhad, Iran, see Meshed
Masira (isl.), Oman 95/H5
Masjed Soleiman, Iran 100/F5
Mask, Lough (lake), Ire. 67/B4
Mason City, Iowa 146/A3
Massachusetts (state), U.S. 136-137
Massawa, Eth. 61/F3
Massena, N.Y. 161/E1
Massillon, Ohio 166/B3
Masurian (lakes), Pol. 87/E2
Matadi, Zaire 62/D5
Matagorda (isl.), Texas 173/E3
Matamoros, Mex. 47/F3
Matane, Que. 185/B2
Matanzas, Cuba 52/D1
Matapan (cape), Greece 85/C4
Mathura, India 102/C2
Mato Grosso (plat.), Braz. 57/D4
Matrah, Oman 95/H5
Matsu (Mazu) (isl.), China 105/F3
Matsumoto, Japan 107/E3
Matsuyama, Japan 106/C3
Matterhorn (mt.), Switz. 80/C3
Mattoon, Ill. 144/C3
Maturín, Ven. 56/C2
Maui (isl.), Hawaii 129/C3
Maumee (riv.), Ohio 166/B1
Mauna Kea (mt.), Hawaii 129/C4
Mauna Loa (mt.), Hawaii 129/C4
Maurepas (lake), La. 150/C3
Mauritania 60/A3
Mauritius 35/M7
May (cape), N.J. 159/B4
Mayagüez, P. Rico 54/A1
Maykop, U.S.S.R. 89/F6
Mayo, Yukon 42/C3
Mayotte 63/G6
Maysville, Ky. 149/E2
Mayville, N. Dak. 164/R4
Mazanillo, Cuba 53/J4
Mazar-i-Sharif, Afghan. 102/B1
Mazatenango, Guat. 48/B3
Mazatlán, Mex. 46/C3
Mazu, China 105/F3
Mbabane (cap.), Swaziland 63/F7
Mbandaka, Zaire 63/D5
Mbeya, Tanz. 63/F5
Mbuji-Mayi, Zaire 63/E5
McAlester, Okla. 168/B4
McAllen, Texas 173/D5
McComb, Miss. 154/B4
McConaughy (lake), Nebr. 157/B2
McCook, Nebr. 157/C2
McDonald (isls.), Austr. 35/M8
McKeesport, Pa. 170/B2
McKinley (mt.), Alaska 129/B2
McKinney, Texas 173/E1
McLean, Va. 139/D1
M'Clintock (chan.), N.W.T. 42/F1
McMinnville, Oreg. 169/A2
McMinnville, Tenn. 149/D3
McPherson, Kans. 147/B3
Mead (lake), U.S. 133/D4
Meade, Kans. 147/C1
Meadow Lake, Sask. 188/B2
Meadville, Pa. 170/A2
Mecca, Saudi Arabia 94/E5
Mecklenburg (state), Ger. 70/D2
Medan, Indon. 112/B5
Medellín, Col. 56/C2
Medford, Mass. 137/F4
Medford, Oreg. 169/A2
Medicine Hat, Alta. 191/F4
Medina, Saudi Arabia 94/E5
Mediterranean (sea) 64-65/D-F5
Meerut, India 102/C2
Megiddo, Isr. 98/C2
Meknès, Mor. 60/B1

Mekong (riv.), Asia 111/D4
Melaka (Malacca), Malaya 111/C7
Melanesia (reg.), Pacific 116/E-H5-8
Melbourne, Austr. 115/D4
Melbourne, Fla. 140/C4
Melfort, Sask. 188/C2
Melilla, Spain 60/B1
Melitopol, U.S.S.R. 89/D5
Melun, France 74/E3
Melville (isl.), Austr. 114/C2
Melville (isl.), N.W.T. 42/E1
Melville (pen.), N.W.T. 43/H2
Melville, Sask. 188/C3
Memphis, Tenn. 148/A3
Memphremagog (lake), N. Amer. 158/B1
Menderes (riv.), Turkey 96/C4
Mendocino (cape), Calif. 132/B1
Mendoza, Arg. 58/C5
Menlo Park, Calif. 133/F1
Menominee, Mich. 152/A2
Menomonee Falls, Wis. 176/A1
Menomonie, Wis. 176/B3
Mentor, Ohio 166/A4
Mequon, Wis. 176/B1
Merced, Calif. 133/D2
Meredith (lake), Texas 172/A1
Mergui (arch.), Burma 111/B5
Mérida, Mex. 47/G4
Mérida, Spain 76/C3
Mérida, Ven. 56/B2
Meriden, Conn. 136/B3
Meridian, Miss. 154/C3
Merowe, Sudan 94/C6
Merriman, Nebr. 157/A2
Merritt, Br. Col. 190/C4
Merritt Island, Fla. 140/C4
Mersâ Matrûh, Egypt 61/E1
Mersey (riv.), Eng. 66/F2
Mersin, Turkey 96/F4
Merthyr Tydfil, Wales 67/E5
Mesa, Ariz. 130/B1
Mesabi (range), Minn. 153/C2
Mesa Verde Nat'l Pk., Colo. 134/C1
Meshed, Iran 101/L2
Mesopotamia (reg.), Iraq 100/B-E3-5
Mesquite, Texas 172/C4
Messina, Italy 79/E5
Meta (riv.), S. Amer. 56/B2
Metairie, La. 150/A4
Metz, France 74/G3
Meuse (riv.), Europe 74/F2
Mexicali, Mex. 46/A1
Mexico 46-47
Mexico, Maine 151/A3
Mexico, Mo. 155/A3
Mexico (gulf), N. Amer. 41/JK7
Mexico City (cap.), Mex. 47/E4
Miami Beach, Fla. 141/D1
Miami, Fla. 141/D1
Miami, Okla. 168/A4
Miass, U.S.S.R. 88/K4
Michigan (lake), U.S. 45/J2
Michigan (state), U.S. 152
Michigan City, Ind. 145/B1
Michurinsk, U.S.S.R. 89/F4
Micronesia, Fed. States of 116/F5
Middelburg, Neth. 73/B5
Middlebury, Vt. 158/A2
Middlesboro, Ky. 149/E3
Middlesbrough, Eng. 67/F3
Middletown, Conn. 136/B3
Middletown, N.Y. 161/E4
Middletown, Ohio 167/D1
Midland, Mich. 152/B3
Midland, Ont. 186/C2
Midland, Texas 172/C2

Midway Islands 116/H3
Midwest City, Okla. 168/B3
Mikonos (isl.), Greece 85/D4
Milan, Italy 78/B2
Milan, Tenn. 148/B4
Milbank, S. Dak. 165/D4
Miles City, Mont. 156/B4
Milford, Conn. 136/B3
Milford, Del. 139/F2
Milford, Mass. 137/D2
Milford Haven, Wales 67/D5
Milk (riv.), N. Amer. 156/A3, 191/F4
Milledgeville, Ga. 142/B3
Mille Lacs (lake), Minn. 153/B3
Millington, Tenn. 148/A4
Millinocket, Maine 151/B2
Millville, N.J. 159/A4
Milpitas, Calif. 133/F2
Milton, Ont. 187/E4
Milton-Freewater, Oreg. 169/A3
Milwaukee, Wis. 176/B3
Milwaukie, Oreg. 180/A4
Minas (basin), N.S. 183/D3
Mindanao (isl.), Phil. 109/DE7
Minden, La. 150/A1
Minden, Nebr. 157/C3
Mindoro (isl.), Phil. 108/C4
Mineola, N.Y. 180/C2
Mineral Wells, Texas 173/D1
Minneapolis, Minn. 153/B3
Minnesota (riv.), Minn. 153/B4
Minnesota (state), U.S. 153
Minnetonka, Minn. 153/B3
Miño (riv.), Spain 76/C1
Minorca (Menorca) (isl.), Spain 77/H2
Minot, N. Dak. 164/B2
Minsk, U.S.S.R. 89/C4
Minya, Egypt, see El Minya
Miramar, Fla. 141/D1
Miramichi (bay), N. Br. 182/C2
Mirim (lag.), Braz. 59/D6
Mishawaka, Ind. 145/B1
Miskolc, Hung. 83/F2
Mississauga, Ont. 187/F4
Mississippi (riv.), U.S. 45/H4
Mississippi (state), U.S. 154
Missoula, Mont. 156/B1
Missouri (riv.), U.S. 45/H3
Missouri (state), U.S. 155
Missouri City, Texas 173/C4
Misti, El (vol.), Peru 56/B4
Misty Fjords Nat'l Mon., Alaska 129/C2
Misurata, Libya 60/B1
Mitchell, Nebr. 157/B3
Mitchell, S. Dak. 165/E4
Mitla (ruin), Mex. 47/F5
Mito, Japan 107/F3
Miyazaki, Japan 106/C5
Moab, Utah 174/C2
Moberly, Mo. 155/A2
Mobile, Ala. 128/A4
Mobile (bay), Ala. 128/A4
Mobridge, S. Dak. 165/D2
Mobutu Sese Seko (lake), Africa 63/E4
Mocha, Yemen 94/E7
Modena, Italy 78/C2
Modesto, Calif. 132/C2
Mogadishu (cap.), Somalia 61/G4
Mogilev, U.S.S.R. 50/C4
Mojave, Calif. 132/D3
Mokp'o, S. Korea 106/B4
Moldau (Vltava) (riv.), Czech. 82/C2
Moldavian S.S.R., U.S.S.R. 89/C5
Moline, Ill. 144/A1
Molise (reg.), Italy 78/E4
Mollendo, Peru 56/B4

Molokai (isl.), Hawaii 129/G3
Moluccas (isls.), Indon. 113/H6
Mombasa, Kenya 63/G5
Mona (passage), W. Indies 51/E3
Monaco 75/G6
Monahans, Texas 172/B2
Mönchengladbach, Ger. 71/B3
Monclova, Mex. 46/E2
Moncton, N. Br. 182/C2
Mongolia 104-105/C-E1
Mono (lake), Calif. 132/C3
Monongahela (riv.), U.S. 170/A4
Monroe (lake), Ind. 145/B3
Monroe, La. 150/A2
Monroe, Mich. 152/C4
Monroeville, Pa. 170/B1
Monrovia (cap.), Liberia 60/A4
Mons, Belg. 72/D7
Mont-Joli, Que. 185/D1
Mont-Laurier, Que. 184/C3
Mont-Royal, Que. 185/E3
Montana (state), U.S. 156
Montauk (pt.), N.Y. 160/C4
Montbéliard, France 74/G4
Montclair, N.J. 180/A2
Montebello, Calif. 179/B2
Montego Bay, Jam. 53/V9
Monterey, Calif. 133/D1
Monterey Park, Calif. 179/B2
Monteria, Col. 56/B2
Monterrey, Mex. 46/E3
Montevideo (cap.), Urug. 59/D6
Montezuma Castle Nat'l Mon., Ariz. 130/C3
Montgomery (cap.), Ala. 128/B3
Monticello, N.Y. 161/E4
Montmagny, Que. 185/E3
Montpelier, Idaho 143/C4
Montpelier (cap.), Vt. 158/A2
Montpellier, France 75/E6
Montréal, Que. 185/D4
Montréal-Nord, Que. 185/D4
Montreux, Switz. 80/B2
Montserrat 51/G3
Monza, Italy 78/B2
Moorcroft, Wyo. 177/A2
Moorea (isl.), Fr. Poly. 117/L7
Moore's Creek Nat'l Battlfld., N.C. 163/E2
Moorhead, Minn. 153/A3
Moosehead (lake), Maine 151/B2
Moose Jaw, Sask. 188/B4
Moosomin, Sask. 189/D4
Mopti, Mali 60/B3
Moradabad, India 102/C2
Moratuwa, Sri Lanka 102/C4
Morava (riv.), Czech. 83/D2
Morava (riv.), Yugo. 84/C2
Moray (firth), Scot. 66/E2
Morecambe (bay), Eng. 67/E4
Morehead, Ky. 149/E2
Morehead City, N.C. 163/E3
Morelia, Mex. 46/E4
Morgan City, La. 150/C2
Morgantown, W. Va. 138/C2
Morioka, Japan 107/F3
Moro (gulf), Phil. 109/D7
Moro Bay, Calif. 133/E2
Morocco 60/B1
Morogoro, Tanz. 63/F5
Moroni (cap.), Comoros 63/G6
Morotai (isl.), Indon. 113/H5
Morrison, Colo. 178/A4
Morristown, N.J. 159/B1
Morristown, Tenn. 149/F1
Moscow, Idaho 143/A2
Moscow (cap.), U.S.S.R. 88/E3
Mosel (Moselle) (riv.), Europe 71/B3
Moses Lake, Wash. 175/B4
Mosi Oa Tunya (Victoria) (falls),

Africa 63/E6
Mosquito (gulf), Pan. 49/D3
Mosquito Coast (reg.), Nic. 49/D2
Moss Point, Miss. 154/C4
Mosul, Iraq 100/C2
Motherwell and Wishaw, Scot. 66/B1
Moulmein, Burma 110/B3
Moultrie, Ga. 142/B4
Moultrie (lake), S.C. 162/C3
Mound City Group Nat'l Mon., Ohio 167/D2
Moundou, Chad 60/D4
Moundsville, W. Va. 138/C2
Mountain Home, Idaho 143/A4
Mountain View, Calif. 133/F1
Mt. Clemens, Mich. 178/D2
Mountlake Terr., Wash. 175/B1
Mt. Lebanon, Pa. 170/A1
Mt. Pearl, Newf. 183/F1
Mt. Pleasant, Iowa 146/C3
Mt. Pleasant, Mich. 152/B3
Mt. Pleasant, S.C. 163/D4
Mount Rainier Nat'l Pk., Wash. 175/B2
Mount Rushmore Nat'l Mem., S. Dak. 165/E1
Mount St. Helens Nat'l Volcanic Mon., Wash. 175/C2
Mt. Vernon, Ill. 144/B4
Mt. Vernon, Ind. 180/C1
Mt. Vernon, N.Y. 180/C1
Mt. Vernon, Ohio 166/C3
Mt. Vernon, Wash. 175/A2
Mouscron, Belg. 73/B6
Mozambique 63/F6-7
Mozambique (chan.), Africa 63/G6-7
Mudanjiang, China 105/G1
Mufulira, Zambia 63/E6
Muir Woods Nat'l Mon., Calif. 133/E1
Mukalla, Yemen 94/F7
Mukden, China, see Shenyang
Mulhacén (mt.), Spain 77/E4
Mulhouse, France 74/G4
Mull (isl.), Scot. 66/D2
Multan, Pak. 102/C1
Muncie, Ind. 145/C2
Mundelein, Ill. 178/A1
Münden, Ger. 70/C3
Munich (München), Ger. 71/D4
Münster, Ger. 70/B3
Muonio (riv.), Europe 68/D1
Mur (Mura) (riv.), Europe 84/A2
Murcia, Spain 77/F4
Mureş (riv.), Rom. 84/C2
Murfreesboro, Tenn. 148/C4
Murmansk, U.S.S.R. 88/D1
Murom, U.S.S.R. 89/F3
Murray (riv.), Austr. 115/D4
Murray, Ky. 148/B3
Murray (lake), S.C. 162/C3
Murray, Utah 174/C1
Mururoa (isl.), Fr. Poly. 117/M8
Muscat (cap.), Oman 95/H5
Muscatine, Iowa 146/C4
Musgrave (ranges), Austr. 114/C3
Muskego, Wis. 176/A1
Muskegon, Mich. 152/A4
Muskingum (riv.), Ohio 167/D3
Muskogee, Okla. 168/B4
Muskoka (lake), Ont. 186/C2
Mutare, Zimb. 63/F6
Mwanza, Tanz. 63/F5
Mweru (lake), Africa 63/E5
Myingyan, Burma 110/A2
Myitkyina, Burma 110/B1
Myrtle Beach, S.C. 163/D3
Mysore, India 102/C3
Mystic, Conn. 136/C3
Mytilini, Greece 85/D4

Index

N

Naberezhnye Chelny, U.S.S.R. 88/H3
Nablus, West Bank 98/C3
Nacala, Moz. 63/G6
Nacogdoches, Texas 173/F2
Naga, Phil. 108/D4
Nagano, Japan 107/E3
Nagaoka, Japan 107/E3
Nagasaki, Japan 106/C4
Nagercoil, India 102/C3
Nagoya, Japan 106/E4
Nagpur, India 102/C2
Nags Head, N.C. 163/F1
Naha, Japan 107/G4
Nahanni Nat'l Pk., N.W.T. 129/C2
Nahariyya, Isr. 98/C1
Nahuel Huapi (lake), Arg. 58/B1
Nairobi (cap.), Kenya 63/F5
Nakhichevan, U.S.S.R. 89/F7
Nakhodka, U.S.S.R. 91/G3
Nakhon Ratchasima, Thai. 110/C4
Naktong (riv.), S. Korea 106/C4
Nakuru, Kenya 63/F5
Nalchik, U.S.S.R. 89/F6
Namangan, U.S.S.R. 90/D3
Namib (des.), Namibia 62/D6-7
Namibe, Angola 62/D6
Namibia 62-63/D7
Nampa, Idaho 143/A3
Namp'o, N. Korea 106/B3
Nampo-Shoto (isls.), Japan 107/G2
Nampula, Moz. 63/F6
Namur, Belg. 73/E7
Nanaimo, Br. Col. 190/B4
Nanchang, China 105/E3
Nanchong, China 104/D3
Nancy, France 74/G3
Nanjing (Nanking), China 105/E2
Nanning, China 104/D3
Nansei Shoto (isls.), Japan 107/G4
Nantes, France 74/C4
Nanticoke, Ont. 186/C4
Nantucket (isl.), Mass. 137/F3
Naolehu, Hawaii 129/C4
Napa, Calif. 132/C1
Naperville, Ill. 178/A2
Napier, N.Z. 115/F4
Naples, Fla. 141/E3
Naples, Italy 79/E4
Napo (riv.), S. Amer. 56/B3
Nara, Japan 107/F4
Narew (riv.), Pol. 87/E2
Narmada (riv.), India 102/C2
Narvik, Nor. 68/C1
Nashua, N.H. 158/C4
Nashville (cap.), Tenn. 148/B1
Nasik, India 102/C3
Nassau (cap.), Bah. 50/C1
Nasser (lake), Egypt 94/C4
Natal, Braz. 57/F3
Natal (prov.), S. Africa 63/F7
Natchez, Miss. 154/A3
Natchitoches, La. 150/A1
Natick, Mass. 137/D2
National City, Calif. 180/C4
N.A.S.A. Space Center, Texas 173/F4
Natuna (isls.), Indon. 112/D5
Nauru 116/G6
Navajo Nat'l Mon., Ariz. 130/C2
Navarin (cape), U.S.S.R. 91/K2
Navarre (reg.), Spain 77/F1
Navassa (isl.), U.S. 50/C3
Náxos (isl.), Greece 85/D4
Nazareth, Isr. 98/C2
N'Djamena (cap.), Chad 60/D3

Ndola, Zambia 63/E6
Neagh (lake), N. Ire. 67/C3
Nebit-Dag, U.S.S.R. 90/C4
Nebo (mt.), Jordan 99/D4
Nebraska (state), U.S. 157
Nebraska City, Nebr. 157/C4
Neckar (riv.), Ger. 71/C4
Needles, Calif. 133/E4
Neenah, Wis. 176/C3
Neepawa, Man. 189/D4
Nefud (des.), Saudi Arabia 94/E4
Negev (reg.), Isr. 99/D5
Negro (riv.), Arg. 58/C6
Negro (riv.), Braz. 56/C3
Negros (isl.), Phil. 109/D6
Nei Monggol Zizhiqu (aut. reg.), China 105/E1
Neisse (riv.), Europe 71/F3
Nejd (reg.), Saudi Arabia 94/D-E4-5
Neligh, Nebr. 157/B3
Nelson, Br. Col. 191/D4
Nelson (riv.), Man. 42/G4
Nelson, N.Z. 115/F4
Neosho (riv.), U.S. 44/G3
Nepal 102/D2
Ness, Loch (lake), Scot. 66/D2
Netanya, Isr. 98/B3
Netherlands 72-73
Netherlands Antilles 51/E4, F3
Neuchâtel, Switz. 80/B2
Neuquén, Arg. 58/C6
Neuse (riv.), N.C. 163/E2
Neusiedler See (lake), Austria 82/D3
Nevada (state), U.S. 132-133
Nevada, Sierra (mts.), Spain 77/E4
Nevada, Sierra (mts.), U.S. 44/C3
Nevis (isl.), St. Kitts & Nevis 51/F3, 55/W
New Albany, Ind. 145/C4
Newark, Calif. 133/F1
Newark, N.J. 180/A2
Newark, Ohio 166/C4
New Bedford, Mass. 137/E3
New Berlin, Wis. 176/H1
New Bern, N.C. 163/E2
Newberry, S.C. 162/B3
New Braunfels, Texas 173/D3
New Britain, Conn. 136/B3
New Britain (isl.), Papua N.G. 116/F6
New Brunswick (prov.), Can. 182
New Brunswick, N.J. 159/B2
Newburgh, N.Y. 161/E4
Newburyport, Mass. 137/E1
New Caledonia & Dependencies 116/G8
New Canaan, Conn. 136/A3
Newcastle, Austr. 115/E4
New Castle, Ind. 145/C3
Newcastle, N. Br. 182/C2
Newcastle, Ont. 187/D3
New Castle, Pa. 170/A4
Newcastle upon Tyne, Eng. 66/E3
New Delhi (cap.), India 102/C2
Newfoundland (isl.), Can. 183/F1
Newfoundland (prov.), Can. 43/L5
New Glasgow, N.S. 183/E3
New Guinea (isl.), Pacific 116/DE6
New Hampshire (state), U.S. 158
New Harmony, Ind. 145/A4
New Haven, Conn. 136/B3
New Hope, Minn. 153/B1
New Iberia, La. 150/C2
New Ireland (isl.), Papua N.G. 116/F6
New Jersey (state), U.S. 159
New Liskeard, Ont. 186/C1

New London, Conn. 136/C3
New Madrid, Mo. 155/C4
Newmarket, Ont. 187/F3
New Mexico (state), U.S. 135
New Milford, Conn. 136/A3
New Milford, Pa. 171/E2
New Orleans, La. 150/A4
New Philadelphia, Ohio 166/C4
New Plymouth, N.Z. 115/F4
Newport, Ky. 149/D1
Newport, N.H. 158/B3
Newport, Oreg. 169/B1
Newport, R.I. 137/D3
Newport, Vt. 158/B1
Newport, Wales 67/E5
Newport Bch., Calif. 133/F3
Newport News, Va. 138/A1
New Port Richey, Fla. 140/C2
New Providence (isl.), Bah. 50/C1
New Rochelle, N.Y. 161/H1
Newry, N. Ire. 67/C3
New Siberian (isls.), U.S.S.R. 91/H2
New Smyrna Bch., Fla. 140/B4
New South Wales (state), Austr. 115/D4
Newton, Iowa 146/B3
Newton, Kans. 147/B3
Newton, Mass. 137/D2
New Ulm, Minn. 153/B4
New Westminster, Br. Col. 190/A1
New York (state), U.S. 160-161
New York City, N.Y. 180/C2
New Zealand 115/F4
Nez Perce Nat'l Hist. Pk., Idaho 143/A2
Nha Trang, Viet. 111/E4
Niagara (riv.), N. Amer. 160/A1
Niagara Falls, N.Y. 160/B3
Niagara Falls, Ont. 187/F4
Niagara-on-the-Lake, Ont. 187/F3
Niamey (cap.), Niger 60/C3
Nias (isl.), Indon. 112/B5
Nicaragua 48/C2
Nicaragua (lake), Nic. 48/C3
Nice, France 75/G4
Nicobar (isls.), India 103/E4
Nicosia (cap.), Cyprus 96/E5
Nicoya (gulf), C. Rica 48/C3
Niger 60/C3
Niger (riv.), Africa 60/C4
Nigeria 60/C4
Niigata, Japan 107/E3
Niihau (isl.), Hawaii 129/A3
Nijmegen, Neth. 72/G4
Nikolayev, U.S.S.R. 89/D5
Nile (riv.), Africa 61/F2
Niles, Ohio 166/B4
Nîmes, France 75/F6
Nineveh (ruins), Iraq 100/C2
Ningbo (Ningpo), China 105/F3
Ningxia (Ningsia) Huizu (aut. reg.), China 104/D2
Niobrara, Nebr. 157/A3
Niobrara (riv.), Nebr. 157/A3
Nipawin, Sask. 188/C2
Nipigon (lake), Ont. 187/D1
Nipissing (lake), Ont. 186/C2
Niš (Nish), Yugo. 84/C3
Nishinomiya, Japan 107/E4
Niterói, Braz. 59/E5
Nitra, Czech. 83/E2
Niue 117/K7
Nizhnevartovsk, U.S.S.R. 90/D2
Nizhniy Tagil, U.S.S.R. 90/D3
Njazidja (isl.), Comoros 63/G6
Nkongsamba, Cam. 60/D4
Noblesville, Ind. 145/B2
Nogales, Ariz. 130/B4
Nome, Alaska 129/A1

Nootka (isl.), Br. Col. 190/A4
Noranda, Que. 184/A2
Nord Ostsee (canal), Ger. 70/C1
Norfolk, Nebr. 157/B3
Norfolk, Va. 138/A1
Norfolk I. (terr.), Austr. 116/G8
Noril'sk, U.S.S.R. 91/E2
Normal, Ill. 144/B2
Norman, Okla. 168/B3
Normandy (prov.), France 74/C3
Norman Wells, N.W.T. 42/D2
Norris (lake), Tenn. 149/E3
Norristown, Pa. 171/D1
Norrköping, Swed. 69/C3
North (sea), Europe 64/E3
North (isl.), N.Z. 115/F4
North (cape), Nor. 68/E1
N. Adams, Mass. 136/B1
North America 40-41
Northampton, Eng. 67/F4
Northampton, Mass. 136/B2
North Atlantic Ocean 35/H4
N. Battleford, Sask. 188/A2
North Bay, Ont. 186/C2
North Bend, Oreg. 169/B1
North Carolina (state), U.S. 162-163
North Cascades Nat'l Pk., Wash. 175/A3
N. Chicago, Ill. 178/B1
N. Conway, N.H. 158/C2
North Dakota (state), U.S. 164
Northern Ireland, U.K. 66/C3
Northern Marianas (isls.), U.S. 116/E4
Northern Territory, Austr. 114/C3
Northern Yukon Nat'l Pk., Yukon 129/K1
Northfield, Minn. 153/B4
North Frisian (isls.), Europe 70/C1
Northglenn, Colo. 178/A3
North Haven, Conn. 136/B3
North Korea 106/C3
N. Las Vegas, Nev. 133/D4
N. Little Rock, Ark. 131/B2
N. Miami Bch., Fla. 141/D1
N. Olmsted, Ohio 167/F3
North Platte, Nebr. 157/B2
North Platte (riv.), U.S. 44/F2
North Rhine-Westphalia (state), Ger. 70-71/B3
North Saskatchewan (riv.), Can. 188/B2
N. Sydney, N.S. 183/F2
Northumberland (str.), Can. 183/D2
N. Vancouver, Br. Col. 190/A1
North West (cape), Austr. 114/A3
Northwest Territories, Can. 42-43/E-J2
Norwalk, Calif. 179/B2
Norwalk, Conn. 136/A4
Norwalk, Ohio 166/B3
Norway 68-69
Norwegian (sea), Europe 35/JK5
Norwich, Conn. 136/C3
Norwich, Eng. 67/G4
Norwood, Mass. 137/D2
Norwood, Ohio 167/F1
Noto (pen.), Japan 106/E3
Nottawasaga (bay), Ont. 186/C2
Nottingham, Eng. 67/F4
Nouadhibou, Maur. 60/A2
Nouakchott (cap.), Mauritania 60/A3
Nouméa (cap.), New Caledonia 116/G8
Nova Iguaçu, Braz. 59/E5
Novara, Italy 78/B3
Nova Scotia (prov.), Can. 182-183

Novato, Calif. 133/D1
Novaya Zemlya (isls.), U.S.S.R. 90/C2
Novgorod, U.S.S.R. 88/D3
Novi Sad, Yugo. 84/C2
Novocherkassk, U.S.S.R. 89/F5
Novokuznetsk, U.S.S.R. 90/D3
Novomoskovsk, U.S.S.R. 88/E4
Novorossiysk, U.S.S.R. 89/E6
Novosibirsk, U.S.S.R. 90/D3
Novyy Urengoy, U.S.S.R. 90/D2
Nubian (des.), Sudan 61/F2
Nueces (riv.), Texas 173/D3
Nuevo Laredo, Mex. 47/F2
Nuku'alofa (cap.), Tonga 117/J8
Nukus, U.S.S.R. 90/C3
Numazu, Japan 107/E4
Nuneaton, Eng. 67/F4
Nuremberg (Nürnberg), Ger. 71/D4
Nutley, N.J. 180/A2
Nuuk (cap.), Greenl. 40/N3
Nyala, Sudan 61/E3
Nyasa (lake), Africa 63/F6
Nyasaland, see Malawi
Nyíregyháza, Hung. 83/F3

O

Oahe (lake), U.S. 165/D2
Oahu (isl.), Hawaii 129/SA
Oak Harbor, Wash. 175/A2
Oakland, Calif. 133/E1
Oakland Park, Fla. 141/D1
Oak Lawn, Ill. 178/B2
Oakley, Kans. 147/B1
Oak Park, Ill. 178/B2
Oak Ridge, Tenn. 149/E4
Oakville, Ont. 187/E4
Oaxaca de Juárez, Mex. 47/F5
Ob' (riv.), U.S.S.R. 90/D2
Oberammergau, Ger. 71/D5
Oberlin, Ohio 166/B3
Oberstdorf, Ger. 71/D5
Ocala, Fla. 140/B3
Ocean (Banaba) (isl.), Kiribati 116/G6
Ocean City, Md. 139/F3
Ocean City, N.J. 159/B4
Oceania 116-117
Oceanside, Calif. 180/B3
Ocean Springs, Miss. 154/C4
Ocho Rios, Jam. 53/V9
Ocracoke, N.C. 163/F2
Odense, Den. 69/B3
Oder (riv.), Europe 70/F2
Odessa, Texas 172/C2
Odessa, U.S.S.R. 89/D5
Offenbach, Ger. 71/C3
Ogaden (reg.), Eth. 61/G4
Ogbomosho, Nigeria 60/C4
Ogden, Utah 174/B2
Ogden Dunes, Ind. 178/C3
Ogdensburg, N.Y. 161/D1
Ogunquit, Maine 151/A4
Ohio (riv.), U.S. 45/J3
Ohio (state), U.S. 166-167
Ohrid (lake), Europe 85/C3
Oil City, Pa. 170/A3
Oise (riv.), France 74/E3
Oita, Japan 106/C4
Ojos del Salado (mt.), S. Amer. 58/C5
Oka (riv.), U.S.S.R. 89/E4
Okayama, Japan 106/D4
Okazaki, Japan 106/E4
Okeechobee (lake), Fla. 141/D4
Okefenokee (swamp), U.S. 142/B4
Okhotsk (sea), U.S.S.R. 91/H3
Oki (isls.), Japan 106/D3

Okinawa (isl.), Japan 107/G4
Oklahoma (state), U.S. 168
Oklahoma City (cap.), Okla. 168/B3
Okmulgee, Okla. 168/B4
Okotoks, Alta. 191/E1
Oktyabr'skiy, U.S.S.R. 89/H4
Öland (isl.), Swed. 69/C3
Olathe, Kans. 147/B4
Oldenburg, Ger. 70/C2
Oldham, Eng. 66/G2
Old Orchard Bch., Maine 151/A4
Old Town, Maine 151/B3
Old Wives (lake), Sask. 188/B4
Olean, N.Y. 160/B3
Olinda, Braz. 57/F3
Olomouc, Czech. 82/D2
Olongapo, Phil. 108/C3
Olsztyn, Pol. 87/E2
Olten, Switz. 80/C1
Olympia (cap.), Wash. 175/B2
Olympic Nat'l Pk., Wash. 175/B2
Olympus (mt.), Greece 84/C3
Omagh, N. Ire. 67/C3
Omaha, Nebr. 157/B4
Oman 95/H6
Oman (gulf), Asia 95/H5
Omdurman, Sudan 61/F3
Omiya, Japan 107/E3
Omsk, U.S.S.R. 90/D3
Omuta, Japan 106/C4
Onega (lake), U.S.S.R. 88/E2
One Hundred Mile House, Br. Col. 190/C3
Oneida (lake), N.Y. 161/D3
O'Neill, Nebr. 157/A3
Oneonta, N.Y. 161/D3
Onitsha, Nigeria 60/C4
Ontario, Calif. 179/B3
Ontario (prov.), Can. 186-187
Ontario (lake), N. Amer. 45/L2
Ontario, Oreg. 169/B4
Oostende (Ostend), Belg. 73/A5
Opelika, Ala. 128/C2
Opelousas, La. 150/B2
Opole, Pol. 86/C3
Oporto, Port. 76/B2
Opportunity, Wash. 175/B4
Oradea, Rom. 84/C2
Oran, Alg. 60/B1
Orange (riv.), Africa 63/D7
Orange, Austr. 115/D4
Orange, Calif. 179/C3
Orange, Texas 173/F3
Orangeburg, S.C. 162/D3
Orange Free State (prov.), S. Africa 63/E7
Orangeville, Ont. 186/C3
Orange Walk Town, Belize 48/B1
Oranjestad (cap.), Aruba 55/O
Ordzhonikidze, U.S.S.R. 89/F6
Örebro, Swed. 69/C3
Oregon (state), U.S. 167
Oregon Caves Nat'l Mon., Oreg. 169/C2
Oregon City, Oreg. 169/A2
Orel, U.S.S.R. 89/E4
Orem, Utah 174/B2
Orenburg, U.S.S.R. 89/J4
Orense, Spain 76/C1
Organ Pipe Cactus Nat'l Mon., Ariz. 130/B4
Orillia, Ont. 186/C3
Orinoco (riv.), S. Amer. 56/C2
Orkney (isls.), Scot. 66/E1
Orlando, Fla. 140/A4
Orléans, France 74/D4
Ormoc, Phi. 109/F3
Ormond Beach, Fla. 140/B3
Oromocto, N. Br. 182/B3

Orono, Maine 151/B3
Orontes (riv.), Syria 97/G5
Orsha, U.S.S.R. 89/D3
Orsk, U.S.S.R. 89/G4
Oruro, Bol. 56/C4
Osaka, Japan 106/D4
Osh, U.S.S.R. 90/B3
Oshawa, Ont. 187/F3
Oshkosh, Wis. 176/D3
Oshogbo, Nigeria 60/C4
Osijek, Yugo. 84/B2
Oslo (cap.), Nor. 69/B2
Osmaniye, Turkey 97/G4
Osnabrück, Ger. 70/C2
Ostend, Belg. 73/A5
Ostrava, Czech. 83/D2
Ostrołęka, Pol. 87/E2
Oswego, N.Y. 161/D2
Oświęcim, Pol. 86/D3
Otaru, Japan 107/F2
Otranto (str.), Europe 85/B4
Otsego (lake), N.Y. 161/E3
Otsu, Japan 107/F4
Ottawa (riv.), Can. 184/A4
Ottawa, Ont. (cap.), Canada 186/A1
Ottumwa, Iowa 146/C3
Ouagadougou (cap.), Burk. Faso 60/B3
Ouargla, Alg. 60/C1
Oujda, Mor. 60/B1
Oulu, Fin. 68/E2
Our (riv.), Europe 73/H7
Ouse (riv.), Eng. 67/G4
Outremont, Que. 184/B1
Oviedo, Spain 76/C1
Owatonna, Minn. 153/B4
Owensboro, Ky. 148/C2
Owen Sound, Ont. 186/B3
Owyhee (lake), Oreg. 169/B4
Oxford, Eng. 67/F5
Oxford, Miss. 154/B6
Oxnard, Calif. 133/E2
Oyapock (riv.), S. Amer. 57/D2
Ozark, Ala. 128/C3
Ozarks, Lake of the (lake), Mo. 155/B2

P

Paarl, S. Africa 63/D8
Pacifica, Calif. 133/F1
Pacific Ocean 116-117
Pacific Rim Nat'l Pk., Br. Col. 190/A4
Padang, Indon. 112/B6
Paderborn, Ger. 71/C3
Padua (Padova), Italy 78/C2
Paducah, Ky. 148/B3
Pago Pago (cap.), Amer. Samoa 117/J7
Pahala, Hawaii 129/C4
Painesville, Ohio 166/A4
Paisley, Scot. 66/B2
Pakistan 102/B-C1-2
Pakse, Laos 110/D4
Palana, U.S.S.R. 91/J3
Palatine, Ill. 178/A1
Palatka, Fla. 140/B3
Palau (isls.) 116/D5
Palawan (isl.), Phil. 109/B6
Palembang, Indon. 112/C6
Palencia, Spain 76/D1
Palermo, Italy 79/D5
Palestine, Texas 173/G7
Palma de Mallorca, Spain 77/H3
Palmas (cape), Liberia 60/B4
Palm Bay, Fla. 140/C4
Palm Beach, Fla. 141/D4
Palmdale, Calif. 133/E3

Palmer Land, Antarc. 118
Palmerston North, N.Z. 115/F4
Palmira, Col. 56/B2
Palm Springs, Calif. 133/F3
Palmyra, Syria, see Tadmor
Palmyra Atoll (isl.), U.S. 117/K5
Palo Alto, Calif. 133/F1
Pamir (plat.), Asia 102/C1
Pamlico (sound), N.C. 163/F2
Pampa, Texas 172/B1
Pampas (plain), Arg. 58/C8
Pamplona, Spain 77/F1
Panama 49/DE3
Panamá (cap.), Pan. 49/E3
Panama (canal), Pan. 49/E3
Panama (gulf), Pan. 49/E4
Panama City, Fla. 141/F2
Panay (isl.), Phil. 109/D5
Panda, Zaire 63/E6
P'anmunjŏm, Korea 106/B3
Pantelleria (isl.), Italy 79/C6
Papeete (cap.), Fr. Poly. 117/M7
Papua New Guinea 116/E6
Pará (riv.), Braz. 57/D3
Paracel (isls.), China 112/E2
Paradise Valley, Ariz. 130/A1
Paragould, Ark. 131/A3
Paraguay 58-59/D5
Paraguay (riv.), S. Amer. 58/D5
Paramaribo (cap.), Suriname 57/D2
Paramus, N.J. 180/B1
Paraná, Arg. 58/C6
Paraná (riv.), S. Amer. 58/D5
Pardubice, Czech. 82/C1
Paria (gulf) 51/F5
Paris (cap.), France 74/B2
Paris, Ky. 149/E2
Paris, Tenn. 148/B3
Paris, Texas 173/G11
Parkersburg, W. Va. 138/B2
Park Forest, Ill. 178/B3
Parkland, Wash. 175/B2
Park Ridge, Ill. 178/B2
Parkville, Md. 139/F1
Parma, Italy 78/C2
Parma, Ohio 167/F4
Parnaíba (riv.), Braz. 57/E3
Parnassus (mt.), Greece 85/C4
Páros (isl.), Greece 85/D4
Parry (chan.), N.W.T. 42/F-G1
Parry Sound, Ont. 186/C3
Parsons, Kans. 147/C4
Pasadena, Calif. 179/A2
Pasadena, Texas 173/F4
Pascagoula, Miss. 154/C4
Pasco, Wash. 175/C4
Passaic, N.J. 180/A2
Pastaza (riv.), S. Amer. 56/B3
Pasto, Col. 56/B2
Patagonia (reg.), Arg. 58/C9
Patapsco (riv.), Md. 139/F2
Paterson, N.J. 180/A1
Patiala, India 102/C1
Pátmos (isl.), Greece 85/D4
Patna, India 102/D2
Patoka (lake), Ind. 145/B4
Patos (lag.), Braz. 59/E6
Pàtrai, Greece 85/C4
Pau, France 75/C6
Pavia, Italy 78/B2
Pavlodar, U.S.S.R. 90/D3
Pawtucket, R.I. 137/D2
Paysandú, Urug. 59/E6
Peace (riv.), Can. 42/E4
Peace River, Alta. 191/D1
Pearl (harb.), Hawaii 129/A4
Pearl City, Hawaii 129/A4
Peary Land, Greenl. 40/Q1
Pechora, U.S.S.R. 88/H1
Pecos, Texas 172/B2

Pecos (riv.), Texas 172/C3
Pecos Nat'l Mon., N. Mex. 135/D3
Pécs, Hung. 83/D3
Pédro Juan Caballero, Par. 59/D5
Pee Dee (riv.), S.C. 163/D3
Peekskill, N.Y. 161/F4
Pegu, Burma 110/B3
Peipus (lake), U.S.S.R. 88/C3
Pekalongan, Indon. 113/J2
Pekin, Ill. 144/B2
Peking (Beijing) (cap.), China 105/E1
Pelée (vol.), Martinique 51/G4, 54/J
Pelée (isl.), Ont. 186/A4
Pelotas, Braz. 59/D6
Pemba, Moz. 63/F6
Pemba (isl.), Tanz. 63/G5
Pembroke, Ont. 187/D2
Pembroke Pines, Fla. 141/D1
Pendleton, Oreg. 169/A3
Pend Oreille (lake), Idaho 143/A1
Pennine Alps (mts.), Europe 80/C3
Pennsylvania (state), U.S. 170-171
Penobscot (riv.), Maine 151/B2
Pensacola, Fla. 141/E4
Penticton, Br. Col. 190/C4
Pentland (firth), Scot. 66/E1
Penza, U.S.S.R. 89/F4
Peoria, Ariz. 130/A1
Peoria, Ill. 144/B2
Percé, Que. 185/F1
Pereira, Col. 56/B2
Perigueux, France 75/D5
Périm (isl.), Yemen 94/E7
Perlas (arch.), Pan. 49/E3
Perm', U.S.S.R. 88/J3
Pernambuco, Braz., see Recife
Pernik, Bulg. 84/C3
Perpignan, France 75/E6
Perry's Victory and Int'l Peace Mem., Ohio 166/A2
Perryton, Texas 172/B1
Perth, Austr. 114/A4
Perth, Ont. 187/E2
Perth, Scot. 66/E2
Perth Amboy, N.J. 180/A2
Perth-Andover, N. Br. 182/B2
Peru 56/B3-4
Peru, Ind. 145/B2
Perugia, Italy 78/D3
Pescara, Italy 78/E3
Peshawar, Pak. 102/C1
Petah Tiqwa, Isr. 99/B3
Petaluma, Calif. 132/C1
Peter I (isl.), Nor. 118
Peterborough, Eng. 67/F4
Peterborough, Ont. 187/D3
Petersburg, Va. 139/E4
Petitcodiac, N. Br. 182/C2
Petoskey, Mich. 152/B2
Petra (ruins), Jordan 99/D5
Petrified Forest Nat'l Pk., Ariz. 130/C3
Petropavlovsk, U.S.S.R. 90/D3
Petropavlovsk-Kamchatskiy, U.S.S.R. 91/J3
Petrozavodsk, U.S.S.R. 88/D2
Pforzheim, Ger. 71/C4
Pharr, Texas 173/D4
Phenix City, Ala. 128/C3
Philadelphia, Miss. 154/C2
Philadelphia, Pa. 171/E1
Philippines 108-109
Phillipsburg, N.J. 159/A2
Phitsanulok, Thai. 110/C3
Phnom Penh (cap.), Camb.

111/D5
Phoenix (cap.), Ariz. 130/A1
Phoenix (isls.), Kiribati 117/J6
Piacenza, Italy 78/B2
Piatra Neamţ, Rom. 84/D2
Piave (riv.), Italy 78/D2
Picayune, Miss. 154/B4
Pickering, Ont. 187/F3
Pico Rivera, Calif. 179/B2
Picton, Ont. 187/D3
Pictou, N.S. 183/E3
Piedmont (reg.), Italy 78/AB2
Pierre (cap.), S. Dak. 165/E2
Pietermaritzburg, S. Africa 63/F7
Pigs, Bay of (bay), see Cochinos (bay)
Pikesville, Md. 139/E1
Pikeville, Ky. 149/F3
Pilar, Par. 58/C5
Pilcomayo (riv.), S. Amer. 58/C5
Pilsen, Czech., see Plzeň
Pinang, Malaysia, see George Town
Pinar del Rio, Cuba 52/B2
Pindus (mts.), Greece 85/C4
Pine Bluff, Ark. 131/B2
Pinellas Park, Fla. 140/C1
Pine Ridge, S. Dak. 165/F1
Pines (Juventud) (isl.), Cuba 50/A2
Pinnacles Nat'l Mon., Calif. 133/D1
Pinsk, U.S.S.R. 89/C4
Pipe Springs Nat'l Mon., Ariz. 130/B2
Pipestone Nat'l Mon., Minn. 153/A4
Piqua, Ohio 166/C1
Piraiévs, Greece 85/C4
Pisa, Italy 78/C3
Pisco, Peru 56/B4
Pitcairn (isl.), Pacific 117/O8
Piteşti, Rom. 84/D2
Pittsburg, Calif. 132/C1
Pittsburg, Kans. 147/C3
Pittsburgh, Pa. 170/A1
Pittsfield, Mass. 136/A1
Piura, Peru 56/A3
Plainfield, N.J. 159/B2
Plainview, Texas 172/C1
Plano, Texas 173/F1
Plantation, Fla. 141/D1
Plant City, Fla. 140/C3
Plata, Rio de la (est.), S. Amer. 59/D6
Platte (riv.), Nebr. 157/C2
Platteville, Wis. 176/B4
Plattsburgh, N.Y. 161/F1
Pleasant Hill, Calif. 133/E1
Pleiku, Viet. 111/E4
Plessisville, Que. 185/E4
Pleven, Bulg. 84/D3
Płock, Pol. 87/D2
Ploieşti, Rom. 84/D2
Plovdiv, Bulg. 84/D3
Plum, Pa. 170/B1
Plymouth, Eng. 67/E5
Plymouth, Mass. 137/E2
Plymouth, N.H. 158/B3
Plzeň, Czech. 82/B2
Po (riv.), Italy 78/C2
Pocatello, Idaho 143/C4
Pocomoke City, Md. 139/F3
P'ohang, S. Korea 106/C3
Pohnpei (Ponape) (isl.), Micronesia 116/F5
Point Pelée Nat'l Pk., Ont. 186/A4
Point Pleasant, N.J. 159/C3
Point Reyes Nat'l Seashore, Calif. 132/C1
Pointe-aux-Trembles, Que.

184/B1
Pointe-Noire, Congo 62/B5
Poitiers, France 75/D4
Poland 86-87
Poltava, U.S.S.R. 89/D5
Polynesia (reg.), Pacific 117/J-N4-8
Pomona, Calif. 179/B3
Pompano Bch., Fla. 141/E4
Ponca City, Okla. 168/A3
Ponce, P. Rico 51/E3, 54/B1
Pondicherry, India 102/D3
Ponoka, Alta. 191/E3
Pontchartrain (lake), La. 150/A4
Pontiac, Mich. 178/C3
Pontianak, Indon. 112/D5
Pontic (mts.), Turkey 97/H2
Pontine (isls.), Italy 79/D4
Poole, Eng. 67/E5
Poona, India 102/C3
Poopó (lake), Bol. 56/C4
Popayán, Col. 56/B2
Poplar Bluff, Mo. 155/C3
Popocatépetl (mt.), Mex. 47/F2
Porcupine (riv.), N. Amer. 42/B2
Pori, Fin. 69/D2
Porsanger (fjord), Nor. 68/E1
Portage la Prairie, Man. 189/E4
Port Alberni, Br. Col. 190/B4
Port Angeles, Wash. 175/A2
Port Arthur, Texas 173/F3
Port-au-Prince (cap.), Haiti 50/D3, P7/S2
Port Charlotte, Fla. 141/D3
Port Chester, N.Y. 180/C1
Port Clinton, Ohio 166/A2
Port Colborne, Ont. 187/F4
Port Coquitlam, Br. Col. 190/B1
Port Elgin, Ont. 186/B3
Port Elizabeth, S. Africa 63/E8
Port-Gentil, Gabon 62/C5
Port Harcourt, Nigeria 60/C4
Port Hardy, Br. Col. 183/A3
Port Hastings, N.S. 183/E3
Port Hawkesbury, N.S. 183/E3
Port Huron, Mich. 152/C4
Portland, Maine 151/A4
Portland Bill (pt.), Eng. 67/E5
Port Lavaca, Texas 173/E3
Port Moresby (cap.), Papua N.G. 112/B7
Portneuf Res., Que. 185/D3
Porto (Oporto), Port. 76/B2
Porto Alegre, Braz. 59/D6
Port-of-Spain (cap.), Trin. & Tob. 51/G5, 55/T
Porto-Novo (cap.), Benin 60/C4
Port Orange, Fla. 140/B3
Port Orford, Oreg. 169/C1
Porto Velho, Braz. 56/C3
Portoviejo, Ecuador 56/A3
Port Said, Egypt 61/F1
Port St. Joe, Fla. 141/F2
Portsmouth, Eng. 67/F5
Portsmouth, N.H. 158/C4
Portsmouth, Ohio 167/E2
Portsmouth, Va. 138/A1
Port Sudan, Sudan 61/F3
Portugal 76
Posadas, Arg. 59/D5
Potholes (res.), Wash. 175/B3
Potomac (riv.), U.S. 139/D2
Potosí, Bol. 56/C4
Potsdam, Ger. 70/E2
Potsdam, N.Y. 161/E1
Pottstown, Pa. 171/E4
Pottsville, Pa. 171/E3
Poughkeepsie, N.Y. 161/F4
Powell (lake), U.S. 174/B4

Powell River, Br. Col. 190/B4
Poyang Hu (lake), China 105/E3
Poznań, Pol. 86/C2
Prague (Praha) (cap.), Czech. 82/C1
Prairie Dog Town Fork (riv.), Texas 172/A1, C1
Prairie du Chien, Wis. 176/A4
Prato, Italy 78/C3
Prattville, Ala. 128/B3
Prescott, Ariz. 130/B3
Prescott, Ont. 187/E2
Presidio, Texas 172/B3
Prešov, Czech. 83/F2
Prespa (lake), Europe 85/C3
Presque Isle, Maine 151/C2
Preston, Eng. 67/E4
Preston, Idaho 143/C4
Prestwick, Scot. 66/D3
Pretoria (cap.), S. Africa 63/E7
Price, Utah 174/B3
Prichard, Ala. 128/A4
Prince Albert, Sask. 188/B2
Prince Albert Nat'l Pk., Sask. 188/B1
Prince Charles (isl.), N.W.T. 43/J2
Prince Edward (isls.), S. Africa 35/L8
Prince Edward Island (prov.), Can. 183/D2
Prince Edward I. Nat'l Pk., P.E.I. 183/D2
Prince George, Br. Col. 190/C2
Prince of Wales (isl.), N.W.T. 42/G1
Prince Patrick (isl.), N.W.T. 34/E2
Prince Rupert, Br. Col. 42/C5
Princeton, Br. Col. 190/C4
Princeton, N.J. 159/B2
Prineville, Oreg. 169/B3
Priština, Yugo. 84/C3
Probolinggo, Indon. 113/K2
Prokop'yevsk, U.S.S.R. 90/E3
Provence (prov.), France 75/F6
Providence (cap.), R.I. 137/D2
Providencia (isl.), Col. 50/B4
Provincetown, Mass. 137/F2
Provo, Utah 174/B2
Prudhoe Land, Greenl. 40/M2
Pryor, Okla. 168/A4
Przemyśl, Pol. 87/F4
Pskov, U.S.S.R. 88/C3
Puebla de Zaragoza, Mex. 47/G2
Pueblo, Colo. 134/B3
Puerto Armuelles, Pan. 49/D3
Puerto Barrios, Guat. 48/B2
Puerto Cabello, Ven. 56/C1
Puerto Cortés, Hond. 48/C2
Puerto La Cruz, Ven. 56/C1
Puerto Montt, Chile 58/B7
Puerto Plata, Dom. Rep. 52/R6
Puerto Rico 51/E3, 54/D2
Puerto Vallarta, Mex. 46/D4
Puget (sound), Wash. 175/B1
Pukaskwa Nat'l Pk., Ont. 187/E1
Pulaski, Va. 138/C4
Pullman, Wash. 175/C4
Pune, see Poona
Puno, Peru 56/B4
Punta Arenas, Chile 58/B8
Puntarenas, C. Rica 48/C3
Punta Gorda, Fla. 141/D3
Punxsutawney, Pa. 170/B3
Puri, India 102/D3
Purus (riv.), S. Amer. 56/C3
Pusan, S. Korea 106/C4
Pushkin, U.S.S.R. 88/D3
Putumayo (riv.), S. Amer. 56/B3
Puuhonua O Honaunau Nat'l Hist. Pk., Hawaii 129/C4

Index

Puy-de-Dôme (mt.), France 75/E5
Puyallup, Wash. 175/C1
Pymatuning (lake), U.S. 166/A4, 170/A2
P'yŏngyang (cap.), N. Korea 106/B3
Pyrenees (mts.), Europe 64/D-E4
Pyu, Burma 110/B3

Q

Qandahar, Afghan. 102/B1
Qatar 95/G4
Qatara (depr.), Egypt 94/A3
Qaqortoq, Greenl. 40/P3
Qazvin, Iran 100/G2
Qeshm (isl.), Iran 101/J7
Qilian Shan (range), China 104/C2
Qingdao, China 105/F2
Qinghai (prov.), China 104/C2
Qinghai Hu (lake), China 104/C2
Qiqihar, China 105/F1
Qiryat Shemona, Isr. 98/C1
Qiryat Yam, Isr. 98/C2
Qom, Iran 100/G3
Quabbin (res.), Mass. 136/C2
Quang Tri, Viet. 110/D3
Quantico, Va. 139/E3
Qu'Appelle (riv.), Sask. 188/C4
Québec (cap.), Que. 185/E3
Québec (prov.), Can. 184-185
Queen Charlotte (isls.), Br. Col. 42/C5
Queens (borough), N.Y. 180/C2
Queensland (state), Austr. 115/D3
Queenstown, S. Africa 63/E8
Quelimane, Moz. 63/F6
Quemoy, China, see Jinmen
Quesnel, Br. Col. 190/B3
Quetta, Pak. 102/B1
Quezaltenango, Guat. 48/B2
Quezon City, Phil. 108/C3
Qui Nhon, Viet. 111/E4
Quill (lakes), Sask. 188/C3
Quincy, Ill. 144/A3
Quincy, Mass. 137/F4
Quito (cap.), Ecua. 56/B2
Qum (Qom), Iran 100/G3
Qumran, West Bank, see Khirbet Qumran

R

Rabat (cap.), Mor. 60/B1
Race (cape), Newf. 43/L6
Racine, Wis. 176/C4
Radcliff, Ky. 149/D2
Radford, Va. 138/C4
Radom, Pol. 87/E3
Rainbow Bridge Nat'l Mon., Utah 174/C4
Rainier (mt.), Wash. 175/B2
Rainy (lake), N. Amer. 153/B2
Raipur, India 102/D2
Rajahmundry, India 102/D3
Rajkot, India 102/C2
Rakata (isl.), Indon. 112/C7
Raleigh (cap.), N.C. 163/D2
Ramadi, Iraq 100/C4
Ramallah, West Bank 99/C4
Ramat Gan, Isr. 99/B3
Ramla, Isr. 99/B4
Ramree (isl.), Burma 110/A3
Rancagua, Chile 58/B6
Ranchi, India 102/D2
Rancho Cucamonga, Calif. 179/B4
Randers, Den. 69/B3
Rangoon (cap.), Burma 110/B3

Rantoul, Ill. 144/C2
Rapa (isl.), Fr. Poly. 117/M8
Rapa Nui (Easter) (isl.), Chile 117/P8
Rapid City, S. Dak. 165/E1
Rappahannock (riv.), Va. 139/D3
Raqqa, Syria, see El Rashid
Rarotonga (isl.), Cook Is. 117/K8
Ras Asér (cape), Somalia 61/H3
Ras Dashan (mt.), Eth. 61/F3
Rasht, Iran 100/F2
Raton, N. Mex. 134/C3
Ravenna, Italy 78/D2
Ravensburg, Ger. 71/C5
Rawalpindi, Pak. 102/C1
Rawlins, Wyo. 177/C2
Rawson, Arg. 58/C7
Raytown, Mo. 155/C1
Reading, Eng. 67/F5
Reading, Pa. 171/E4
Recife, Braz. 57/F5
Recklinghausen, Ger. 70/B3
Red (sea) 94/D5-6
Red (riv.), Asia 110/C2
Red (riv.), U.S. 45/H4
Red Bank, N.J. 159/C2
Red Bank, Tenn. 149/D4
Red Cloud, Nebr. 157/C3
Red Deer, Alta. 191/E3
Red Deer (riv.), Alta. 191/E3
Redding, Calif. 132/B1
Redfield, S. Dak. 165/D3
Red Lake, Minn. 153/A2
Redlands, Calif. 133/E3
Redmond, Oreg. 169/B3
Redmond, Wash. 175/B1
Redondo Bch., Calif. 179/C1
Red River of the North (riv.), N. Amer. 153/A3, 164/A4, 189/F4
Red Wing, Minn. 153/C4
Redwood City, Calif. 133/F1
Redwood Nat'l Pk., Calif. 132/A1
Ree, Lough (lake), Ire. 67/C4
Reedsport, Oreg. 169/B2
Regensburg, Ger. 71/D4
Reggio di Calabria, Italy 79/E5
Reggio nell'Emilia, Italy 78/C2
Regina (cap.), Sask. 188/C4
Rehoboth Bch., Del. 139/F3
Rehovot, Isr. 99/B4
Reims, France 74/F3
Reina Adelaida (arch.), Chile 58/B8
Reindeer (lake), Can. 42/F4
Reisterstown, Md. 139/E2
Rennes, France 74/C3
Reno, Nev. 132/B2
Renton, Wash. 175/C1
Repentigny, Que. 184/B1
Republican (riv.), U.S. 147/A1
Resistencia, Arg. 58/C5
Reşiţa, Rom. 84/C2
Resolution (isl.), N.W.T. 43/K3
Restigouche (riv.), N. Br. 182/B1
Réunion 35/L7
Reus, Spain 77/G2
Reutlingen, Ger. 71/C4
Revelstoke, Br. Col. 191/D4
Revillagigedo (isls.), Mex. 46/B4
Rexburg, Idaho 143/C3
Reykjavik (cap.), Iceland 64/B2
Reynosa, Mex. 47/E3
Rhaetian Alps (mts.), Europe 81/E2
Rhine (riv.), Europe 64/E4
Rhinelander, Wis. 176/B3
Rhode Island (state), U.S. 137/D3
Rhodes, Greece 85/E4
Rhodope (mts.), Europe 85/D3
Rhondda, Wales 67/E5
Rhône (riv.), Europe 75/F5

Rialto, Calif. 179/B4
Riau (arch.), Indon. 112/C5
Ribeirão Preto, Braz. 59/E5
Richardson, Texas 172/C4
Richfield, Minn. 153/B1
Richfield, Utah 174/B3
Richibucto, N. Br. 182/C2
Richland, Wash. 175/C4
Richmond, Br. Col. 190/A1
Richmond, Calif. 133/E1
Richmond, Ind. 145/C3
Richmond, Ky. 149/E2
Richmond (cap.), Va. 139/E3
Richmond Hill, Ont. 187/E3
Riding Mtn. Nat'l Pk., Man. 189/D3
Riga, U.S.S.R. 88/B3
Rigi (mt.), Switz. 81/D1
Rijeka, Yugo. 84/A2
Rimini, Italy 78/D2
Rimouski, Que. 185/F2
Riobamba, Ecua. 56/B3
Rio Branco, Braz. 56/C3
Rio de Janeiro, Braz. 59/E5
Rio Gallegos, Arg. 58/C8
Rio Grande (riv.), N. Amer. 44/F5, 46/D1
Rio Grande, Braz. 59/D8
Riohacha, Col. 56/B1
Ripon, Wis. 176/C4
Rishon Le Ziyyon, Isr. 99/B4
Riverside, Calif. 179/B4
Riverton, Wyo. 177/B3
Riverview, N. Br. 182/C3
Riviera (reg.), Europe 75/G6
Riviera Beach, Fla. 141/D4
Rivière-du-Loup, Que. 185/D1
Riyadh (cap.), Saudi Arabia 94/F5
Road Town (cap.), V.I (Br.) 54/F
Roanne, France 75/F4
Roanoke (riv.), U.S. 139/D4, 163/E1
Roanoke, Va. 138/C4
Roanoke Rapids, N.C. 163/E1
Roatán, Hond. 48/C1
Rochdale, Eng. 66/B2
Rochester, Minn. 153/C4
Rochester, N.H. 158/C3
Rochester, N.Y. 160/C3
Rockford, Ill. 144/B1
Rockhampton, Austr. 115/E3
Rock Hill, S.C. 162/C2
Rock Island, Ill. 144/A1
Rockland, Maine 151/B4
Rock Springs, Wyo. 177/C3
Rockville, Md. 139/E2
Rocky (mts.), N. Amer. 40-41/F-G4-6
Rocky Mount, N.C. 163/E1
Rocky Mountain House, Alta. 191/E3
Rocky Mountain Nat'l Pk., Colo. 134/A2
Roeselare (Roulers), Belg. 73/A6
Rogers, Ark. 131/A1
Rogue (riv.), Oreg. 169/C2
Rolla, Mo. 155/B3
Romania 84/CD2
Rome, Ga. 142/A3
Rome (cap.), Italy 78/D3
Rome, N.Y. 161/D2
Ronda, Spain 76/D4
Roosevelt (isl.), Antarc. 118
Roosevelt (riv.), Braz. 56/C3
Roosevelt Campobello Int'l Pk., N. Amer. 151/C3
Roraima (mt.), S. Amer. 56/C2
Rosa (mt.), Europe 78/A2
Rosario, Arg. 58/C6
Roseau (cap.), Dominica 51/G4, 55/K

Roseburg, Oreg. 169/C2
Rosenburg, Texas 173/E3
Rosetown, Sask. 188/A3
Roseville, Minn. 153/C1
Ross (sea), Antarc. 118
Rostock, Ger. 70/E1
Rostov-na-Donu, U.S.S.R. 89/F5
Roswell, Ga. 142/A2
Roswell, N. Mex. 135/E3
Rothenberg, Ger. 71/D4
Rotherham, Eng. 67/F4
Rotterdam, Neth. 72/D4
Rotuma (isl.), Fiji 116/H7
Roubaix, France 74/E2
Rouen, France 74/D3
Roundup, Mont. 156/B3
Rouyn, Que. 184/A2
Rovno, U.S.S.R. 89/C4
Rovuma (riv.), Africa 63/F6
Roxas, Phil. 109/D5
Royal Oak, Mich. 178/C4
Rub' al Kahli (des.), Asia
  94-95/F5
Rubtsovsk, U.S.S.R. 90/E3
Ruda-Slaska, Pol. 86/A4
Rudolf (lake), Africa, see Turkana
Rufiji (riv.), Tanz. 63/F5
Rugby, N. Dak. 164/B3
Rügen (isl.), Ger. 70/E1
Ruhr (riv.), Ger. 70/C3
Rukwa (lake), Tanz. 63/F5
Rum (Rhum) (isl.), Scot. 66/C2
Rumford, Maine 151/A3
Rurutu (isl.), Fr. Poly. 117/L8
Ruse, Bulg. 84/D3
Russell Cave Nat'l Mon., Ala.
  128/E1
Russellville, Ark. 131/B2
Russellville, Ky. 148/C3
Russian S.F.S.R., U.S.S.R. 88-91
Ruston, La. 150/A2
Rutland, Vt. 158/A3
Rwanda 63/F5
Ryazan', U.S.S.R. 89/E4
Rybinsk, U.S.S.R. 88/E3
Rybnik, Pol. 86/D3
Ryukyu (isls.), Japan 107/F-G3-4
Rzeszow, Pol. 87/F3
Rzhev, U.S.S.R. 88/D3

S

Saale (riv.), Ger. 70/D3
Saar (riv.), Europe 71/B4
Saarbrücken, Ger. 71/B4
Saaremaa (isl.), U.S.S.R. 88/B3
Saarland (state), Ger. 71/B4
Saba (isl.), Neth. Ant. 51/F3
Sabadell, Spain 77/H2
Sabah (state), Malaysia 112/F4
Sabine (riv.), U.S. 150/B1, 173/F2
Sable (cape), Fla. 141/E4
Sable (cape), N.S. 43/K7
Sable (isl.), N.S. 43/L7
Sacajawea (lake), Wash. 175/C4
Sackets Harbor, N.Y. 161/D2
Sackville, N.S. 183/D3
Saco, Maine 151/A4
Sacramento (cap.), Calif. 132/C2
Sacramento (riv.), Calif. 132/B1
Sacramento (mts.), N. Mex.
  135/E2
Sado (isl.), Japan 107/G3
Safad (riv.), see Zefat
Safi, Mor. 60/B1
Saga, Japan 106/C4
Saginaw, Mich. 152/C3
Saguaro Nat'l Mon., Ariz. 130/B4
Sahara (des.), Africa 60-61/B-E3
Saharanpur, India 102/C2
Saida, Leb. 96/F6

Saigon, Viet., see Ho Chi Minh
  City
St. Albans, Eng. 67/F5
St. Albans, Vt. 158/A2
St. Albans, W. Va. 138/B3
St. Albert, Alta. 191/F1
St. Andrews, Scot. 66/E2
St. Anthony, Newf. 183/F1
St. Augustine, Fla. 140/A3
Saint Bernard (pass), Europe
  80/C3
St-Brieuc, France 74/B3
St. Catharines, Ont. 187/F4
St. Charles, Mo. 155/A4
Saint Christopher, see Saint Kitts
St. Clair (lake), N. Amer. 152/C4,
  186/A4
St. Clair Shores, Mich. 178/C4
St. Cloud, Minn. 153/B3
St. Croix, U.S. 153/C3,
  176/A2
Saint Croix (isl.), V.I. (U.S.)
  51/H2, 54/G
St-Denis, France 74/B1
Ste. Anne, Man. 189/F4
Ste-Foy, Que. 185/E3
Sainte-Marie (cape), Madag., see
  Vohimena
Ste-Thérèse, Que. 184/A1
St-Étienne, France 75/F5
St-Eustache, Que. 184/A1
Saint Eustatius (isl.), Neth. Ant.
  51/F3
St-Félicien, Que. 185/D2
Saint George (cape), Newf.
  183/E1
St. George, Utah 174/A4
Saint George's (chan.), Europe
  67/C5
St. George's (cap.), Grenada
  51/F5, 55/R
Saint Georges (bay), N.S. 183/E3
St. Gotthard (tunnel), Switz.
  81/D2
Saint Helena (isl.), U.K. 35/J6
St. Helens, Eng. 66/G2
St. Helens (vol.), Wash. 175/C2
St-Hubert, Que. 184/B1
St-Hyacinthe, Que. 185/D4
St. Ignace, Mich. 152/B2
St. Ignatius, Mont. 156/B1
St-Jean, Que. 185/D4
Saint-Jean (lake), Que. 185/D2
St-Jérôme, Que. 184/A1
St. John, N. Br. 182/C3
Saint John (riv.), N. Bruns.
  182/A2
Saint John (isl.), V.I. (U.S.) 54/F
St. Johns (cap.), Antigua &
  Barbuda 51/G3, 55/V
Saint Johns (riv.), Fla. 140/A3
St. John's (cap.), Newf. 183/F1
St. Johnsbury, Vt. 158/B2
St. Joseph, Mo. 155/A2
Saint Joseph (isl.), Ont. 186/A1
Saint Kitts (isl.), St. Kitts & Nevis
  51/F3, 55/W
Saint Kitts and Nevis 51/F3
St-Laurent, Que. 184/A1
Saint Lawrence (isl.), Alaska
  40/A3
Saint Lawrence (gulf), Can. 43/K6
Saint Lawrence (riv.), N. Amer.
  185/F2
Saint Lawrence Is. Nat'l Pk., Ont.
  187/D2
St-Lô, France 74/C3
St. Louis, Mo. 155/A4
St-Louis, Sen. 60/A3
St. Louis Park, Minn. 153/B1
Saint Lucia 51/G4

Saint-Malo (gulf), France 74/B3
Saint Martin (isl.), Fr., Neth. Ant.
  51/F3
St. Marys, Ohio 166/C1
St. Matthews, Ky. 149/F1
St. Moritz, Switz. 81/E2
St-Nazaire, France 74/B4
St. Paul (cap.), Minn. 153/C1
Saint Paul (isl.), Fr. 35/M7
St. Petersburg, Fla. 140/C1
St-Pierre, Mart. 54/J
Saint Pierre & Miquelon 43/L6
St-Siméon, Que. 185/E3
St. Stephen, N. Br. 182/B3
St. Thomas, Ont. 186/B4
Saint Thomas (isl.), V.I. (U.S.)
  51/F3, 54/F
St-Tropez, France 75/G6
Saint Vincent (cape), Port. 76/B4
Saint Vincent & the Grenadines
  51/G4, 55/P
Saipan (isl.), N. Marianas 116/E4
Sakai, Japan 107/E5
Sakakawea (lake), N. Dak.
  164/B1
Sakarya (riv.), Turkey 96/D2
Sakhalin (isl.), U.S.S.R. 91/H3
Sakishima (isls.), Japan 107/F4
Salaberry-de-Valleyfield, Que.
  184/C4
Salado (riv.), Arg. 58/C6
Salala, Oman 95/G6
Salamanca, N.Y. 160/B3
Salamanca, Spain 76/D2
Sala y Gómez (isl.), Chile 117/Q8
Salekhard, U.S.S.R. 90/D2
Salem, India 102/C3
Salem, Mass. 137/E1
Salem, N.J. 159/A3
Salem (cap.), Oreg. 169/C2
Salem, Va. 138/C4
Salerno, Italy 79/E4
Salford, Eng. 66/G2
Salgitter, Ger. 70/D2
Salida, Colo. 134/B3
Salina, Kans. 147/B3
Salinas, Calif. 133/D1
Salinas Nat'l Mon., N. Mex.
  135/E2
Salisbury, Eng. 67/F5
Salisbury, Md. 139/F3
Salisbury, N.C. 162/C2
Salisbury, Zimb., see Harare
Salmon, Idaho 143/B3
Salmon (riv.), Idaho 143/A3
Salmon Arm, Br. Col. 190/C3
Salonika, Greece, see
  Thessaloniki
Sal'sk, U.S.S.R. 89/F5
Salt, Jordan, see Es Salt
Salta, Arg. 58/C5
Saltillo, Mex. 46/E3
Salt Lake City (cap.), Utah
  174/C1
Salto, Urug. 59/D6
Salton Sea (lake), Calif. 133/F4
Saluda (riv.), S.C. 162/B2
Salvador, Braz. 57/F4
Salween (riv.), Asia 110/B2
Salzach (riv.), Europe 82/B2
Salzburg, Austria 82/B3
Samar (isl.), Phil. 108/D5
Samaria (reg.), West Bank 98/C3
Samarinda, Indon. 112/F6
Samarkand, U.S.S.R. 90/B4
Samarra, Iraq 100/C3
Samoa 117/J7
Sámos (isl.), Greece 85/D4
Samothráki (isl.), Greece 85/D3
Sam Rayburn (res.), Texas
  173/F2

Index

Samsun, Turkey 97/G2
San (riv.), Pol. 87/F3
San'a (cap.), Yemen 94/E6
San Andrés (isl.), Col. 5/B4
San Angelo, Texas 172/C2
San Antonio, Texas 173/D3
San Bernardino, Calif. 179/B4
San Bernardino (mts.), Calif. 179/A4
San Bernardino (str.), Phil. 108/E4
San Blas (gulf), Pan. 49/E3
San Bruno, Calif. 133/F1
San Carlos, Phil. 109/D5
San Carlos de Bariloche, Arg. 58/B7
San Clemente, Calif. 133/F3
San Clemente (isl.), Calif. 133/F3
San Cristóbal, Ven. 56/B2
San Cristóbal, Dom. Rep. 52/R7
Sancti Spiritus, Cuba 52/F3
Sand (hills), Nebr. 157/A1
Sandakan, Malaysia 110/F4
San Diego, Calif. 180/C4
Sandpoint, Idaho 143/A1
Sand Springs, Okla. 168/A3
Sandusky, Ohio 166/A3
Sandy, Utah 174/B2
Sandy Hook (spit), N.J. 159/C2
San Fernando, Calif. 179/A1
San Fernando, Phil. 108/D5
San Fernando, Trin. & Tob. 55/T
Sanford, Fla. 140/B3
Sanford, Maine 151/A4
Sanford, N.C. 163/D2
San Francisco, Calif. 133/E1
San Francisco (bay), Calif. 133/E1
San Gabriel, Calif. 179/B2
San Gabriel (mts.), Calif. 179/A2
Sanibel (isl.), Fla. 141/E3
San Jacinto Mon., Texas 173/F4
San Joaquin (riv.), Calif. 133/D2
San Jorge (gulf), Arg. 58/C7
San Jose, Calif. 133/F2
San José (cap.), C. Rica 49/D3
San José, Guat. 48/B2
San Juan, Arg. 58/C6
San Juan (riv.), Cent. Amer. 48/C3
San Juan (cap.), P. Rico 51/G1, 54/C1
San Juan Capistrano, Calif. 133/F3
San Juan del Norte, Nic. 49/D3
San Juan del Sur, Nic. 48/C3
Sankt Gallen, Switz. 81/E1
Sankt Pölten, Austria 82/C2
San Leandro, Calif. 133/E1
San Lucas (cape), Mex. 46/B3
San Luis, Arg. 58/C6
San Luis Obispo, Calif. 133/E2
San Luis Potosí, Mex. 46/E3
San Marcos, Texas 173/D3
San Marino 78/D3
San Mateo, Calif. 133/F1
San Matias (gulf), Arg. 58/C7
San Miguel, El Sal. 48/C2
San Miguel de Tucumán, Arg. 58/C5
San Pedro, Calif. 179/C2
San Pedro de Macoris, Dom. Rep. 53/S7
San Pedro Sula, Hond. 48/B2
Sandpoint, Idaho 143/A1
San Rafael, Calif. 133/E1
San Remo, Italy 78/A3
San Salvador (isl.), Bah. 50/C1
San Salvador (cap.), El Sal. 48/B2
San Sebastián, Spain 77/E1
San Simeon, Calif. 133/D2
Santa Ana, Calif. 179/C3

Santa Ana, El Sal. 48/B2
Santa Barbara, Calif. 133/E2
Santa Catalina (isl.), Calif. 133/F3
Santa Clara, Calif. 133/F1
Santa Clara, Cuba 52/F3
Santa Cruz, Bol. 56/C4
Santa Cruz, Calif. 133/D1
Santa Cruz (isls.), Sol. Is. 116/G6
Santa Cruz de Tenerife, Spain 76/B4
Santa Fe, Arg. 58/C6
Santa Fe (cap.), N. Mex. 135/D3
Santa Inés (isl.), Chile 58/B8
Santa Maria, Braz. 59/D5
Santa Maria, Calif. 133/E3
Santa Marta, Col. 56/B1
Santa Monica, Calif. 179/B1
Santander, Spain 76/D1
Santanilla (isls.), Hond. 48/C1
Santa Rosa, Arg. 58/C6
Santa Rosa, Calif. 132/C1
Santee (riv.), S.C. 163/D3
Santiago (cap.), Chile 58/B6
Santiago, Dom. Rep. 50/D3, 52/R6
Santiago, Panama 49/D3
Santiago de Compostela, Spain 76/B1
Santiago de Cuba, Cuba 53/J5
Santiago del Estero, Arg. 58/C5
Säntis (mt.), Switz. 81/E1
Santo Domingo (cap.), Dom. Rep. 52/S7
Santos, Braz. 59/E5
São Francisco (riv.), Braz. 57/E4
São Luis, Braz. 57/E3
Saône (riv.), France 75/F4
São Paulo, Braz. 59/E5
São Roque (cape), Braz. 57/F3
São Tomé e Príncipe 62/C4
São Vincent (cape), Port. 76/B4
Sapporo, Japan 107/F2
Sapulpa, Okla. 168/B3
Saragossa, Spain 77/F2
Sarajevo, Yugo. 84/B3
Saranac Lake, N.Y. 161/E2
Saransk, U.S.S.R. 89/F4
Sarapul, U.S.S.R. 88/H3
Sarasota, Fla. 141/D2
Saratoga Sprs., N.Y. 161/E3
Saratov, U.S.S.R. 89/G4
Sarawak (state), Malaysia 112/E5
Sardinia (isl.), Italy 79/B4-5
Sardis (lake), Miss. 154/D1
Sargodha, Pak. 102/C1
Sari, Iran 101/H2
Sarnia, Ont. 186/A4
Sasebo, Japan 106/B3
Saskatchewan (riv.), Can. 188/B3
Saskatchewan (prov.), Can. 188-189
Saskatoon, Sask. 188/B3
Sassari, Italy 79/B4
Satu Mare, Rom. 84/C2
Saudi Arabia 94/E-F4-5
Sauk Center, Minn. 153/B3
Sault Ste. Marie, Mich. 152/B2
Sault Ste. Marie, Ont. 187/F1
Sausalito, Calif. 133/E1
Sava (riv.), Yugo. 84/A2
Savannah, Ga. 142/C3
Savannah (riv.), U.S. 126/K4
Savannakhet, Laos 110/D3
Save (riv.), Moz. 63/F7
Savu (sea), Indon. 113/G7
Sawtooth Nat'l Rec. Area, Idaho 143/B3
Sawu (isl.), Indon. 113/G7
Saxony (state), Ger. 71/E3
Sayre, Pa. 171/D2

Scapa Flow (chan.), Scot. 66/E1
Scarborough, Eng. 67/F3
Scarsdale, N.Y. 180/C1
Schaffhausen, Switz. 81/D1
Scheldt (riv.), Belg. 73/D5
Schenectady, N.Y. 161/E3
Scheveningen, Neth. 72/D3
Schleswig-Holstein (state), Ger. 70/C1
Schofield Barracks, Hawaii 129/A4
Schuylkill (riv.), Pa. 171/E3
Schwarzwald (Black) (for.), Ger. 71/C4
Schweinfurt, Ger. 71/D3
Schwerin, Ger. 70/D2
Schwyz, Switz. 81/D1
Scilly (isls.), Eng. 67/C6
Scioto (riv.), Ohio 167/E2
Scotia (sea), Antarc. 35/H8
Scotland, U.K. 66/D-E2-3
Scott (isl.), Antarc. 118
Scottsbluff, Nebr. 157/B1
Scotts Bluff Nat'l Mon., Nebr. 157/B1
Scottsboro, Ala. 128/C1
Scottsdale, Ariz. 130/A1
Scranton, Pa. 171/E3
Scunthorpe, Eng. 67/F4
Scutari (lake), Europe 84/B3
Scutari (Shkodër), Alb. 84-85/B3
Sea (isls.), U.S. 142/C4
Seaford, Del. 139/F3
Seal Beach, Calif. 179/C2
Searcy, Ark. 131/B3
Searsport, Maine 151/B3
Seaside, Oreg. 169/A1
Seattle, Wash. 175/B1
Sebago (lake), Maine 151/A4
Sebha, Libya 60/D2
Sebring, Fla. 141/D3
Sedalia, Mo. 155/B2
Ségou, Mali 60/B3
Segovia, Spain 76/D2
Seguin, Texas 173/D3
Seine (riv.), France 74/D3
Sekondi, Ghana 60/B4
Selkirk, Man. 189/F4
Selma, Ala. 128/C2
Semarang, Indon. 113/J2
Semeru (mt.), Malaysia 113/K2
Seminole, Okla. 168/B3
Semipalatinsk, U.S.S.R. 90/D3
Sendai, Japan 107/F3
Seneca (lake), N.Y. 160/C3
Senegal 60/A3
Senegal (riv.), Africa 60/A3
Sennar, Sudan 61/F3
Seoul (cap.), S. Korea 106/B3
Sepik (riv.), Papua N.G. 112/B6
Sept-Iles, Que. 43/K5
Sequoia Nat'l Pk., Calif. 133/D3
Seremban, Malaysia 111/C7
Serov, U.S.S.R. 90/D3
Serowe, Bots. 63/E7
Serpents Mouth (str.) 55/T
Serpukhov, U.S.S.R. 89/E4
Sétif, Alg. 60/C1
Setúbal, Port. 76/B3
Sevastopol', U.S.S.R. 89/D6
Severn (riv.), U.K. 67/E5
Severnaya Zemlya (isls.), U.S.S.R. 91/F1
Severodvinsk, U.S.S.R. 88/E2
Sevier (riv.), Utah 174/B3
Seville, Spain 76/C4
Seward, Alaska 129/B2
Seward (pen.), Alaska 129/A1
Seychelles 93/E6
Seyhan (riv.), Turkey 97/F4
Seymour, Ind. 145/B3

Sfax, Tun. 60/D1
'sGravenhage (The Hague) (cap.), Neth. 72/D3
Shaanxi (prov.), China 104/D2
Shaba, Zaire, see Katanga
Shahjahanpur, India 102/D2
Shaker Hts., Ohio 167/F4
Shakhty, U.S.S.R. 89/F5
Shamokin, Pa. 171/D3
Shan (plat.), Burma 110/B2
Shandong (Shantung) (prov.), China 105/E2
Shanghai, China 105/E3
Shannon (riv.), Ire. 67/B4
Shantou, China 105/E3
Shanxi (Shansi) (prov.), China 105/E2
Shari (riv.), Africa 61/D4
Sharon, Pa. 170/A3
Shasta (lake), Calif. 132/B1
Shawinigan, Que. 185/D3
Shawnee, Okla. 168/B3
Sheboygan, Wis. 176/C4
Sheffield, Eng. 67/F4
Shelby, Mont. 156/A2
Shelby, N.C. 162/C2
Shelbyville, Ind. 145/C3
Shelbyville, Tenn. 148/C4
Shellbrook, Sask. 188/B2
Shelton, Conn. 136/B3
Shenandoah, Pa. 171/E3
Shenandoah Nat'l Pk., Va. 139/D3
Shensi, China, see Shaanxi
Shenyang, China 105/F1
Sherbrooke, Que. 185/E4
Sheridan, Wyo. 177/A2
Sherman, Texas 173/E1
's Hertogenbosch, Neth. 72/F4
Sherwood Park, Alta. 191/F1
Shetland (isls.), Scot. 66/G1
Shevchenko, U.S.S.R. 90/C3
Sheyenne (riv.), N. Dak. 164/B3
Shijiazhuang, China 105/E2
Shikoku (isl.), Japan 106/D4
Shikotan (isl.), Japan 107/G3
Shiloh Nat'l Mem. Pk., Tenn. 148/B4
Shimizu, Japan 107/E4
Shimonoseki, Japan 106/C4
Shippegan, N. Br. 182/C1
Shiraz, Iran 101/H6
Shively, Ky. 149/E1
Shizuoka, Japan 107/E4
Shkodër, Alb. 84-85/B3
Sholapur, India 102/C3
Shorewood, Wis. 176/B1
Shoshone (riv.), Wyo. 177/A3
Shreveport, La. 150/A1
Shrewsbury, Eng. 67/E4
Shumen, Bulg. 84/D3
Shushtar, Iran 100/F4
Sialkot, Pak. 102/C1
Siam, see Thailand
Si'an, China, see Xi'an
Siauliai, U.S.S.R. 88/B3
Siberia (reg.), U.S.S.R. 90-91/D-H2
Siberut (isl.), Indon. 112/B6
Sibiu, Rom. 84/C2
Sibley Prov. Pk., Ont. 187/D1
Sibuyan (sea), Phil. 108/D3
Sichuan (prov.), China 104/D2
Sicily (isl.), Italy 79/D6
Sidi Bel Abbès, Alg. 60/B1
Sidon, Leb., see Saida
Sidra (gulf), Africa 61/D1
Siedlce, Pol. 87/F2
Siegen, Ger. 71/C3
Siena, Italy 80/C4
Sierra Leone 60/A4

Sierra Nevada (mts.), U.S. 44/C3
Sierra Vista, Ariz. 130/C4
Sikasso, Mali 60/B3
Sikeston, Mo. 155/C4
Si Kiang, China, see Xi Jiang
Silver Bay, Minn. 153/C2
Silver City, N. Mex. 135/D1
Silver Spring, Md. 139/D1
Silverton, Colo. 134/C2
Simcoe, Ont. 186/C4
Simcoe (lake), Ont. 186/C3
Simferopol', U.S.S.R. 89/D6
Simi Valley, Calif. 179/A1
Simla, India 102/C1
Simplon (tunnel), Europe 80/D2
Simpson (des.), Austr. 114/C3
Sinai (pen.), Egypt 94/C4
Singapore 111/E6
Singapore (cap.), Sing. 111/E6
Sinkiang, China, see Xinjiang Uygur Zizhiqu
Sint-Niklaas, Belg. 73/C5
Sinŭiju, N. Korea 106/B2
Sion, Switz. 80/C2
Sioux City, Iowa 146/A1
Sioux Falls, S. Dak. 165/E4
Siracusa (Syracuse), Italy 79/E6
Siret (riv.), Rom. 84/D2
Sitka, Alaska 129/C2
Sitka Nat'l Hist. Pk., Alaska 129/C2
Sittard, Neth. 73/G5
Sittwe, Burma 110/A2
Sivas, Turkey 97/G3
Siwa (oasis), Egypt 94/B4
Skagerrak (str.), Europe 69/E3
Skagit (riv.), Wash. 175/A3
Skeena (riv.), Br. Col. 190/A2
Skien, Nor. 69/B3
Skikda, Alg. 60/C1
Skokie, Ill. 178/B1
Skopje, Yugo. 85/C3
Skowhegan, Maine 151/A3
Skye (isl.), Scot. 66/C2
Slave Lake, Alta. 191/E2
Sleeping Bear Dunes Nat'l Lakeshore, Mich. 152/A3
Slidell, La. 150/A4
Sligo, Ire. 67/B3
Slupsk, Pol. 86/C1
Smithers, Br. Col. 190/A2
Smiths Falls, Ont. 187/E2
Smoky (riv.), Alta. 191/D2
Smoky Hill (riv.), Kans. 147/B2
Smolensk, U.S.S.R. 89/D4
Smyrna, Del. 139/F2
Smyrna, Ga. 142/B1
Smyrna, see Izmir
Snake (riv.), U.S. 44/D2
Snoqualmie (pass), Wash. 175/B3
Snowdon (mt.), Wales 67/E4
Sochi, U.S.S.R. 89/E6
Society (isls.), Fr. Poly. 117/L7
Socorro, N. Mex. 135/E2
Socotra (isl.), Yemen 95/G7
Södertälje, Swed. 69/D3
Sofia (cap.), Bulg. 84/C3
Sognafjord (fjord), Nor. 69/A2
Sohâg, Egypt 94/C4
Sokoto, Nigeria 60/C3
Solomon Islands 116/G6
Solothurn, Switz. 80/C1
Solway (firth), U.K. 67/E3
Somalia 61/E4
Somerset (isl.), Berm. 51/G3
Somerset, Ky. 149/D3
Somerset (isl.), N.W.T. 42/G1
Somerville, Mass. 137/F4
Somme (riv.), France 74/D2
Songhua Jiang (riv.), China 105/F1

Songkhla, Thai. 111/C6
Sonora, Texas 172/C5
Soochow, China, see Suzhou
Sorel, Que. 43/K7
Sorocaba, Braz. 59/E5
Sorrento, Italy 79/E4
Sosnowiec, Pol. 86/B4
Soufrière (vol.), Guad. 55/H5
Souris, Man. 189/D4
Souris (riv.), N. Amer. 164/B2, 189/D4
Souris, P.E.I. 183/E2
Sousse, Tun. 60/D1
South (isl.), N.Z. 115/F4
South Africa 63/E7-8
South America 56-59
Southampton, Eng. 67/F5
Southampton, N.Y. 160/C4
South Atlantic Ocean 35/J7
South Australia (state), Austr. 114/C3
S. Baymouth, Ont. 186/B2
S. Bend, Ind. 145/B1
South Carolina (state), U.S. 162-163
South China (sea), Asia 93/H5
South Dakota (state), U.S. 165
S. Elgin, Ill. 178/A2
Southend-on-Sea, Eng. 67/G5
Southern Alps (mts.), N.Z. 115/F4
Southern Pines, N.C. 163/D2
S. Euclid, Ohio 167/F4
Southfield, Mich. 178/A5
S. Gate, Calif. 179/B2
South Georgia (isl.), Antarc. 35/H8
South Korea 106/C3
S. Lake Tahoe, Calif. 132/C2
South Orkney (isls.), Antarc. 118
South Platte (riv.), U.S. 157/C1
South Pole 118
Southport, Eng. 66/F1
S. Portland, Maine 151/A4
S. San Francisco, Calif. 133/E1
South Sandwich (isl.), Antarc. 35/J8
South Saskatchewan (riv.), Can. 188/B3
South Shetland (isls.), Antarc. 118
S. Shields, Eng. 66/F3
S. Sioux City, Nebr. 157/A4
S. St. Paul, Minn. 153/C1
South-West Africa, see Namibia
Spa, Belg. 73/G7
Spain 76-77
Spandau, Ger. 70/E2
Spanish Fork, Utah 174/B3
Spanish Town, Jam. 53/V10
Sparks, Nev. 132/B2
Sparrows Point, Md. 139/F2
Sparta, Greece 85/C4
Spartanburg, S.C. 162/B2
Spassk-Dal'niy, U.S.S.R. 91/G3
Spearfish, S. Dak. 165/E1
Spencer (gulf), Austr. 114/C4
Spey (riv.), Scot. 66/E2
Spirit Lake, Iowa 146/A2
Spirit River, Alta. 190/C1
Spitsbergen (isl.), Nor. 68/A1
Split, Yugo. 84/B3
Spokane, Wash. 175/B4
Spratly (isl.) 112/E4
Spree (riv.), Ger. 70/F3
Springdale, Ark. 131/A1
Springfield (cap.), Ill. 144/B3
Springfield, Mass. 136/B2
Springfield, Mo. 155/C2
Springfield, Ohio 166/C1
Springfield, Oreg. 169/B2
Springfield, Tenn. 148/C3

Index

Springfield, Vt. 158/B3
Spring Hill, Fla. 140/C2
Springhill, N.S. 183/D3
Springville, Utah 174/B3
Spruce Grove, Alta. 191/E1
Spruce Knob Nat'l Rec. Area, W.
  Va. 138/C3
Squamish, Brit. Col. 190/B4
Squaw (valley), Calif. 132/C2
Sri Lanka 102/F7
Srinagar, India 102/C1
Stafford, Eng. 67/E4
Stalingrad, U.S.S.R., see
  Volgograd
Stamford, Conn. 136/A4
Stanley (cap.), Falkland Is. 59/D8
Stanley (Boyoma) (falls), Zaire
  63/E5
Stanovoy (range), U.S.S.R. 91/G3
Stara Zagora, Bulg. 84/D3
Starkville, Miss. 154/C2
State College, Pa. 170/C3
Staten (isl.), Arg., see Estados
Staten Island (borough), N.Y.
  180/A3
Statesboro, Ga. 142/C3
Statesville, N.C. 162/C2
Statue of Liberty Nat'l Mon., U.S.
  180/B2
Staunton, Va. 139/D3
Stavanger, Nor. 69/A3
Stavropol', U.S.S.R. 89/F5
Steamboat Springs, Colo. 134/A2
Stepanakert, U.S.S.R. 89/G7
Stephenville, Newf. 183/E1
Stephenville, Texas 173/D2
Sterling, Colo. 134/A4
Sterling, Ill. 144/B1
Sterling Hts., Mich. 178/C3
Sterlitamak, U.S.S.R. 89/J4
Stettin, Pol., see Szczecin
Stettler, Alta. 191/E3
Steubenville, Ohio 166/C4
Stevens Point, Wis. 176/B3
Stewart (isl.), N.Z. 115/F4
Steyr, Austria 82/C1
Stillwater, Okla. 168/A3
Stirling, Scot. 66/B1
Stockholm (cap.), Swed. 69/D3
Stockport, Eng. 66/G2
Stockton, Calif. 132/C2
Stockton (plat.), Texas 172/C2
Stockton-on-Tees, Eng. 67/F3
Stoke-on-Trent, Eng. 67/E4
Stones River Nat'l Battlfld., Tenn.
  148/C4
Stornoway, Scot. 66/C1
Storrs, Conn. 136/C2
Stoughton, Mass. 137/E2
Stowe, Vt. 158/A2
Strabane, N. Ire. 67/C3
Strasbourg, France 74/G3
Stratford, Conn. 136/B3
Stratford, Ont. 186/B3
Stromboli (isl.), Italy 79/E5
Strongsville, Ohio 167/F3
Stroudsburg, Pa. 171/E4
Stuart, Fla. 141/D4
Sturbridge, Mass. 136/C2
Sturgeon Bay, Wis. 176/C3
Sturgeon Falls, Ont. 186/C1
Sturgis, S. Dak. 165/E1
Stuttgart, Ark. 131/D3
Stuttgart, Ger. 71/C4
Subic (bay), Phil. 108/B3
Subotica, Yugo. 84/B2
Sucre (cap.), Bol. 56/C4
Sudan 61/E-F5
Sudan (reg.), Africa 60-61/B-F3
Sudbury, Ont. 186/B1
Sudd (swamp), Sudan 61/F4

Sudeten (mts.), Europe 82/C1
Suez, Egypt 94/H4
Suez (canal), Egypt 94/C3
Suez (gulf), Egypt 94/C4
Suffolk, Va. 139/E4
Suir (riv.), Ire. 67/C4
Suita, Japan 107/E4
Sukabumi, Indon. 113/H2
Sukhumi, U.S.S.R. 89/F6
Sukkur, Pak. 102/B2
Sula (isls.), Indon. 113/H6
Sulaimaniya, Iraq 100/D3
Sulawesi (Celebes) (isl.), Indon.
  113/G6
Sulphur, La. 150/C1
Sulu (sea), Asia 113/G4
Sulu (arch.), Phil. 113/G4
Sumatra (isl.), Indon. 112/B-C5-6
Sumba (isl.), Indon. 113/F7
Sumbawa (isl.), Indon.
  112-113/F7
Sumter, S.C. 162/C3
Sumy, U.S.S.R. 89/D4
Sunbury, Pa. 171/D3
Sun City, Ariz. 130/B3
Sunda (str.), Indon. 112/C7
Sunderland, Eng. 66/F3
Sundsvall, Swed. 69/C2
Sungari, China, see Songhua
  Jiang
Sunnyvale, Calif. 133/F1
Sunrise, Fla. 141/D1
Sunset Crater Nat'l Mon., Ariz.
  130/B3
Sun Valley, Idaho 143/B3
Suo (sea), Japan 106/C4
Superior (lake), N. Amer. 40/K5
Superior, Wis. 176/A2
Sur, Leb. 96/F6
Surabaya, Indon. 113/K2
Surakarta, Indon. 113/J2
Surat, India 102/C2
Surgut, U.S.S.R. 90/D2
Surigao (str.), Phil. 109/E6
Suriname 57/D2
Surrey, Br. Col. 190/B1
Susquehanna (riv.), U.S. 171/D4
Sutlej (riv.), Asia 102/C1
Suva (cap.), Fiji 116/H7
Suwalki, Pol. 87/F1
Suwannee (riv.), U.S. 140/B2
Suzhou, China 105/F3
Svalbard (isls.), Nor. 68/A1
Sverdlovsk, U.S.S.R. 90/D3
Sverdrup (isls.), N.W.T. 40/H2
Svobodnyy, U.S.S.R. 91/G3
Swakopmund, Namibia 62/D7
Swan (Santanilla) (isls.), Hond.
  48/C1
Swan River, Man. 189/D3
Swansea, Wales 67/D5
Swarthmore, Pa. 171/D2
Swatow, China, see Shantou
Swaziland 63/F7
Sweden 68-69
Sweetwater, Texas 172/C2
Sweetwater (riv.), Wyo. 177/B3
Swift Current, Sask. 188/B4
Swilly, Lough (inlet), Ire. 66/C3
Swindon, Eng. 67/F5
Switzerland 80-81
Sydney, Austr. 115/E4
Sydney, N.S. 183/F2
Syktyvkar, U.S.S.R. 88/H2
Sylacauga, Ala. 128/B2
Sylt (isl.), Ger. 70/C1
Syracuse, Italy 79/E6
Syracuse, N.Y. 161/D3
Syrdar'ya (riv.), U.S.S.R. 90/D3
Syria 97/G-H5
Syrian (des.), Asia 100/B4

Syzran', U.S.S.R. 89/G4
Szczecin, Pol. 86/B2
Szechwan, China, see Sichuan
Szeged, Hung. 83/E3
Székesfehérvár, Hung. 83/D3
Szolnok, Hung. 83/E3
Szombathely, Hung. 82/D3

T

Taber, Alta. 191/F4
Table Rock (lake), Mo. 155/C2
Tabora, Tanz. 63/F5
Tabriz, Iran 100/D2
Tabuaeran (isl.), Kiribati 117/L5
Tacloban, Phil. 109/E5
Tacna, Peru 56/B4
Tacoma, Wash. 175/C1
Tadmor, Syria 97/H5
Tadzhik S.S.R., U.S.S.R. 90/D4
Taebaek (mt.), S. Korea 106/D3
Taedong (riv.), N. Korea 106/B3
Taegu, S. Korea 106/C4
Taejŏn, S. Korea 106/B3
Taganrog, U.S.S.R. 89/E5
Tagus (Tajos) (riv.), Europe 76/B3
Tahiti (isl.), Fr. Poly. 117/L7
Tahoe (lake), U.S. 132/C2
Tahoua, Niger 60/C3
Taichung, China 105/F3
Taif, S. Arabia 94/E5
Tainan, China 105/E2
Taipei (cap.), Taiwan (Rep. of
  China) 105/F3
Taitao (pen.), Chile 58/B7
Taiwan (isl.), China 105/F3
Taiwan (str.), China 105/E3
Taiyuan, China 105/E2
Ta'izz, Yemen 94/E7
Takamatsu, Japan 106/D4
Takaoka, Japan 106/E3
Takasaki, Japan 107/E3
Takatsuki, Japan 107/E4
Takoma Park, Md. 139/D1
Takoradi, Ghana 60/B4
Talca, Chile 58/B6
Talcahuano, Chile 58/B6
Taldy-Kurgan, U.S.S.R. 90/D3
Talladega, Ala. 128/C2
Tallahassee (cap.), Fla. 140/A1
Tallinn, U.S.S.R. 88/C3
Tamali, Ghana 60/B4
Tamanrasset, Alg. 60/C2
Tamaqua, Pa. 171/E3
Tamatave, Madag., see
  Toamasina
Tambov, U.S.S.R. 89/F4
Tampa, Fla. 140/C3
Tampa (bay), Fla. 140/C1
Tampere, Fin. 69/D2
Tampico, Mex. 47/F3
Tamworth, Austr. 115/E4
Tana (lake), Eth. 61/F3
Tana (riv.), Kenya 63/G5
Tandil, Arg. 58/D6
Tanega (isl.), Japan 107/H2
Tanezrouft (des.), Africa 60/C2
Tanga, Tanz. 63/F5
Tanganyika (lake), Africa 63/F5
Tangier, Mor. 60/B1
Tangshan, China 105/E2
Tanimbar (isls.), Indon. 113/J7
Tanjungkarang, Indon. 112/D7
Tanta, Egypt 94/C3
Tanzania 63/F5
Taos, N. Mex. 134/C3
Tapachula, Mex. 47/G5
Tapajós (riv.), Braz. 57/D3
Tar (riv.), N.C. 163/D1
Tarabulus, Leb. 97/F5
Tarakan, Indon. 113/F5

Taranto, Italy 79/F4
Tarawa (atoll), Kiribati 116/H5
Tarhuna, Libya 60/D1
Tarija, Bol. 58/C5
Tarim He (riv.), China 104/B1
Tarnów, Pol. 83/E4
Tarpon Sprs., Fla. 140/C2
Tarragona, Spain 77/G2
Tarrasa, Spain 77/G2
Tarsus, Turkey 96/F4
Tartu, U.S.S.R. 88/C3
Tartus, Syria 97/F5
Tashkent, U.S.S.R. 90/D3
Tasman (sea), Pacific 116/F9
Tasmania (state), Austr. 115/D5
Tata, Hung. 83/E3
Tatar (str.), U.S.S.R. 91/H3
Tatra, High (mts.), Europe 83/E2
Taunton, Eng. 67/E5
Taunton, Mass. 137/E3
Taunus (range), Ger. 71/C3
Taurus (mts.), Turkey 96/DE4
Tavoy, Burma 111/B4
Tawi Tawi (isl.), Phil. 109/C8
Tay (firth), Scot. 66/E2
Taylor, Mich. 157/B3
Taymyr (pen.), U.S.S.R. 91/E2
Tbilisi, U.S.S.R. 89/F6
Teaneck, N.J. 180/B1
Tegal, Indon. 113/H2
Tegucigalpa (cap.), Hond. 48/C2
Tehran (cap.), Iran 101/G3
Tehuantepec, Mex. 47/F5
Tejo (Tagus) (riv.), Port. 76/B3
Tel Aviv-Jaffa, Isr. 99/B3
Tela, Hond. 48/C2
Tema, Ghana 60/C4
Temirtau, U.S.S.R. 90/D3
Tempe, Ariz. 130/A1
Temple, Texas 173/E2
Temuco, Chile 58/B6
Tenerife (isl.), Spain 76/B4
Tennessee (state), U.S. 148-149
Tennessee (riv.), U.S. 45/J3
Ten Thousand (isls.), Fla. 141/E3
Tepic, Mexico 46/D4
Teresina, Braz. 57/F3
Ternate, Indon. 113/H5
Terni, Italy 78/D3
Ternopol, U.S.S.R. 89/C5
Terrace, Br. Col. 190/A2
Terra Nova Nat'l Pk., Newf. 183/F1
Terrebonne (bay), La. 150/C3
Terre Haute, Ind. 145/A3
Tete, Moz. 63/F6
Tétouan, Mor. 60/B1
Tetovo, Yugo. 84/C3
Texarkana, Ark. 131/C1
Texarkana, Texas 173/F1
Texas (state), U.S. 172-173
Texas City, Texas 173/F3
Texel (isl.), Neth. 72/E1
Texoma (lake), U.S. 168/C3, 173/E1
Thailand 110/C2
Thames (riv.), Eng. 67/G5
Thames (riv.), Ont. 186/B4
Thanjavur, India 102/C3
Thásos (isl.), Greece 85/D3
The Dalles, Oreg. 169/A3
Thedford, Nebr. 157/B2
The Hague (cap.), Neth. 72/D3
Theodore Roosevelt (lake), Ariz. 130/B3
Theodore Roosevelt Nat'l Pk., N. Dak. 164/BC1
The Pas, Man. 189/D2
Thermopolis, Wyo. 177/B3
Thessaloníki, Greece 85/C4
Thetford Mines, Que. 185/F4

Thibodaux, La. 150/C3
Thiès, Sen. 60/A3
Thika, Kenya 63/F5
Thimphu (cap.), Bhutan 103/E2
Thionville, France 74/G3
Thira (isl.), Greece 85/D4
Thívai (Thebes), Greece 85/C4
Thomasville, Ga. 142/A4
Thomasville, N.C. 162/C2
Thompson (riv.), Br. Col. 190/C3
Thompson, Man. 189/E3
Thompsonville, Conn. 136/C2
Thon Buri, Thai. 111/C4
Thornton, Colo. 178/A4
Thorold, Ont. 187/F4
Thule Air Base, Greenl. 40/L2
Thun, Switz. 80/C2
Thunder Bay, Ont. 187/D1
Thuringia (state), Ger. 70/D3
Thurrock, Eng. 67/C5
Thurso, Scot. 66/E1
Tian (Tien) Shan (mts.), China 104/B1
Tianjin, China 105/E2
Tiber (riv.), Italy 78/D3
Tiberias, Isr. 98/C2
Tibesti (mts.), Chad 60/D2
Tibet (reg.), China 104/B2
Ticonderoga, N.Y. 161/F2
Tientsin, China, see Tianjin
Tierra del Fuego (isl.), S. Amer. 58/C8
Tiête (riv.), Braz. 59/E5
Tiffin, Ohio 166/B2
Tifton, Ga. 142/B4
Tigris (riv.), Asia 94/E2
Tihama (reg.), Asia 94/D-E5-6
Tijuana, Mex. 46/A1
Tilburg, Neth. 73/F5
Tilbury, Ont. 186/A4
Timaru, N.Z. 115/F4
Timbuktu, Mali 60/B3
Timişoara, Rom. 84/C2
Timmins, Ont. 187/F1
Timor (isl.), Indon. 113/H7
Tinian (isl.), N. Marianas 116/E4
Tinley Park, Ill. 178/B3
Tippecanoe (riv.), Ind. 145/B2
Tipperary, Ire. 67/B4
Tiranë (Tirana) (cap.), Albania 85/B3
Tîrgovişte, Rom. 84/D2
Tîrgu Mureş, Rom. 84/D2
Tiruchirappalli, India 102/C3
Tirunelveli, India 102/C4
Tisza (riv.), Hung. 83/F3
Titicaca (lake), S. Amer. 56/C4
Titograd, Yugo. 84/B3
Titusville, Fla. 140/C4
Titusville, Pa. 170/B2
Tiverton, R.I. 137/D3
Tivoli, Italy 78/D4
Tlemcen, Alg. 60/B1
Toamasina, Madag. 63/G6
Tobago (isl.), Trin. & Tob. 51/G5, 55/U
Tobermory, Ont. 186/B2
Tobol (riv.), U.S.S.R. 90/D3
Tobol'sk, U.S.S.R. 90/D3
Tobruk, Libya 61/E1
Tocantins (riv.), Braz. 57/E3
Togliatti, U.S.S.R. 90/F5
Togo 60/C4
Toiyabe (range), Nev. 132/B-C3
Tokelau 116/J6
Tokushima, Japan 106/D4
Tokyo (cap.), Japan 107/E4
Toledo, Ohio 166/A2
Toledo, Spain 76/D3

Toledo Bend (res.), U.S. 150/A1
Toliara, Madag. 63/G7
Tolima (mt.), Col. 56/B2
Toluca, Mex. 46/E4
Tomakomai, Japan 107/F2
Tombigbee (riv.), U.S. 154/C2
Tombouctou, Mali, see Timbuktu
Tombstone, Ariz. 130/C4
Toms River, N.J. 159/C3
Tomsk, U.S.S.R. 90/E3
Tonawanda, N.Y. 160/B3
Tonga 117/J8
Tongareva (atoll), Cook Is. 117/L6
Tongatapu (isl.), Tonga 117/J8
Tongue (riv.), U.S. 156/C4
Tonkin (gulf), Asia 110/D3
Tonle Sap (lake), Camb. 111/C4
Tooele, Utah 174/B2
Toowoomba, Austr. 115/E3
Topeka (cap.), Kans. 147/B4
Torbay, Eng. 67/E5
Torino, Italy, see Turin
Tornio (riv.), Europe 68/D1
Toronto (cap.), Ont. 187/F3
Torquay, Eng., see Torbay
Torrance, Calif. 133/F3
Torrens (lake), Austr. 114/C4
Torreón, Mex. 46/D3
Torres (str.) 116/E7
Torrington, Conn. 136/B2
Tortola (isl.), V.I. (Br.) 54/F
Tortuė (Portuga) (isl.), Haiti 52/P6
Toruń, Pol. 86/D2
Totowa, N.J. 180/A1
Tottori, Japan 106/D3
Touggourt, Alg. 60/C1
Toulon, France 75/F6
Toulouse, France 75/D6
Tourcoing, France 74/E2
Tournai, Belg. 73/B6
Tours, France 74/D4
Townsville, Austr. 115/D2
Towson, Md. 139/F1
Toyama, Japan 106/E3
Toyohashi, Japan 106/E4
Toyonaka, Japan 107/E4
Trabzon, Turkey 97/H2
Tracy, Que. 185/D4
Trafalgar (cape), Spain 76/C4
Trail, Br. Col. 191/D4
Tralee, Ire. 67/B4
Transkei (aut. rep.), S. Africa 63/E8
Transvaal (prov.), S. Africa 63/E7
Transylvanian Alps (mts.), Rom. 84/D2
Traverse City, Mich. 152/B3
Treasure Island, Fla. 140/C4
Trent (riv.), Eng. 67/F4
Trentino-Adige (reg.), Italy 78/C1
Trento, Italy 78/C1
Trenton (cap.), N.J. 159/B2
Trenton, Ont. 187/D3
Trier, Ger. 71/B4
Trieste, Italy 78/E2
Trincomalee, Sri Lanka 102/D4
Trinidad, Bol. 56/C4
Trinidad, Colo. 134/C3
Trinidad (isl.), Trin. & Tob. 51/G5, 55/T
Trinidad and Tobago 51/G5
Trinity (riv.), Calif. 132/B1
Trinity (riv.), Texas 173/E2
Tripoli (Tarabulus), Leb. 97/F5
Tripoli (cap.), Libya 60/D1
Tripolitania (reg.), Libya 60/B1-2
Tristan da Cunha (isl.), St. Helena 35/J7
Trivandrum, India 102/C4
Trobriand (isls.), Papua N.G. 112/C7

Index

Trois Rivières, Que. 185/D4
Tromso, Nor. 68/D1
Trondheim, Nor. 68/B2
Troy, Ala. 128/C3
Troy, N.Y. 161/F3
Troyes, France 74/F3
Trujillo, Peru 56/B3
Trujillo, Spain 76/D3
Truk (isls.), Micronesia 116/F5
Truro, N.S. 183/D3
Tselinograd, U.S.S.R. 90/D3
Tsinan, China, see Jinan
Tsinghai, China, see Qinghai
Tsingtao, China, see Qingdao
Tsu (isls.), Japan 106/C4
Tsugaru (str.), Japan 107/E2
Tsumeb, Namibia 63/D6
Tuamotu (arch.), Fr. Poly. 117/M7
Tübingen, Ger. 71/C4
Tubuai (isls.), see Austral (isls.)
Tucson, Ariz. 130/C4
Tucumán, San Miguel de, Arg. 58/C3
Tucumcari, N. Mex. 135/D3
Tula, U.S.S.R. 89/E4
Tulare, Calif. 133/D2
Tulkarm, West Bank 98/C3
Tullahoma, Tenn. 148/C4
Tullamore, Ire. 67/C4
Tulsa, Okla. 168/A4
Tumacacori Nat'l Mon., Ariz. 130/B4
Tumen (riv.), Asia 106/C2
Tunis (cap.), Tun. 60/D1
Tunisia 60/C1
Tupelo, Miss. 154/C1
Tupelo Nat'l Battlfld., Miss. 154/C1
Turin, Italy 78/A2
Turkana (lake), Africa 61/F4
Turkey 96-97
Turkmen S.S.R., U.S.S.R. 90/C4
Turks & Caicos Is. 50-51/D-E2
Turku, Fin. 69/D2
Turlock, Calif. 132/C2
Turneffe (isls.), Belize 48/C1
Turnhout, Belg. 73/E5
Tuscaloosa, Ala. 128/C2
Tuscany (reg.), Italy 78/A3
Tuskegee, Ala. 128/C3
Tuticorin, India 102/C4
Tutuila (isl.), Amer. Samoa 117/J7
Tuvalu 116/H6
Tuz (lake), Turkey 96/E3
Tuzigoot Nat'l Mon., Ariz. 130/B3
Tver, see Kalinin
Twin Falls, Idaho 143/B4
Two Harbors, Minn. 153/C3
Two Rivers, Wis. 176/C3
Tychy, Poland 86/B4
Tyler, Texas 173/F2
Tyre (Sur), Leb. 96/F6
Tyrone, Pa. 170/C3
Tyrrhenian (sea), Italy 79/C-D4-5
Tyumen, U.S.S.R. 90/D3

U

Ubangi (riv.), Africa 63/D4
Ube, Japan 106/C4
Uberaba, Braz. 57/E4
Uberlândia, Braz. 57/E4
Ucayali (riv.), Peru 56/B3
Uchiura (bay), Japan 107/F2
Udaipur, India 102/C2
Udine, Italy 78/D1
Udon Thani, Thai. 110/C3
Uele (riv.), Zaire 61/E4
Ufa, U.S.S.R. 89/J4
Uganda 61/F4
Uinta (mts.), Utah 174/C2

Uist, North and South (isls.), Scot. 66/C2
Uitenhage, S. Africa 63/E8
Ujiji, Tanz. 63/F5
Ujjain, India 102/C2
Ujpest, Hung. 83/E3
Ujung Pandang, Indon. 113/F7
Ukhta, U.S.S.R. 90/C2
Ukrainian S.S.R., U.S.S.R. 89/C5
Ulaanbaatar (cap.), Mong. 104/D1
Ulan-Ude, U.S.S.R. 91/F3
Ulithi (isl.), Micronesia 116/D4
Ullŭng (isl.), S. Korea 106/C3
Ulm, Ger. 71/C4
Ulsan, S. Korea 106/C4
Ul'yanovsk, U.S.S.R. 89/G4
Umbria (reg.), Italy 78/D3
Umeå, Swed. 68/D2
Umpqua (riv.), Oreg. 169/B2
Umtata, S. Africa 63/E8
Ungava (bay), Que. 43/K4
Union, N.J. 180/A2
Union City, Calif. 133/F1
Union City, N.J. 180/B2
Union City, Tenn. 148/B3
Union of Soviet Socialist Republics 88-91
Uniontown, Pa. 170/A4
United Arab Emirates 95/G5
United Kingdom 66-67
United States of America 44-45, 126-127
University City, Mo. 155/A4
University Park, Texas 172/A4
Upland, Calif. 179/A3
Upper Darby, Pa. 171/E1
Upper Klamath (lake), Oreg. 169/C2
Upper Red (lake), Minn. 153/B2
Upper Volta, see Burkina Faso
Uppsala, Swed. 69/C3
Urabá (gulf), Col. 56/B2
Ural (mts.), U.S.S.R. 90/C3
Ural (riv.), U.S.S.R. 90/C3
Uralsk, U.S.S.R. 90/C3
Urawa, Japan 107/H2
Urbana, Ill. 144/C2
Urbandale, Iowa 146/B2
Urfa, Turkey 97/H4
Urgench, U.S.S.R. 90/D3
Urmia, Iran 100/D2
Urmia (lake), Iran 100/D2
Uruapan, Mex. 46/E4
Uruguay 59/D5
Uruguay (riv.), S. Amer. 59/D5
Ürümqi (Urumchi), China 104/B1
Ushuaia, Arg. 58/C9
Usk (riv.), Wales 67/D5
Üsküdar, Turkey 96/D6
Usol'ye-Sibirskoye, U.S.S.R. 91/F3
Ussuri Wusuli (riv.), Asia 105/G1
Ussuriysk, U.S.S.R. 91/G3
Usti nad Labem, Czech. 82/C1
Ust-Kamenogorsk, U.S.S.R. 90/D3
Utah (state), U.S. 174
Utah (lake), Utah 174/B3
Utica, N.Y. 161/E3
Utrecht, Neth. 72/F3
Utsunomiya, Japan 107/F3
Uvalde, Texas 173/D3
Uxmal (ruins), Mex. 47/H4
Uzbek S.S.R., U.S.S.R. 90/D3

V

Vaal (riv.), S. Africa 63/E7
Vaasa, Fin. 68/D2
Vacaville, Calif. 132/C1
Vadodara, India, see Baroda

Vaduz (cap.), Liechtenstein 81/E1
Vail, Colo. 134/B2
Valais (canton), Switz. 80/C2
Valdés (pen.), Arg. 58/C7
Valdez, Alaska 129/B2
Valdivia, Chile 58/B6
Val-d'Or, Que. 184/B2
Valdosta, Ga. 142/B4
Valence, France 75/F5
Valencia, Spain 77/F3
Valencia, Ven. 56/C2
Valenciennes, France 74/E2
Valentine, Nebr. 157/A2
Valera, Ven. 56/B2
Valladolid, Spain 76/D2
Valledupar, Col. 56/B1
Vallejo, Calif. 133/D1
Valletta (cap.), Malta 79/E7
Valley City, N. Dak. 164/C4
Valley Stream, N.Y. 180/C2
Valleyview, Alta. 191/D2
Valparaiso, Chile 58/B6
Valparaiso, Ind. 145/A1
Van, Turkey 97/K3
Van (lake), Turkey 97/K3
Van Buren, Ark. 131/B1
Vancouver, Br. Col. 190/A1
Vancouver (isl.), Br. Col. 42/D6
Vancouver, Wash. 175/C2
Vandalia, Ill. 144/B3
Vanderhoof, Br. Col. 190/B2
Vänern (lake), Swed. 68/C3
Vanier, Ont. 186/A1
Vanua Levu (isl.), Fiji 116/J7
Vanuatu 116/G2
Varanasi, India 102/D2
Varangerfjord (fjord), Nor. 68/F1
Vardar (riv.), Europe 85/C3
Varna, Bulg. 84/E3
Vashon (isl.), Wash. 175/C1
Västeras, Swed. 69/C3
Vatican City 78/D4
Vättern (lake), Swed. 69/C3
Vaupés (riv.), S. Am. 56/B2
Vegreville, Alta. 191/F2
Velikiye Luki, U.S.S.R. 88/D3
Vellore, India 102/C3
Venda (aut. rep.), S. Africa 63/E7
Veneto (reg.), Italy 78/C2
Venezuela 56/C2
Venezuela (gulf), Ven. 56/B1
Venice, Fla. 141/D3
Venice (Venezia), Italy 78/D2
Ventura, Calif. 133/E3
Veracruz, Mex. 47/F4
Verde (cape.), Sen. 60/A3
Verdun, France 74/F3
Vereeniging, S. Africa 63/E7
Verkhoyansk (range), U.S.S.R. 91/G2
Vermillion, S. Dak. 165/F4
Vermont (state), U.S. 158
Vernal, Utah 174/C2
Vernon, Br. Col. 190/C4
Vero Beach, Fla. 141/C4
Verona, Italy 78/C2
Versailles, France 74/A2
Vestfjord (fjord), Nor. 68/C1
Vesuvius (vol.), Italy 79/E4
Veszprém, Hung. 83/E3
Vevey, Switz. 80/B2
Vicenza, Italy 78/C2
Vichy, France 75/E4
Vicksburg, Miss. 154/A3
Victoria (falls), Africa 63/E6
Victoria (lake), Africa 63/F5
Victoria (state), Austr. 115/D4
Victoria (cap.), Br. Col. 190/B4
Victoria (cap.), Hong Kong 105/E3
Victoria (isl.), N.W.T. 42/E1

Victoria, Texas 173/E3
Victoria Beach, Man. 189/F3
Victoriaville, Que. 185/E4
Vidalia, Ga. 142/B3
Viedma, Arg. 58/C7
Vienna (Wien) (cap.), Austria 82/D2
Vientiane (cap.), Laos 110/C3
Vieques (isl.), P. Rico 54/E1
Vietnam 110/D3
Vigo, Spain 76/B1
Vijayawada, India 102/C3
Vila (cap.), Vanuatu 116/G7
Villach, Austria 82/B3
Villahermosa, Mex. 47/G5
Villa Park, Ill. 178/A2
Villavicencio, Col. 56/B2
Vilnius (Vilna), U.S.S.R. 89/C4
Viña del Mar, Chile 58/B6
Vinalhaven (isl.), Maine 151/B4
Vincennes, Ind. 145/A4
Vindhya (range), India 102/C2
Vineland, N.J. 159/B4
Vinita, Okla 168/A4
Vinnitsa, U.S.S.R. 89/C5
Vinson Massif (mt.), Antarc. 118
Virden, Man. 189/D4
Virginia (state), U.S. 138-139
Virginia, Minn. 153/C2
Virginia Beach, Va. 138/B1
Virginia City, Mont. 156/D1
Virginia City, Nev. 132/B2
Virgin Is. (Br.) 51/H1, 54/F
Virgin Is. (U.S.) 51/H1, 54/F, G
Virgin Is. Nat'l Pk., V.I. (U.S.) 54/F
Visakhapatnam, India 102/D3
Visalia, Calif. 133/D2
Visayan (sea), Phil. 109/D5
Vista, Calif. 133/F3
Vistula (riv.), Pol. 87/D2
Vitebsk, U.S.S.R. 88/D3
Viti Levu (isl.), Fiji 116/H7
Vitoria, Braz. 59/F5
Vitoria, Spain 77/E1
Vladimir, U.S.S.R. 88/F3
Vladivostok, U.S.S.R. 91/G3
Vlorë, Alb. 85/B3
Vltava (Moldau) (riv.), Czech. 82/C2
Vohimena (cape), Madag. 63/G7
Volcano (isls.), Japan 107/G3
Volga (riv.), U.S.S.R. 89/G5
Volgograd, U.S.S.R. 89/F5
Vologda, U.S.S.R. 88/E3
Vólos, Greece 85/C4
Volta (lake), Ghana 60/B4
Volta (riv.), Ghana 60/B4
Volta Redonda, Braz. 59/E5
Volturno (riv.), Italy 79/E4
Vorkuta, U.S.S.R. 88/K1
Voronezh, U.S.S.R. 89/E4
Voroshilovgrad, U.S.S.R. 89/E5
Vosges (mts.), France 74/G3
Voyageurs Nat'l Pk., Minn. 153/C2

W

Wabash, Ind. 145/B2
Wabash (riv.), U.S. 144/C3, 145/A3
Waco, Texas 173/E2
Waddenzee (sound), Neth. 72/F1
Wad Medani, Sudan 61/F3
Wahiawa, Hawaii 129/A4
Wahpeton, N. Dak. 164/C4
Wailuku, Hawaii 129/C3
Wainwright, Alta. 191/F2
Waipahu, Hawaii 129/A4
Wakayama, Japan 106/D4

Wake (isl.), Pacific 116/G4
Wakefield, Eng. 67/F4
Wake Forest, N.C. 163/D1
Walbrzych, Pol. 86/C3
Walcheren (isl.), Neth. 73/B5
Wales, U.K. 67/E5
Wall, S. Dak. 165/E1
Wallaceburg, Ont. 186/A4
Wallasey, Eng. 66/F2
Walla Walla, Wash. 175/C4
Wallingford, Conn. 136/B3
Wallis & Futuna 117/J7
Walnut Canyon Nat'l Mon., Ariz. 130/B3
Walnut Creek, Calif. 133/E1
Walsall, Eng. 67/F4
Waltham, Mass. 137/F4
Walvis Bay, S. Africa 62/D7
Wapakoneta, Ohio 166/C1
Warangal, India 102/D3
Warren, Mich. 178/C3
Warren, Ohio 166/B4
Warren, Pa. 170/B2
Warrington, Eng. 66/G2
Warrnambool, Austr. 115/D4
Warsaw (cap.), Pol. 87/E2
Warta, Pol. 86/B2
Warwick, R.I. 137/D3
Wash, The (bay), Eng. 67/G4
Washington (mt.), N.H. 158/C2
Washington, N.C. 163/E2
Washington, Pa. 170/A4
Washington, D.C. (cap.), U.S. 139/D1
Washington (state), U.S. 175
Waterbury, Conn. 136/B3
Waterbury, Vt. 136/A2
Waterford, Ire. 67/C4
Waterloo, Belg. 73/D6
Waterloo, Iowa 146/B3
Waterloo, Ont. 187/D4
Waterton-Glacier Int'l Peace Pk., N. Amer. 156/C1
Waterton Lakes Nat'l Pk., Alta. 191/E4
Watertown, Conn. 136/A3
Watertown, N.Y. 161/B2
Watertown, S. Dak. 165/D4
Watertown, Wis. 176/C4
Waterville, Maine 151/B3
Watford, Eng. 67/B5
Watkins Glen, N.Y. 160/C3
Watling (isl.), see San Salvador (isl.)
Watsonville, Calif. 133/D1
Watts Barr (lake), Tenn. 149/D4
Wau, Sudan 61/E4
Waukegan, Ill. 178/B1
Waukesha, Wis. 176/A1
Wausau, Wis. 176/B3
Wawatosa, Wis. 176/C4
Waxahachie, Texas 173/E2
Waycross, Ga. 142/B4
Waynesboro, Va. 138/D3
Weatherford, Okla. 168/B2
Webster, N.Y. 160/C2
Weddell (sea), Antarc. 118
Weimar, Ger. 71/F3
Weirton, W. Va. 138/C1
Weiser, Idaho 143/A3
Welkom, S. Africa 63/E7
Welland, Ont. 187/F4
Wellington (isl.), Chile 58/B7
Wellington (cap.), N.Z. 115/F4
Wellsboro, Pa. 171/D2
Wels, Austria 82/B2
Wenatchee, Wash. 175/B3
Wendover, Utah 174/A2
Wenzhou, China 105/F3
Weser (riv.), Ger. 70/C2
Weslaco, Texas 173/D4

W. Allis, Wis. 176/A1
West Bank 98-99/C3
W. Bend, Wis. 176/C4
Westbrook, Maine 151/A4
W. Chester, Pa. 171/E4
W. Covina, Calif. 179/B3
W. Des Moines, Iowa 146/B2
Westerly, R.I. 137/D3
Western Australia (state), Austr. 114/B3
Western Sahara 60/A2
Western Samoa 117/J7
Westerville, Maine 151/B3
Westerville, Ohio 166/C2
W. Fargo, N. Dak. 164/C4
Westfield, Mass. 136/B2
W. Hartford, Conn. 136/B2
W. Haven, Conn. 136/B3
W. Helena, Ark. 131/B3
West Indies 50-51
W. Jordan, Utah 174/C4
W. Lafayette, Ind. 145/A2
Westland, Mich. 178/B4
W. Memphis, Ark. 131/B3
W. Mifflin, Pa. 170/A1
Westminster, Calif. 179/C2
Westminster, Colo. 158/A2
Westminster, Eng. 67/B5
W. Monroe, La. 150/A3
Westmount, Que. 184/B1
W. Palm Bch., Fla. 141/D4
W. Point, Miss. 154/C2
Westport, Conn. 136/A3
W. Seneca, N.Y. 160/B1
W. Springfield, Mass. 136/B2
W. Valley City, Utah 174/C1
W. Vancouver, Br. Col. 190/A1
West Virginia (state), U.S. 138-139
W. Warwick, R.I. 137/D3
Westwego, La. 150/B4
Wetar (isl.), Indon. 113/H7
Wetaskiwin, Alta. 191/D2
Wewak, Papua N.G. 112/B6
Wexford, Ire. 67/C4
Weyburn, Sask. 188/C4
Whalsay (isl.), Scot. 66/G1
Whangarei, N.Z. 115/F3
Wheat Ridge, Colo. 178/A4
Wheeling, Ill. 178/A1
Wheeling, W. Va. 138/C2
Whiskeytown-Shasta-Trinity Nat'l Rec. Area, Calif. 132/A1
Whitby, Ont. 187/F3
White (riv.), Ind. 145/A4
White (mts.), N.H. 158/C3
White (sea), U.S.S.R. 88/E1
White Bear Lake, Minn. 153/C1
Whitecourt, Alta. 191/D2
Whitefish, Mont. 156/A1
Whitefish Bay, Wis. 176/B1
Whitehorse (cap.), Yukon 42/C3
White Mtns. Nat'l Rec. Area, Alaska 129/B1
White Nile (riv.), Africa 61/F4
White Plains, N.Y. 180/C1
White River Junction, Vt. 158/B3
White Rock, Br. Col. 190/B1
White Russian S.S.R. (Byelo-russian S.S.R.), U.S.S.R. 89/C4
White Sands Nat'l Mon., N. Mex. 135/F2
White Sulphur Sprs., W. Va. 138/C3
Whitewater, Wis. 176/C4
Whitney (mt.), Calif. 133/D3
Whittier, Calif. 179/B2
Whyalla, Austr. 114/C4
Wichita, Kans. 147/C3
Wichita Falls, Texas 173/D1
Wicklow, Ire. 67/C4

Index

Wien, see Vienna
Wiener Neustadt, Austria 82/C3
Wiesbaden, Ger. 71/B3
Wigan, Eng. 66/G2
Wight (isl.), Eng. 67/F5
Wildwood, N.J. 159/B4
Wilkes-Barre, Pa. 171/E3
Wilkinsburg, Pa. 170/B1
Willamette (riv.), Oreg. 169/B2
Willapa (bay), Wash. 175/C1
Willemstad (cap.), Neth. Ant. 51/E4
William H. Taft Nat'l Hist. Site,
 Ohio 167/F1
Williamsburg, Va. 139/E4
Williams Lake, Br. Col. 190/C3
Williamsport, Pa. 171/D3
Williamstown, Mass. 136/B1
Willimantic, Conn. 136/C3
Williston (lake), Br. Col. 190/B1
Williston, N. Dak. 164/B1
Willmar, Minn. 153/B4
Wilmette, Ill. 178/B1
Wilmington, Del. 139/F2
Wilmington, N.C. 163/E2
Wilson, N.C. 163/E2
Winchester, Eng. 67/F5
Winchester, Ky. 149/E2
Winchester, Va. 139/D2
Wind (riv.), Wyo. 177/B3
Wind Cave Nat'l Pk., S. Dak.
 165/E1
Windhoek (cap.), Namibia 63/D7
Windsor, Conn. 136/B2
Windsor, Ont. 186/B4
Windward (isls.), W. Indies 51/G4
Winfield, Kans. 147/C3
Winkler, Man. 189/E4
Winnebago (lake), Wis. 176/C4
Winnemucca, Nev. 132/A1
Winner, S. Dak. 165/F3
Winnetka, Ill. 178/B1
Winnibigoshish (lake), Minn.
 153/B2
Winnipeg (cap.), Man. 189/F4
Winnipeg (lake), Man. 189/E2
Winnipegosis (lake), Man. 189/D2
Winnipesaukee (lake), N.H. 158/C3
Winona, Minn. 153/C4
Winooski, Vt. 158/A2
Winslow, Ariz. 130/C3
Winston-Salem, N.C. 163/E1
Winter Haven, Fla. 140/D3
Winter Park, Fla. 140/A4
Winterthur, Switz. 81/D1
Wiscasset, Maine 151/B4
Wisconsin (riv.), Wis. 176/B4
Wisconsin (state), U.S. 176
Wisconsin Dells, Wis. 176/B4
Wisconsin Rapids, Wis. 176/B3
Wittenberg, Ger. 70/E3
Woburn, Mass. 137/F4
Woking, Eng. 67/B6
Wolfsburg, Ger. 70/D2
Wollongong, Austr. 115/E4
Wolverhampton, Eng. 67/E4
Wŏnju, S. Korea 106/C3
Wŏnsan, N. Korea 106/B3
Woodbridge, N.J. 180/B3
Woodbridge, Ont. 187/E3
Woodland, Calif. 132/C1
Woods, Lake of the (lake), N.
 Amer. 153/B2, 186/C1
Woods Hole, Mass. 137/E3
Woodstock, N. Br. 182/B2
Woodstock, Ont. 186/B4
Woodward, Okla. 168/C2
Woonsocket, R.I. 137/D2
Wooster, Ohio 166/B3
Worcester, Eng. 67/F4

Worcester, Mass. 136/C2
Worcester, S. Africa 63/D8
Worland, Wyo. 177/A3
World 34-35
Worms, Ger. 71/C4
Worthing, Eng. 67/F5
Worthington, Minn. 153/A4
Wrangel (isl.), U.S.S.R. 91/K2
Wrangell, Alaska 129/C2
Wrangell-St. Elias Nat'l Pk.,
 Alaska 129/B2
Wrexham, Wales 67/E4
Wright Brothers Nat'l Mem., N.C.
 163/F1
Wrightsville Bch., N.C. 163/E3
Wroclaw, Pol. 86/C3
Wuhan, China 105/E2
Wuhu, China 105/E2
Wupatki Nat'l Mon., Ariz. 130/B2
Wuppertal, Ger. 70/B3
Würzburg, Ger. 71/D4
Wusuli Jiang, China, see Ussuri
Wuxi, China 105/E2
Wyoming, Mich. 152/B4
Wyoming (state), U.S. 177

X

Xenia, Ohio 167/D1
Xiamen, China 105/E3
Xi'an, China 105/D2
Xiangtan, China 105/E3
Xingu (riv.), Braz. 57/D3
Xining, China 104/D2
Xinjiang Uygur Zizhiqu (aut. reg.),
 China 104/B1
Xinxiang, China 105/E2
Xizang (aut. reg.), China 104/B2
Xuzhou, China 105/E2

Y

Yablonovyy (range), U.S.S.R.
 91/H3
Yakutsk, U.S.S.R. 91/G2
Yalu (riv.), Asia 106/B2
Yamagata, Japan 107/F3
Yambol, Bulg. 93/C3
Yamoussoukro (cap.), Ivory
 Coast 61/C4
Yanbo, S. Arabia, see Yenbo
Yakima, Wash. 175/C3
Yangtze (Chang Jiang) (riv.),
 China 105/E2
Yankton, S. Dak. 165/F4
Yantai, China 105/F2
Yao, Japan 107/E4
Yaoundé (cap.), Camb. 60/D4
Yap (isl.), Micronesia 116/D5
Yarmouth, Mass. 137/F2
Yarmouth, N.S. 182/B4
Yarmuk (riv.), Asia 98/D2
Yaroslavl', U.S.S.R. 88/E3
Yazd, Iran 101/J5
Yazoo (riv.), Miss. 154/B2
Yazoo City, Miss. 154/A2
Yelets, U.S.S.R. 89/E4
Yellow (Huang He) (riv.), China
 105/E2
Yellow (sea), Asia 105/F2
Yellowknife (cap.), N.W.T. 42/E3
Yellowstone (riv.), U.S. 156/B4
Yellowstone Nat'l Pk., U.S.
 177/A4
Yemen 94/D6
Yenbo, S. Arabia 94/D5
Yenisey (riv.), U.S.S.R. 90/E3
Yerevan, U.S.S.R. 89/F6
Yerington, Nev. 132/C2
Yichang, China 105/E2
Yinchuan, China 104/D2

Yogyakarta, Indon. 113/J2
Yoho Nat'l Pk., Br. Col. 191/D3
Yokkaichi, Japan 106/E4
Yokohama, Japan 107/E4
Yokosuka, Japan 107/E4
Yonkers, N.Y. 180/B1
Yorba Linda, Calif. 179/C3
York (cape), Austr. 115/D2
York, Eng. 67/F3
York, Nebr. 157/B3
York, Pa. 171/D4
Yorkton, Sask. 189/D3
Yorktown, Va. 139/E4
Yosemite Nat'l Pk., Calif. 132/C2
Yoshkar-Ola, U.S.S.R. 88/G3
Youghal, Ire. 67/B5
Youghiogheny (riv.), U.S. 170/A4
Youngstown, Ohio 166/B4
Ypres (leper), Belg. 73/A6
Yucatán (pen.), Mex. 47/H4
Yugoslavia 84/B2
Yukon (terr.), Can. 42/C3
Yukon (riv.), N. Amer. 40/C3
Yuma, Ariz. 130/A4
Yumen, China 104/C2
Yunnan (prov.), China 104/D3
Yuzhno-Sakhalinsk, U.S.S.R.
 91/H3

Z

Zaandam, Neth. 72/B4
Zabrze, Pol. 86/A4
Zacapa, Guat. 48/B2
Zacatecas, Mex. 46/D3
Zagreb, Yugo. 84/A2
Zagros (mts.), Iran 100/E4
Zahedan, Iran 101/M6
Zahle, Leb. 97/G6
Zaire 63/E5
Zaire (riv.), Zaire 63/E4
Zákinthos (Zante) (isl.), Greece
 85/C4
Zalaegerszeg, Hung. 82/D3
Zambezi (riv.), Africa 63/E6
Zambia 63/E6
Zamboanga, Phil. 109/C7
Zanesville, Ohio 166/C3
Zanjan, Iran 100/F2
Zanzibar (is.), Tanz. 63/F5
Zaporozh'ye, U.S.S.R. 89/E5
Zaragoza, Spain, see Saragossa
Zaria, Nigeria 60/C3
Zarqa, see Ez Zarqa
Zawia, Libya 60/D1
Zefat, Isr. 98/C2
Zermatt, Switz. 80/C2
Zhangjiakou, China 105/E1
Zhejiang (prov.), China 105/E3
Zhengzhou, China 105/E2
Zhitomir, U.S.S.R. 89/C4
Zibo, China 105/E2
Zielona Gora, Pol. 86/B3
Zigong, China 104/D3
Ziguinchor, Sen. 60/A3
Zilina, Czech. 83/E2
Zimbabwe 63/E-F6
Zinder, Niger 60/C3
Zion, Ill. 144/C1
Zion Nat'l Pk., Utah 174/A4
Zlatoust, U.S.S.R. 90/C3
Zlin, Czech. 83/D2
Zomba, Malawi 63/F6
Zonguldak, Turkey 96/D2
Zrenjanin, Yugo. 84/C2
Zuni, N. Mex. 135/D1
Zug, Switz. 81/D1
Zugspitze (mt.), Europe 71/D5
Zürich, Switz. 81/D1
Zwickau, Ger. 71/E3
Zwolle, Neth. 72/H3